Urban Dynamics: A Real Estate Perspective

An institutional analysis of the production of the built environment

Urban Dynamics:
A Real Estate Perspective

An institutional analysis of the production of the built environment

Erwin van der Krabben

THESIS PUBLISHERS
AMSTERDAM 1995

CIP-DATA KONINKLIJKE BIBLIOTHEEK, DEN HAAG

Krabben, Erwin van der

Urban dynamics: a real estate perspective : an
institutional analysis of the production of the built
environment / Erwin van der Krabben. - Amsterdam : Thesis
Publishers. - Fig., tab.
Also publ. as thesis Katholieke Universiteit Nijmegen,
1995. - With ref. - With summary in Dutch.
ISBN 90-5170-390-2
NUGI 681
Subject headings: urban dynamics / housing market / urban economics.

Cover design: Pijnenburg Communicatie Tilburg

© 1995 Erwin van der Krabben

All rights reserved. Save exceptions stated by the law no part of this publication may be reproduced, stored in a retrieval system of any nature, or transmitted in any form or by means, electronic, mechanical, photocopying, recording or otherwise, included a complete or partial transcription, without the prior written permission of the publisher, application for which should be addressed to Thesis Publishers, P.O. Box, 1001 LG Amsterdam, the Netherlands.

In so far it is permitted to make copies from this publication under the provision of article 16B and 17 of the Auteurswet 1912 (Copyright Act), you are obliged to make the payments required by law to the Stichting Reprorecht (Repro Law Foundation), P.O. Box 882, 1180 AW Amstelveen, the Netherlands. To use any part or parts of this publication in anthologies, readers and other compilations (article 16 Auteurswet 1912) you are obliged to contact the publisher.

ISBN 90-5170-390-2
NUGI 681

"... 'Ik probeer te overtuigen, mensen te beïnvloeden. Dat is de politiek, de macht; het is allemaal verbaal, een onafgebroken sneeuwjacht van woorden. Maar het is niet gewoon spreken, nee, het is het doen van uitspraken. Het is handelen; het is iets doen zonder iets te doen. Het is natuurlijk prachtig als je dingen kunt veranderen en verbeteren, daar zul je mij niet over horen, - maar het besef, dat het op die manier gebeurt, begint langzamerhand aan mij te vreten.' 'Waarom? Wat is er nu mooier dan iets doen met woorden? Doet een schrijver iets anders? Of neem God'."

(uit: Harry Mulisch, De Ontdekking van de Hemel: hoofdstuk 40, De Woordenwereld)

ACKNOWLEDGEMENTS

This dissertation is the product of four years working in the Department of Social Economics of Tilburg University. At the beginning of these four years, one imagines that there is time to spare; at the end, one knows better. I also realise now that the support of several people has been indispensable to be able to finish this job. Therefore, I would like to extend my gratitude to a number of people who got me on the right track and kept me there.
First of all, I want to thank my two supervisors. Jan Lambooy has especially guided me in developing the theoretical perspective of this book. Frans Boekema has always been there to comment on earlier drafts of this book. Moreover, he has stimulated me to finish this book in time.
I want to address a special word of gratitude to Barrie Needham who has probably been my most rigorous critic during these four years. However, I have always considered his criticism as constructive and I don't know what would have become of this book without it.
During my Ph.D. I spent three months at the Centre for Research of the European Urban Environment at the University of Newcastle-upon-Tyne. My discussions with Patsy Healey and other colleagues of the CREUE have helped me in forming my opinion.
Furthermore, I want to thank my colleagues at the Department of Social Economics, in particular my fellow Ph.D students, for making those four years in Tilburg a pleasant time. I want to thank Henk van Houtum and Rob Aalbers also for commenting on earlier drafs of this book. I am grateful to Jan-Kees Helderman and Marc van der Meer who both have spent a lot of time on reading parts of this book.
My final expression of gratitude addresses Brigitte, "Johnnie" (although he/she has not yet realised that he/she has been of any help), and my parents for their never-ending support, and Silvia van der Cammen and Frans de Man for helping me to put the finishing touches to this book.

Nijmegen, June 24, 1995

CONTENTS

Acknowledgements 7

Contents 9

List of figures & tables 13

Introduction 17

PART I   REAL ESTATE DEVELOPMENT AND URBAN DYNAMICS 23

1 THE TRANSFORMATION OF THE BUILT ENVIRONMENT 25
   1.1. Introduction 25
   1.2. The Real Estate Market: a Special Type of Market 27
   1.3. The Malfunctioning of the Urban Real Estate Market: Empirical Evidence 29
   1.4. Definition of the Problem Area and Research Questions 32

2 MISSING LINKS BETWEEN URBAN ECONOMIC THEORY AND PROPERTY DEVELOPMENT PROCESSES 35
   2.1. International Differences with Respect to Property Development 35
   2.2. The Provision of the Built Environment 39
   2.3. Land and Property Development and the Urban Economy 41
   2.4. A Vacuum in Urban Economic Theory; Clues for Analysis 43
       2.4.1.   Basic premises of urban economic theories 44
       2.4.2.   Clues for analysis 46
       2.4.3.   Operationalisation 49
   2.5. The Malfunctioning of Urban Real Estate Markets: Theoretical Explanations . . . 49
   2.6. Summary: Theoretical Explanations of Urban Economic Growth, Dynamics of Urban Change and Real Estate Development Processes 52

PART II   THEORIES OF URBAN CHANGE 55

3 MODELS OF THE DEVELOPMENT PROCESS: EXISTING APPROACHES 59
   3.1. Theories of Urban Change: Goals and Perspectives 59
   3.2. A Neo-classical Model of the Real Estate Development Process 59
   3.3. Marxist Approaches: Circuits of Capital 62
   3.4. Institutional Models of the Development Process 64
   3.5. The Blind Alley of Descriptive Models 65
   3.6. Conclusions: Explanations of Urban Dynamics 66

4 INSTITUTIONAL ECONOMIC THEORY: A REALISTIC APPROACH 67
   4.1. Introduction 67
   4.2. Institutional Economic Theory: Rejecting Neo-classical Assumptions 68
   4.3. Markets and Coordination 74
   4.4. Basic Premises of New Institutional Economics; problems of coordination 76
   4.5. Institutional change 79
   4.6. A Framework for analysis: basic elements 81

5 THE INSTITUTIONAL ORGANISATION OF THE REAL ESTATE MARKET: FRAMEWORK FOR ANALYSIS 85
   5.1. Analysing the institutional context 85
   5.2. Spatial Variations with respect to the Organisation of the Real Estate Market ... 86
   5.3. Consequences for the Outcome of Market Processes 93
   5.4. Temporal variation with respect to the organisation of the development industry . 98
   5.5. Changing strategies 102
   5.6. Changes in the outcome of development processes 104
   5.7. Conclusions 106

PART III   THE HOUSING MARKET: A CASE STUDY OF ORGANISATIONAL STRUCTURE, INSTITUTIONAL CHANGE AND PATH DEPENDENCY 109

6 THE HOUSING DEVELOPMENT INDUSTRY: ORGANISATIONAL STRUCTURE AND INSTITUTIONAL CHANGE 115
   6.1. The Aims of the Case Study 115
   6.2. Propositions: guidelines for study 120
   6.3. The Agents involved in House Building 121
   6.4. Government Intervention 125
   6.5. Strategies of the actors 130
   6.6. Institutional Economic Relations between the Agents 136
   6.7. Summary 138

7 TRENDS IN HOUSING PRODUCTION AND STRATEGIES OF MARKET PARTIES 141
   7.1. Introduction 141
   7.2. The Production of New Buildings and Renovations: Investment Trends 142
   7.3. The Number of New Dwellings, by Year and by Way of Financing 146
   7.4. Changes in the Housing Stock: Age, Tenure and Quality 151
   7.5. House Price Fluctuations and Changing Land Prices 155
   7.6. The Consumption of Housing 162
   7.7. Conclusions 163

8 A CRISIS IN HOUSING PRODUCTION: INSTITUTIONAL CHANGES, PATH DEPENDENCY AND FUTURE TRENDS 167
   8.1. Introduction 167
   8.2. Sources of Institutional Change 167
   8.3. Institutional Changes with respect to Housing Development 179
   8.4. Development Gains in Housebuilding Development Processes 193
   8.5. Explanations for the Crisis in Housing Production 199
   8.6. Conclusions: A Qualification of the Dutch Property System 201

PART IV TOWARDS A BETTER UNDERSTANDING OF PROPERTY DEVELOPMENT PROCESSES ... 203

9 THE INSTITUTIONAL ORGANISATION OF THE DUTCH REAL ESTATE MARKET: EVALUATION ... 207
  9.1. Evaluating the Dutch Property System ... 207
  9.2. The Institutional Organisation of Urban Real Estate Markets: Criteria of Allocative Efficacy and Productive Efficiency ... 208
  9.3. How Well Does the Dutch Housing Market Work? ... 210
  9.4. The Dutch Real Estate Market: Examples of Allocative Inefficacy and Productive Inefficiency? ... 214
  9.5. Concluding Remarks ... 216

10   DIRECTIONS FOR URBAN REGENERATION POLICIES ... 219
  10.1.   Introduction ... 219
  10.2.   The Real Estate Sector and Urban Economic Growth: Conceptual Links   221
  10.3.   The British Experience: property-led urban regeneration policies ... 224
  10.4.   The Dutch Experience: Conditions for Economic Growth ... 227
  10.5.   Synthesis: Public Policy, the Real Estate Sector and the Urban Economy   230

Samenvatting ... 233

References ... 239

LIST OF FIGURES & TABLES

LIST OF FIGURES

CHAPTER FOUR
fig. 4.1   The scope and boundaries of, respectively, orthodox economic theory and institutional economic theory
fig. 4.2   Institutional economic theory: subjects of study

CHAPTER FIVE
fig. 5.1   An institutional approach to real estate development processes: subjects of study

CHAPTER SEVEN
fig. 7.1   Gross investments in housebuilding, by principal, 1975-1993 (current prices)
fig. 7.2   Indices for gross investments in housing, business buildings and total building investments, 1974-1993 (1980 = 100; current prices)
fig. 7.3   Gross investments in housing, business buildings and total building investments, annual % of change, 1974-1993
fig. 7.4   International comparison of gross fixed capital formation in building construction, as a percentage of gross domestic product, 1980-1992
fig. 7.5   International comparison of gross fixed capital formation in residential buildings as a percentage of gross fixed capital formation in building construction, 1980-1991/1992
fig. 7.6   Dwellings completed, by tenure status and by way of financing, 1960-1993
fig. 7.7   Dwellings completed, by tenure status and by way of financing, as a percentage of the total, 1960-1993
fig. 7.8   Dwellings completed, by principal as a percentage of the total, 1960-1993
fig. 7.9   International comparison: dwellings completed and rate of change of population, 1980-1992
fig. 7.10   Dwellings stock, by date of building, 1 January 1992
fig. 7.11   Average estimated value per dwelling, by date of building, 1 January 1992 (prices 1992)
fig. 7.12   Annual % of change of the total stock of dwellings and the number of households, 1960-1994
fig. 7.13   Owner-occupied dwellings, as a percentage of the total building stock, 1970-1994
fig. 7.14   Trend of average selling prices of owner-occupied dwellings, 1975-1993 (current prices)
fig. 7.15   Development of average house prices and average loan capacity, 1975-1993
fig. 7.16   Price indices of the average selling price of owner-occupied dwellings, 1975-1993 (1975 = 100; current prices)
fig. 7.17   Average selling prices of owner-occupied dwellings and rate of inflation: annual % of change, 1975-1993 (current prices)
fig. 7.18   Average building plot prices for owner-occupied single-family dwellings in

fig. 7.19   new expansion areas, by way of financing, 1982-1991 (prices 1990)
Average building plot prices for social sector dwellings, 1965-1993 (prices 1993)
fig. 7.20   Average building plot prices per m2 for owner-occupied single-family dwellings in new expansion areas, by way of financing, 1982-1991 (prices 1990)
fig. 7.21   Indices for the development of housing expenses for tenants and owner-occupiers and rate of inflation, 1981-1992 (1981 = 100; current prices)
fig. 7.22   Relative frequency distribution of housing rents, per 1 July 1992

CHAPTER EIGHT

fig. 8.1   Variations in building costs per m3 of new dwellings, by degree of 'urbanity' and by tenure status
fig. 8.2   International comparison: price indices for average building costs of new dwellings, 1980-1992
fig. 8.3   Variations in building costs per m3 of new dwellings, by project size (by share in total of new dwellings) and by tenure status, 1992
fig. 8.4   Average building costs of new dwellings, by sector, 1975-1993 (current prices)
fig. 8.5   Mutations of average building costs per dwelling, by sector, 1975-1993 (corrected for inflation)
fig. 8.6   Average building costs of new dwellings per m3, by sector, 1975-1993 (current prices)
fig. 8.7   Mutations of average building costs per m3, by sector, 1975-1993 (corrected for inflation)
fig. 8.8   The total costs of new dwellings in the owner-occupied sector (with one-time allocation and premium-assisted), versus average selling prices of all owner-occupied dwellings, 1984-1992 (current prices)
fig. 8.9   Price indices for the total costs of new social-sector dwellings and new subsidised owner-occupied dwellings, 1975-1993 (1984 = 100; current prices)
fig. 8.10   Investments per Dfl. 1,000 added value, average for 1983-1989
fig. 8.11   Developments in interest and inflation
fig. 8.12   Gross expenditures Ministry of Housing with respect to housing, 1970-1994 (current prices)
fig. 8.13   Gross expenditures Ministry of Housing with respect to housing, as a percentage of net national income, 1970-1991
fig. 8.14   Development of gross government expenditures with respect to housing, per dwelling (total housing stock), 1975-1993 (prices 1990)
fig. 8.15   Development of gross government expenditures with respect to housing, per newly built dwelling, 1975-1993 (prices 1990)
fig. 8.16   Development of gross government subsidies with respect to the owner-occupied sector per newly built dwelling, 1975-1993 (prices 1990)
fig. 8.17   Development of gross government subsidies with respect to the social rented sector per dwelling (total social-housing stock), 1975-1993 (prices 1990)
fig. 8.18   Average building investments per project (including renovations), by type of building, 1988-1993 (current prices)

fig. 8.19   Average building investments per m3 (including renovations), by type of building, 1988-1993 (current prices)
fig. 8.20   Average number of dwellings per project, 1988-1993
fig. 8.21   Average number of dwellings per project (single dwellings built by private persons excluded), 1988-1993
fig. 8.22   Trend of newly registered mortgages on real estate and average rate of interest on newly registered mortgages on real estate, 1970-1993
fig. 8.23   Number of firms in the construction industry, by size of firm, 1973-1988
fig. 8.24   Gross turnover by firms in construction industry, by size of firm, 1981-1987 (current prices)
fig. 8.25   Trend in labour productivity, by size of firm (average turnover per employee), in 1980, 1983, and 1988 (current prices)
fig. 8.26   Index numbers of the trends of land acquisition costs, land servicing costs and building plot prices for dwellings, 1965-1991 (1972 = 100; current prices)
fig. 8.27   Index numbers of the profitability of speculative house building, owner-occupied dwellings, non-subsidised sector: development of returns versus development of costs, 1975-1993 (1983 = 100; current prices)
fig. 8.28   Index numbers of the profitability of speculative house building, owner-occupied dwellings, premium-assisted sector: development of returns versus development of costs, 1975-1993 (1983 = 100; current prices)
fig. 8.29   Index numbers of the total costs per m2 of speculative housebuilding, owner-occupied premium-assisted sector, with and without government subsidies, 1975-1993 (current prices)

LIST OF TABLES

CHAPTER SIX
tab. 6.1   Dwellings completed, by type of financing and by principal in 1993 (in absolute figures)
tab. 6.2   Newly built owner-occupied dwellings, by type of financing 1991-1993 (in absolute figures)
tab. 6.3   Composition and number of firms involved in the building-construction industry in 1991 (residential and non-residential building)
tab. 6.4   Gross expenditures by the Ministry of Housing with respect to housing, 1993 and 1994
tab. 6.5   Gross investments in buildings, by type of financing and by principal, 1993
tab. 6.6   Gross investments in housebuilding, by type of financing and by principal, 1993
tab. 6.7   Number of dwellings owned by housing associations and municipal housing departments, 1989-1991
tab. 6.8   Newly registered mortgagees on real estate, by total number of registrations and total amounts and by market share of mortgagees, 1990-1993

CHAPTER SEVEN
tab. 7.1   Average building plot prices and building plot sizes for owner-occupied single-family houses, by type of area, by region and by way of financing, 1990/1991

CHAPTER EIGHT
tab. 8.1   Average project size (A) and annual number of projects in progress, by building construction firms (B), by size of firm in 1980, 1983, and 1988 (prices 1987)

INTRODUCTION

This study investigates processes of development and redevelopment in cities -- in Dutch cities in particular. Development processes refer to *urban real estate* development processes. On urban real estate markets land and buildings are being developed, land and buildings are traded, and land and buildings are, ultimately, demolished, to make place for redevelopment projects. This study focuses especially on the way land and buildings are *developed*, the supply-side of the real estate market -- but then exclusively on the supply of land and new buildings. Who are the builders and the developers, who finances new development projects, what does it cost, who gains by it and how much, which strategies are pursued both by market parties and government organisations, etc. More precisely, the subject of this study is to investigate the way in which the supply of land and buildings is influenced by the typical organisational structure of real estate markets.

Two different observations underlie my choice to draw attention to this subject. First, in the Netherlands the factor 'land' has recently gained in relevancy, with respect to the functioning of urban or regional economies. The present debate concentrates, on the one hand, on the question where to locate new economic activities, and, on the other hand, on the question whether the amount of land is still sufficient to meet future demand for expansion areas by, for instance, the economic sector and the housing sector. Moreover, it is likely that the future land claims by different sectors will be conflicting with each other. To be able to answer these questions properly, I believe that we should pay more attention to the way building land is developed -- the production of land -- and to potential obstructions to land development. Likewise, more attention is needed for the processes underlying the development of the building. In other words, the development of land and buildings and the way real estate development processes, possibly, hinder regional and urban economic growth should receive more attention.

Second, many municipalities focus, in their attempts to realise urban economic policy goals, on the real estate sector. Municipalities make plans for new commercial real estate projects, they develop new business sites, they enter into alliances with market parties to develop new building schemes (public private partnerships), and they finance development projects in different sectors of the real estate market (government subsidies). The public sector not only supports, financially, the development of business sites, commercial real estate projects and housebuilding schemes, but in many cases she bears the risks as well. This calls into question the social efficiency of public sector investments in real estate development and in urban/regional economic development.

The results of many studies of real estate development processes - also with respect to the Dutch context - are already available. This information can be used to find answers to the above mentioned questions. However, I wonder whether these analyses have been sufficiently profound, particularly regarding the meaning of the institutional organisation of the real estate market. In many cases the typical institutional context and its impact on market processes has been taken into consideration, but the institutional organisation of the real estate market was not the prime subject of study. The intention of the present study is just to find out the significance of institutional factors to real estate development. What does the concept of *institutional organisation of the market* mean, which aspects are relevant to the discussion of real estate market processes, how does this institutional organisation comes about, what kind of changes take place with respect to the institutional context, what is the significance of spatial and temporal variations in the institutional organisation, and what is the impact of the institutional organisation on development processes, etc.? To clear up one misunderstanding already, the concept of institutional context includes much more than only public sector interventions in markets. Regarding the institutional organisation of the real estate market, we must also take into consideration the composition of the group of actors that take part in the development industry, the different strategies of market parties, the institutional (non-market) relations between market parties and the public sector (e.g. public private partnerships, informal networks), the meaning of property ownership and property rights in general, the impact of various 'rules' -- not only legislation, but also norms and values -- on market processes, the significance of new ideas and new technologies, etc. Studying the institutional context we must also examine the role of uncertainty or incomplete information in market processes. The concept of uncertainty is crucial in economics. Many market processes are influenced by the degree of uncertainty. For instance, the uncertainty with respect to future returns of commercial real estate investments influences the developers' decisions about the development of new real estate projects.

The impact of the institutional organisation of real estate markets on real estate development can best be assessed by taking into consideration the changes that take place on these markets or the international variations in market performances. Both these changes in market processes and international variations can only be understood properly by focusing on *institutional* changes and international *institutional* differences. For instance: the fact that Dutch municipalities have been satisfied for a long time with selling building land against cost price (land acquisition costs, increased by the costs of servicing the land), while the market value of land on some locations probably was substantially higher. The consequences of the specific role of Dutch municipalities on land markets have been studied by other authors. Therefore, I do not want to suggest that an institutional approach to this subject implies a shift to a totally new area of study. However, I *do* aim to analyse certain aspects of the institutional organisation of the Dutch real estate market that have been ignored in other studies. Referring again to the land price issue: when land prices suddenly increase, it should be investigated whether this rise is the result of a suddenly growing demand for building land or whether institutional changes are responsible for the change in land prices. In the latter case, many municipalities could have decided, for instance, to charge market prices for land (according to the market value of the land) instead of being satisfied with a price that just covers the costs (the costs to 'produce' building land). As a consequence, fundamental shifts in the division of development gains on urban land markets may occur (with the result that market parties change their strategies as well).

This study aims (I) to study the institutional organisation of urban real estate markets - with a special interest in the Dutch case; (II) to analyse the meaning of spatial and temporal variation in this institutional organisation; and (III) to examine the impact of the institutional organisation of the market on development processes that actually take place. To be able to interpret correctly the institutional aspects of real estate markets we need, in my opinion, an analytical framework. Institutional economic theory aims to explain the significance of institutions, institutional differences and changes with respect to market processes. In this study I will make use of institutional economic theory to develop a framework for the analysis of the institutional organisation of the Dutch real estate market. With help of the analytical framework I intend to investigate the impact of the typical institutional organisation of the Dutch real estate market on real estate development.

I will analyse in particular the functioning of the urban land market and the owner-occupied housing market. These sectors of the real estate market are of interest for several reasons. At present the land market receives much attention, both from policy-makers and academics, mainly because the availability of land for building purposes is not as obvious as it used to be in the Netherlands. Municipalities see it as their duty to supply always sufficient building land; however, this task is not so easy to perform any more. With respect to the owner-occupied housing market several events direct our attention to the functioning of this market. The market prices of owner-occupied dwellings have risen sharply in the 1990s, with important consequences for both the owners of existing dwellings, future owners, and developers of new dwellings. Moreover, the public sector has withdrawn itself financially from the social housing sector. As a result, the larger part of the total amount of new dwellings that have to be built in the next years (to fulfil housing needs) must now be developed in the owner-occupied sector. (Note that until now the share of owner-occupied dwellings in the total housing stock is, in an international context, relatively low in the Netherlands.) Finally, both policy-makers and pressure groups have warned that the number of new dwellings that is currently developed is insufficient to fulfil the demand/need for housing. They claim that this is mainly due to a shortage of building land. However, in my opinion, other reasons play a role as well. The aim of the case study is to add to a better understanding of these processes -- the way they occur in the Netherlands -- by focusing especially on institutional aspects related to the supply side of the real estate market.

My choice to use the insights of institutional economic theory to develop a framework for analysis is a conscious choice, but needs more explanation. First, institutional-economic theory is clearly a theory that is still in the making. Its explanatory power in empirical analyses has not yet been proven sufficiently and should therefore be treated with some reservations. Second, as a result the use of institutional economic theory in this study is limited. I use institutional economic theory to develop a framework for the analysis of the functioning of urban real estate markets. I do not aim to develop a new theory of real estate development (and I do not explicitly test the theory in my case study). Third, my choice for institutional theory does explicitly not imply a rejection of mainstream neo-classical theory. Neo-classical economics has proven its value in numerous studies of real estate market functioning. Nevertheless, it is a fact that in academic literature a growing interest for institutional theory can be noted, leading to an intense debate about the nature of markets in general. It is also clear that in the field of real estate studies numerous issues still need to be resolved. From these perspectives I believe it is worthwhile to find out whether applying institutional-economic theory to this field of research will improve our knowledge of real estate development processes. The challenge of this study is to show the value of institutional economic theory to the analysis of real estate market issues *and* to add to a better understanding of real estate development processes in general and the Dutch land and housing market in particular.

The book consists of ten chapters, divided into four parts. Chapter One presents the social relevancy of the study. Among other things, a number of real estate issues in Dutch cities, that are socially unwanted, will be discussed. In these examples, so it will be argued, *institutional constraints* play an important role. Furthermore, in Chapter One the problem area will be defined, as well as the way the problem area is further handled.

Chapter Two discusses relevant literature in the field of real estate market research. Most attention will be paid to institutional analyses of urban real estate developments. Moreover, the *missing links* between urban economic theory and real estate market functioning will be addressed. It will be argued that in many theoretical explanations of urban dynamics the way land and buildings -- the materials of urban development -- are actually produced are ignored.

Part II consists of Chapters Three, Four, and Five and aims to clarify the theoretical foundation of the study. First, in Chapter Three a number of alternative approaches to the analysis of real estate development processes are mentioned. The intention is to make clear that the goals and subjects of study in these analyses differ from the perspective that has been chosen in the present study. Chapter Four deals with the state of affairs with respect to institutional-economic theory. The basic elements of this theoretical tradition will be discussed shortly. The ultimate goal of this chapter is to develop a framework for analysis. This framework will direct our attention to a number of issues of which it is believed that an institutional-economic approach will add to a better understanding of them. Four main issues are analysed: the meaning of *information problems* or *uncertainty* in economic life, the *rationalities* behind the strategies of market participants, *institutional change*, and the meaning of *path dependency*. Chapter Five aims to apply the framework for analysis to a study of real estate development processes. In this institutional framework for analysis the concepts of spatial variation and temporal variation, with respect to the institutional organisation of real estate markets, are central. The meaning of these concepts to the functioning of urban real estate markets in the Netherlands will be illustrated. The intention of Chapter Five is to use the insights of institutional economic theory to analyse a number of issues that seem to be significant to the present functioning of real estate markets.

Part III presents the results of a case study of the functioning of the urban land and housing market in the Netherlands. This case study deals with, subsequently, the characteristics of the organisational structure of the Dutch housebuilding market (Chapter Six), trends in housebuilding production and in the strategies of market parties (Chapter Seven), and the (meaning of) institutional changes that took place in the past twenty five years (Chapter Eight). The framework for analysis that has been developed in Chapter Five is used as a guideline for research, to interpret the relevance of institutional factors to the functioning of the market. The case study aims to demonstrate the significance of the housing market's organisational structure to housebuilding production. The present debate about the supposed shortages of building production is the immediate reason for carrying out this case study. It is argued that the usual explanation for the present shortages - a shortage of building land - misses the point. Other reasons, related to the role of municipalities on urban land markets, the strategies of private developers, and structural characteristics of the housebuilding market, are at least as important.

Finally, Part IV aims to evaluate the study. Chapter Nine assesses the Dutch *property system* both on its allocative efficacy and on its productive efficiency (the production of land and buildings). This chapter pays attention on the one hand to the conditions for effective public sector policy on urban land and property markets and on the other hand to the conditions for an efficiently operating real estate market. Chapter Ten discusses various directions with respect to regional/urban regeneration policies. This discussion takes place on base of the analysis of the relations between processes underlying real estate development and regional/urban economic growth. Chapter Ten concentrates on two different themes. First, it will be discussed whether *property-led* urban regeneration strategies contribute to general public sector policy directed at regional/urban economic growth. Second, the various ways in which municipalities may try to stimulate private sector real estate development will be examined. By discussing both themes I hope to gather more information on, first, the conditions the real estate sector claims with respect to a -- in their view -- successful regional/urban economic policy, and, second, on the social efficiency of the public sector's spatial investments.

PART I REAL ESTATE DEVELOPMENT AND URBAN DYNAMICS

1 THE TRANSFORMATION OF THE BUILT ENVIRONMENT

1.1. Introduction

To claim that the urban built environment is characteristically subject to transformation processes, resulting in a continually changing spatial-economic structure, would be to state the obvious. Nevertheless, it forms the motivation to write this book about property development processes: new developments taking place on the edges of cities, redevelopment projects of inner-city areas, renovation or demolishment of obsolete buildings, new housing schemes and business parks, infrastructural projects, etc. I intend to look for conformity in these processes in an international context, but, more explicitly, I will investigate property development in the particular context of Dutch cities.

The Dutch planning system is often considered -- together with the planning systems in Scandinavian countries -- as a classic example of successful government intervention.[1] The same goes for the functioning of urban land and property markets in these countries, which are strongly regulated by government control and active government intervention. Perhaps because of these considerations, the Dutch urban real estate market has been widely neglected as a study object in the academic world. In the Netherlands this situation has only recently been changed (as we will see in the next chapter).

This study stems from a fascination for cities: the city on the one hand as a phenomenon of the contemporary world, and on the other hand as the historical result of centuries of building activities. Moreover, the city is constantly and apparently, with ever-increasing speed, being converted into new forms, sometimes not even leaving enough time for us to ask ourselves whether or not the transformation is a desirable one. For instance, within the last decade, the Netherlands has undergone the development of a large number of new representative business parks near motorways and railway stations, inner-city areas have been redeveloped, the housing stock has expanded with almost one hundred thousand dwellings per year, while at the same time some housing estates dating from the 1960s have been demolished. In the meantime, the financing of new development projects has sometimes changed completely, government involvement has altered, the profitability of real estate development and (related to this) the possibility of making development gains constantly fluctuates, etc.

The fascination for urban dynamics may have a tinge of philosophy; nevertheless, the present study is mainly economic in essence. The urban spatial structure is considered to be the outcome of processes taking place on the urban real estate market where demand for land and property by firms, households and institutions meets with the supply of land and property by the groups of actors that are part of the so-called property development industry. As opposed to many studies of *urban economics*, this survey does not assume implicitly these supply and demand relations to be unproblematic -- that is, many studies of urban economies pay no attention to the effect of the nature of demand and supply relations on the real estate market for the outcome of urban restructuring processes. This study, however, will investigate explicitly the functioning of the real estate market following, as we will see

---

1   A detailed description of the Dutch planning system falls uitside the scope of this study. However, see for instance Faludi and Van der Valk (1990, 1994) and Dieleman and Musterd (1992).

in Chapter Two, a recently developed theoretical interest for property development processes in Great Britain.

The real estate market is not portrayed as a smoothly functioning service-hatch; it is placed at the centre of analysis and the development processes are *problematised*. One of the starting points is the assumption that the real estate market, because of its technical *and* economic characteristics, is *imperfect by nature*. The real estate market in Dutch cities is no exception to this. For instance, in many situations the outcome of market processes is not optimal to all parties that are involved, supply is not always able to meet demand despite the fact that the market price exceeds production costs, negative side-effects often occur, and substantial government expenditures are demanded to guarantee a sufficient level of building production. Moreover, the urban real estate market is considered to be both a complicated and dynamic market. This implies, among other things, that the institutional organisation of the real estate market is characterised by a large variety of groups of agents that are involved in property development and of institutional relations between them, and that a whole range of rules, norms and values determine market functioning. I assume not only that the organisation of the real estate market varies in an (inter)national context, but also that it characteristically changes through time, as well.

Several points of view have motivated my study of real estate development processes in Dutch cities. First, real estate development 'matters' with respect to regional and urban economic growth patterns. I claim, for instance, that the success of public-sector urban policy should substantially increase when we take better account of the interrelationship between real estate development processes and urban economic growth. Second, it can easily be observed that the outcome of real estate market processes continually changes through time. It is interesting to understand the 'mechanisms' underlying these changes. Third, it is obvious that the institutional organisation of real estate markets differs between the Netherlands and other countries. Differences with respect to the organisational structure of the market are assumed to lead to different outcomes of market processes. In other words, I want to demonstrate the link between the institutional organisation of the market and the outcome of urban development processes. Fourth, in some situations urban development processes are 'socially unwanted'. That is, they bring forward situations that harm some groups of agents, they cause negative side-effects, or they just fail to fulfil demand in a proper way.[2] Would a better understanding of real estate development processes, and more specifically, of the impact of the institutional organisation of the market on these processes, help to prevent these situations occurring? Finally, I believe that many studies of urban development neglect the above issues. They fail to pay sufficient attention to the actual production of the built environment, thus possibly missing both vital sources of urban change and clear constraints to the smooth functioning of urban economies.[3]

---

2   The issue of 'social problems', related to the malfunctioning of urban real estate markets, will be discussed below.

3   Of course, real estate development studies are just concerned with built-environment production. What I intend to say is that many studies of the urban economy take no account of the results of these real estate studies.

In the subsequent parts of Chapter One I will further elaborate these points. This chapter aims to introduce the theme of the book, to sketch its social relevance -- the motivation for writing this book -- and ultimately to define the exact problem area. Section 1.2 considers the real estate market as a special type of market, with particular attention paid to aspects that are related to the typical organisational structure of this market. Subsequently, section 1.3 will cover a number of spatial-economic developments that currently occur in urban areas. These developments have in common that the 'outcome' is problematic: they lead to situations that are, from a social point of view, unwanted; they harm certain groups in the society; they cause negative side-effects, etc. Finally, based on the discussion in the previous paragraphs, section 1.4 will define the problem tackled by the study and formulate the research questions.

1.2. The Real Estate Market: a Special Type of Market

A way to extend our knowledge of *urban dynamics* is to concentrate on actual land and building development processes and to analyse the strategies of the groups of actors that are involved in property development. In this respect, the *organisation of the property development industry*, the *rules, ownership rights* and the *institutional relations* between the developers, financial institutions, real estate investment companies, building construction companies, real estate agents, etc. have to be investigated. This branch of industry is interesting apart from its academic attractions; several reasons are on hand which plead for more attention. A better understanding of the functioning of urban land and property markets (1) will contribute to a more effective government policy with respect to urbanisation processes, (2) will make up a better basis for financial spending with respect to land and property by both the public and the private sector, and (3) will help to improve the quality of the built environment -- or at least recognise that improving this quality should be an issue in urban politics.

In general, urban spatial-economic policy -- either by local or national governments -- is extremely influential in shaping urban spatial (re-)structuring processes because of the powerful instruments that governments have at their disposal. In this case, the effectiveness of urban policy obviously improves when sufficient knowledge of the issues to which this policy is directed can be obtained.[4]

Urban development and redevelopment is 'big business' and it involves a substantial amount of money.[5] According to Van Gool *et al.* (1993), the replacement value of the built environment in the Netherlands, leaving aside uncultivated land, can be estimated at Dfl.

---

4   In Part IV of this book I will pay attention to the efficiency of the Dutch property system and its impact on spatial restructuring processes.

5   For example, in 1988 half of new capital formation in the Netherlands were in land and property (see Brouwer, 1990).

1650 billion in 1991.[6] Compared to the total national debt in the Netherlands of Dfl. 403 billion and the total value of the Stock Exchanges of all Dutch limited liability companies of Dfl. 224 billion in 1991 (see also Van Gool *et al.*, 1993), this is a high figure.

Local authorities, the national government, private property developers and financiers benefit from minimalising the risks related to property development (risks concern, for instance, the future returns from a certain project). Again, a better understanding of the property development process will certainly be of help in this respect. Finally, and perhaps the most important argument for studying the property development process, is that the production of space, in the form of both buildings and sites, ultimately determines the quality of the built environment. In this respect, it is important to be able to predict whether property development will bring us a desired quality of the built environment. Elsewhere, I have argued that the quality of commercial property in the Netherlands is, in an international context, rather poor -- due to relatively low office rents and commercial property values (Van der Krabben, 1993a).

The functioning of the real estate market in Dutch cities is a relatively unknown field of research.[7] We do know that in an international context substantial differences exist with respect to the way real estate markets function. It is also clear that all sectors of the real estate market -- the markets for dwellings, office buildings, buildings for the manufacturing industry, retail property, hotels and recreational projects -- operate according to their own unique dynamics. But do we really understand these differences?

In Great Britain and the US much more attention is paid to the mechanisms underlying real estate development as compared to the Netherlands. This attention in Great Britain and the US -- but in other countries as well -- has only recently led to attempts to *theorise* the functioning of real estate markets, viz. the property development process. I will argue in the next chapter that a clear distinction should be made between theoretical approaches to property market functioning that explain property development taking the price mechanism as a starting point -- *property prices* and *rent levels* are explained in the first place -- and an approach that takes institutional relations underlying market processes as a starting point -- the *institutional organisation of the market* and its impact on development processes are explained in the first place.

These two approaches do not, in fact, conflict, but, rather, can complement each other. This implies, among other things, that a theoretical explanation of property prices that includes *institutional factors* in the analysis -- belonging to the first type of analysis -- should be distinguished from a theoretical explanation of the institutional organisation of the real estate market, including its dynamics and spatial variations -- the second type of analysis. The former takes the institutional context as given in its explanation of prices; the latter explicitly explains the relation between (changes in) the institutional context and urban development. For instance, under the first approach the price mechanism on the office market -- the development of office rents -- may be studied. A plausible conclusion may be that the imperfect working of the real estate market blocks a smooth functioning of market

---

6   In May 1995 £1 equals Dfl. 2.47.

7   However, in recent years a number of interesting studies have changed this situation; among them are a number of PhD-theses: Janssen (1992), De Wit (1993), Lie (1994), Grootendorst (1994), Brouwer (1994).

processes on commercial property markets -- the price mechanism does not properly regulate the supply; high vacancy rates may be the result. The second approach explores why the development industry produces too much office space -- this may be due, for instance, to the imperfect organisation of the development industry (e.g. poor institutional relations within a locality), information problems for the developers, uncertainty because of opportunistic behaviour of the demanders, etc.

In my opinion, these two approaches are fundamentally different, each leading to specific insights in urban development, but not necessarily conflicting. Chapters Two and Three elaborate this point and argue that the second approach -- the institutional one -- can add valuable insight to our understanding of urban development. In neo-classical models, belonging to the first approach, institutional matters are either neglected or taken as given. Institutional models explicitly analyse the institutional organisation of the market in order to explain real estate development processes.

Anticipating the discussion in Chapter Two, my study aims, basically, to explain the link between the institutional organisation of real estate markets, the outcome of real estate market processes and the spatial-economic restructuring of urban areas. In order to achieve this goal I will use the concepts of institutional economic theory to interpret the institutional organisation of the real estate market and the differences with respect to this organisation, as well as to explain institutional change.

1.3.   The Malfunctioning of the Urban Real Estate Market: Empirical Evidence

From research carried out in Great Britain we know that the smooth functioning of the real estate market in most cities is impeded by different kinds of supply-side constraints, most commonly the failure to supply a sufficient amount of building land.[8] Most authors seem to agree on the imperfect nature of urban real estate markets. However, they vary in their view of what might be the significance of the malfunctioning of these markets. Is it an expression of the market being temporarily out of equilibrium or is it a problem that is structural to the functioning of real estate markets?

The starting point for the investigation of property development processes in Dutch cities is that problematic situations are certainly common to urban real estate markets. I leave aside whether these problematic situations are to be considered as market failures or not. I prefer to call them socially unwanted aspects of real estate development processes.

The concept of market failure is misleading because of the meaning that is ascribed to this perception in neo-classical economics. For, using this concept supposes in the first place that a perfect market should always be preferred above situations in which the market is by definition not perfect, in the second place that it should always be possible to make a distinction between optimal and non-optimal situations, and in the third place that problematic situations are only *recognized* as such, when they fit in this restricted definition of 'failure.' Instead, I assume that socially unwanted situations may occur in all kinds of

---

[8]   See, for instance, several studies by Adams (*et al.*, 1988; with May, 1991; 1991, *et al.*, 1992; *et al.*, 1993). I will discuss this and other work related to this issue in Chapter Two.

markets, be they perfect or not. It is much more interesting to analyse and explain these situations, taking them as the starting point of analysis. Vice versa, imperfect market conditions may result in more acceptable outcomes of market processes than would be the case under perfect market conditions. Therefore, an analysis of real estate market functioning in terms of imperfections and failures is in the context of the present study not useful.

Next to a discussion of the nature of these socially unwanted aspects of real estate development processes -- be they temporary or structural -- it is also interesting to analyse when and where they can be found. Moreover, it is important to find out whether different types of social problems can be distinguished, how they can be identified, and how they "structure" urban development and urban economic growth.

Several examples are on hand that show that these social problems are, undeniably, not an unknown phenomenon to the Dutch real estate market.[9]

(1) the present high vacancy rates on the office market, which may cause difficulties for the owners of vacant buildings and which is considered as socially undesirable (because vacant buildings occupy locations that cannot be used for alternative purposes);

(2) the failure to supply a sufficient amount of building land for the development of new residential property (municipalities make no use of the available government money to build new dwellings, because there is not enough land to build on), blocking new developments;

(3) the recent break-off of the development of the Y-bank project in Amsterdam; a large amount of office space, in combination with new dwellings, shops, hotels and cultural buildings has not been developed, because the investors have withdrawn from the project. This means, among other things, that a substantial amount of government money has been wasted during the preparation period. Reasons for this break off are the 'sudden' reduction of demand for office space, and perhaps the complexity of the project. The Y-bank project is a large-scale development, involving among other things a large group of participants in both the preparation and development phase. It is conceivable that this complexity obstructed optimal collaboration of the participants -- that is, institutional relations may have been weak!

(4) some of the Dutch financial institutions and the real estate investment companies made enormous losses on their real estate assets in recent years. Scandinavian investors who entered the Dutch commercial property market in the late 1980s even made bigger losses. Apparently, it is difficult to estimate the need for future property development. This may deter other potential investors. This issue directs attention to the significance of the concept of uncertainty on real estate markets;

(5) the property development industry complains that in the four large cities -- Amsterdam, Rotterdam, The Hague and Utrecht -- office development is far too decentralized. As a result, international top locations are missing and high returns are not feasible:

---

9 See also Bos *et al.* (1987) on failures of the Dutch planning system. This study concentrates on a number of principles underlying the Dutch planning system, such as government policy with respect to office locations, new industrial business parks, parking problems in inner cities, the spatial order of shopping centres and housing. Contrary to the concept of social problems in the present study, in Bos *et al.* the starting point is the government and not the market. The study focuses particularly on public-sector policy failures.

since the returns on property investments are low, land prices stay low as well. Because for local governments land development costs are relatively high, in many cases redevelopment of inner-city areas can only take place if subsidized by the central government;

(6) in the 1980s a large amount of commercial property was developed near motorways. Because of changed government policy with respect to the location of working places, commercial property may no longer be developed on these locations (instead, the government now encourages commercial property development near public transport junctions). However, the already developed locations will be in use for many years, being jointly responsible for an extra load on the overburdened Dutch transport system;

(7) in many cities, the older industrial areas struggle with the consequences of technical obsolescence. Furthermore, the location of these business sites may no longer be optimal from an economic point of view. As such these areas have become less attractive for companies. The areas become run-down and either a large amount of government money is needed to revitalise them, or the areas are not improved, thus being responsible for a degradation of the quality of the built environment;

(8) the special spatial characteristics of the Dutch property market are responsible for the fact that office rents and property values are -- in an international context -- low and stable. Two different problems are related to this. On the one hand, though the price mechanism may function smoothly, the outcome may nevertheless be unfavourable. In some cities the demand for office space exceeds the supply of office space, but new developments do not take place because development costs exceed property values. In this case we would expect a rise in office rents. However, this does not happen, because of an oversupply of building land and office buildings due to the tough competition between municipalities. On the other hand, low property values necessarily go hand in hand with (relatively) cheap building construction. Because property values are low and not rising, there is a limit to the building costs. As a result, the quality of the built environment is in danger. In an earlier paper I investigated this phenomenon (Van der Krabben, 1993b). The results of the analysis support this hypothesis.

(9) the valuation of land and property is often problematic because it involves an assessment of future returns that are yet unknown, and because the real estate market is characteristically diversified. Therefore, in some situations it is difficult to fix the right market price. This may result, for instance, in unnecessary government subsidies, when municipalities charge land prices that do not cover the costs of (re)developing the land;

(10) Some of the recently developed business parks in various cities have been only partly developed, due to the current economic recession. That is, not all building sites may have been sold, being responsible for capital losses for municipalities. Furthermore, these business parks face the risk of becoming less attractive, since a considerable part of them is undeveloped;

(11) Schiphol Airport in Amsterdam has become one of the most attractive locations as a place of business for internationally operating firms in the Netherlands. This brings in the possibility of monopoly landownership, as is indeed the case at this moment. Land speculation by a private developer blocks new developments.

This should not be considered as a complete enumeration of social problems related to real estate market functioning in the Netherlands. Alternative examples could easily be added. However, it gives an indication of what might -- and does -- go wrong on real estate markets. At the end of the book, in Chapter Ten, I will come back to these examples. The starting point taken in this study is that urban real estate markets are characterised by various types of social problems. There are mismatches between demand and supply, institutional relations between the actors who take part in the development industry are problematic, and market processes cause negative side-effects. These social problems -- be they structural or incidental -- deserve our attention. From a policy viewpoint we would like to be able to prevent these situations from happening; from an academic viewpoint we would like to improve our knowledge of the reasons underlying these social problems. In this study I choose to develop an institutional approach to explain the complicated market processes that are characteristic to urban real estate markets.

The latter point is the subject of the next chapter. To be able to interpret the above-mentioned problematic situations on real estate markets, I will argue in Chapter Two that the (imperfect) functioning of the price mechanism is only one of the explanatory variables. I believe that property development processes -- complicated as they are -- cannot be simply *embraced* within a simple set of land rent postulates.[10] Also important are institutional factors -- notably the organisation of the development industry, ownership rights, the planning system and government intervention on land and property markets. Neo-classical theory does not deem these facts unimportant, but rather takes these issues as given. For one thing, neo-classical theory pays less attention to the meaning of institutional changes. Moreover, in the present study the *strategies of the agents* are problematised; opportunistic behaviour of some of them, uncertainty and information problems, expectations and different kind of social norms like trust and habits influence them under certain conditions. It should be understood clearly that the present study's objective is not to reject neo-classical explanations of real estate development, but to find out what an institutional approach to these issues could contribute to what we already know.

Numerous studies of property development have shown the relevance of institutional factors to property development processes. However, I feel that most of these studies lack a theoretical framework to explain the meaning of the institutional context. *Institutional Economics* offers such a framework. In Chapter Five I will develop a framework for analysis, based on institutional economic theory, meant to interpret the impact of (changes and variations in) the institutional organisation of the real estate market on property development processes. My aim is to explain how the institutional context influences the functioning of urban property markets and what the significance is of both temporal and spatial variation in the institutional context.

1.4. Definition of the Problem Area and Research Questions

Having explained the various motivations that underlie this study, I will now provide a definition of the problem which will then be further explored -- both theoretically and

---

10 See Ball and Harloe (1993) on this point. They argue that mainstream neo-classical urban economics focusses one-sidedly on the effects of the (imperfect) functioning of the price mechanism in analysing property development processes.

empirically -- in Chapter Two. This book aims to investigate the processes that underlie the functioning of urban real estate markets in general and the Dutch urban real estate market in particular. An attempt will be made to explain why these property development processes are changing over time, why they are different in each sector of the urban property market, why they vary between locations both within a city and between different cities, and why -- in an international context -- urban property market functioning diverges so greatly. I intend to provide both theoretical explanations and empirical evidence for the hypothesis that, apart from the nature of demand and supply in a local real estate market, the institutional organisation of that market plays a significant role with respect to the outcome of real estate market processes. Therefore, I will particularly focus on the influence of the institutional organisation of the market on real estate development. Special attention will be given to situations in which the outcome of development processes is felt to be socially undesirable. Differences in the institutional organisation of the real estate market, including, particularly, the organisation of the development industry, the strategies of the 'property developers' and the institutional relations between the actors that are involved in this industry, property ownership, (active) government intervention and regulation are believed to be vital parameters with respect to the explanations for these variations.

Furthermore, I aim to study the way in which institutional-economic theory can be applied to a study of urban real estate market functioning. The supposition that is at the basis of this choice for institutional-economic theory is that the dynamic character of urban land and property markets, the meaning of institutional relations and institutional change, and the relevance of the strategies and decisions of the various groups of agents that are involved in property development should be studied explicitly; institutional-economic theory may contribute to a better understanding of them.

The framework for analysis, based on institutional-economic theory, will be used to analyse the functioning of the housing market in the Netherlands. The production of new dwellings, roughly between 1970 and 1995, will be related to, among other things, the organisational structure of the real estate development industry, government intervention, the functioning of the second-hand owner-occupied housing market, trends in production costs, development gains and the profitability of speculative housing development, and the spatial structure of Dutch cities. I will investigate the relation between the 'structure of house building provision' that is typical to the Dutch situation and (the outcome of) development processes on the housing market. With respect to housing production I refer to, among other things, the amount, type, quality and location of new dwellings, the ownership of the new dwellings, the building costs and the profitability of speculative housing development. Moreover, I will analyse the institutional changes that have taken place on the Dutch housing market and the sources of these institutional changes. Thus, it will be possible to address a number of issues that are at present subject of both political and academic debates of the housing market. Of note will be the following: the supposed crisis in housing production, the increasing costs of house building construction, the consequences of the restructuring of government intervention in the housing market, the fluctuations in the profitability of speculative housing development and the sharp price increases on the owner-occupied housing market.

The next step in the analysis is a study of the efficacy and efficiency of national property systems. This study focuses especially on the nature of the Dutch property system and its impact on real estate development processes. Finally, I will investigate the relation between real estate development processes and the urban economy. The ultimate objective is then to link this issue to a discussion of public-sector urban-economic regeneration policies (with special attention to so-called property-led urban regeneration).

Summarising, the thesis' problem definition reads as follows:

In what sense is the functioning of urban real estate markets influenced by the institutional organisation of the market, what are the effects for the outcome of urban spatial-economic development processes, and what kind of changes have occurred with respect to the nexus of institutions and institutional relations that structure urban real estate markets?

This leads to a number of research questions that serve to guide the research. First, which factors influence the functioning of real estate markets? More specifically, what is the significance of, respectively, the nature of demand and supply and the institutional organisation of the real estate market for urban development?

Second, which theoretical explanations are given by standard urban-economic theories with respect to the transformation of the built environment? What are the shortcomings of these theoretical concepts and what are their strengths?

Third, is it possible to operationalise institutional-economic theory into a framework for analysis of urban development processes? Can we explain, on the one hand, both temporal and spatial variation in the institutional organisation of local and/or national real estate markets, and on the other hand the impact of these variations on the outcome of real estate development processes?

Fourth, with respect to the Dutch housing market, what kind of institutional changes have taken place as far as they are relevant to real estate development processes and what are the sources of these changes?

Fifth, again with respect to the Dutch housing market, in what sense does the institutional organisation of the Dutch real estate market differ from other systems of housing provision, and what are the consequences of these differences?

Sixth, how can we assess the efficacy and efficiency of national property systems and how efficient is the Dutch property system?

Seventh, what kind of relations exist between real estate development and the urban economy and how can the public sector influence these relations and intervene in real estate development processes?

Finally, what are the chances of so-called property-led urban regeneration policies, and which conditions must be met to guarantee the success of these public-sector policies?

2 MISSING LINKS BETWEEN URBAN ECONOMIC THEORY AND PROPERTY DEVELOPMENT PROCESSES

2.1. International Differences with Respect to Property Development

In an international context substantial differences can be observed with respect to the way property development takes place. The following examples confirm this assertion. First, the locational pattern of the retail trade in the Netherlands is remarkably different from, for instance, that in Great Britain, France, Belgium and Germany. In the Netherlands, retail trade is almost completely concentrated in inner-city areas and, in addition to this, in some shopping subcentres in the neighbourhoods. Shopping centres on peripheral locations on the urban fringe, which are characteristic of the retail structure in many West-European countries, are missing.

Second, both the price-setting processes and the locational structure on the office market vary considerably in West-European countries. Confining ourselves again to the situation in the Netherlands, we note relatively low office rents in Dutch cities -- even on top locations in the four large cities Amsterdam, Rotterdam, The Hague and Utrecht, only small variations in office rents between top locations and peripheral locations, a relatively low quality of office buildings and a spreading of office buildings over many locations within cities, instead of a concentration on a few locations, as is characteristic of most West-European countries.[11] In the Netherlands, international top locations, measured from the level of office rents, the amount of office space, and the number of international firms, are said to be missing.[12]

Third, in contrast with the situation in, for instance, Great Britain, in the Netherlands the property-development industry shows hardly any interest in investing in new buildings for the manufacturing industry, let alone that they should build speculatively for this market. As a result, in the Netherlands the industrial building stock is almost entirely 'produced' by industrial companies building for their own use (of course, they contract building companies for the building activities, but it is not possible for them to rent buildings). Furthermore, the industrial building stock in the Netherlands is far less obsolete compared to the building stock in Great Britain. Studies in Great Britain have shown that the obsolete industrial building stock acts as a constraint to economic growth (Fothergill *et al.*, 1987); in the Netherlands this problem hardly occurs.

Fourth, it is remarkable that in the Dutch housing market new dwellings are usually developed in large quantities by property developers, while in other countries -- Germany and Belgium are perhaps the extreme examples in this respect -- many more owners build their own dwellings in more or less isolated locations. The consequences for urban spatial structures may be far more drastic than generally seems to be assumed -- at least when we review the lack of attention for this phenomenon in the international literature on urban dynamics. Dutch cities are characterized by large, uniform, but high-quality new expansions; in Germany and Belgium, for instance, these are not developed in such large quantities.

---

11 See Brouwer (1989, 1994) on the spatial structure of the Dutch office market.

12 See Lie and Bongenaar (1990) on the issue of 'top locations' in the Netherlands.

It is not coincidental that some examples of international differences in all sectors of the urban property market are mentioned here. By providing these examples, I intend to show that variations in real estate development are not exceptions, but rather *a sine qua non* to urban development processes in an international context. It is not difficult at all to find more striking dissimilarities in urban-property-market functioning in West-European countries and, even to a larger extent, between West- and East-European and Third World countries (of which we know much less). These variations in the outcome of development processes cannot fully be understood within of the concept of optimal allocation that is central to standard neo-classical models of urban development. This concept implies that the demand of firms, institutions and households for buildings is met by supply and that market mechanisms lead to an equilibrium in which all these firms, institutions and households, given their budgets and their preferences, are situated on an optimal location in a wished for building.[13] This would imply that the above-listed international variations in urban development processes are the result of differences in budget constraints and preferences of the actors that are looking for new locations and new buildings, and of differences in geography and history. Perhaps, in some cases budgets and preferences *are* different, but it is unlikely that they differ on such a large scale as is shown in the above examples. Surely, many neo-classical studies of urban development are concerned with supply-side constraints on the production of land and property and on the way public regulation of property supply affects land and property prices (see for instance Evans, 1987; Needham, 1981, 1992; Needham and Lie, 1993; and the discussion of them in Chapter Three), but these studies do not take account of several aspects of property development that are, in my view, vital to an understanding of development processes. For instance, according to Healey, neo-classical models do not recognise the relevance to urban property development of existing tenure patterns, strategies of agents based on irrational behaviour (i.e. non-maximising strategies-EvdK), environmental quality, and inefficient institutional relations in the development industry inherited from the past (Healey, 1992: p. 24,25). To these points it can be added that neo-classical models in general take the institutional context -- acting as a 'constraint' -- as given, while I consider it important, actually, to study the dynamic character of the institutional organisation of the real estate market.

The fact that the spatial dispersal of the retail trade in the Netherlands is so different from the structure in the other countries mentioned is more likely due to the more influential municipal power in the Netherlands. Dutch municipalities prohibit new retail developments on peripheral locations because they want to protect the economic continuity of the inner-city shopping areas. Perhaps municipalities in other countries would like to do the same, but they do not have the same influential set of instruments.

Furthermore, the argument that price-setting processes on urban property markets are only a matter of demand and supply is hard to defend. For instance, the way office rents evolve is a much more complicated process than is sometimes assumed in basic neo-classical models. Low office rents in Dutch cities are closely related to the lack of scarcity that is characteristic to urban land markets. Municipalities supply almost all building land and consider it as their task to care for an invariably sufficient amount of available building plots

---

13 Deliberately, to make clear the differences between neo-classical and institutional theory, I have referred to *standard* neo-classical models. Below I will pay attention to more advanced neo-classical models that are more realistic with respect to the meaning of the neo-classical assumptions.

(see Needham, 1992). This issue focuses our attention to the different kinds of rationality that may underlie the strategies of actors. Moreover, the rationality of human behaviour may be limited because of information problems (see Chapter Four and Five). The result of all this is that property developers and financial institutions are now complaining that development gains on office markets are too small (as a consequence of the lack of scarcity). At the same time, the national government complains that urban redevelopment plans can only be carried out heavily subsidised, because the revenues from land sales by municipalities are disappointing. Both market parties and the national government believe that the problems can be solved by creating an artificial scarcity on urban land markets -- although they seem to differ in their view as to whether the government is indeed able to create this scarcity.

The influence of public regulation on office rents can be explained in a neo-classical model.[14] I do not question the value of such a model for an understanding of property development processes. However, the neo-classical approach does not aim to explain the *institutional change* that underlies the change in government policy on this point -- it takes the institutional change as a starting point of the analysis. Furthermore, the consequences of this change for, e.g., the organisational structure of the development industry and their strategies is not *problematised* in neo-classical models. Scarcity on the land market would mean, for instance, increasing land rents, making -- in turn -- land development more profitable. In such a case, land development may become attractive to private companies. This would imply a considerable change in the organisation of the development industry, which is not considered in the neo-classical model.

The above is an outstanding example of a situation in which market parties try to influence demand and supply without making use of market processes: they try to change *the rules* that are part of the institutional structure.[15]

Another issue that deserves our attention is the significance of institutional relations within the development industry for real estate development. Healey has shown that the kind of institutional relations within the development industry in a region certainly matter (Healey; 1993b).[16] She holds that many sources of variation in regional property markets can be found:

'One dimension is clearly the nature of demand in the local economy. However, this itself is multidimensional, with variations not merely between sectors (industrial, commercial, retail) but between segments (small, local firms seeking new premises for expansion;

---

14 For applying such a model to the situation in the Netherlands, see Needham and Lie (1993) and the discussion of this paper in Chapter Three.

15 It must be noted that, in this case, they lobbied successfully. The content of the national planning report (the VINEX report) has been changed according to their wishes: the creation of a few international top locations for office developments is now official government policy. Note, however, that the shifts in national government policy were mainly due to transport and environmental problems and not really the result of the property industry's complaints.

16 See also Scott and Storper (1992); they claim that a 'technological-institutional system exists, which can differ between regions and countries'.

outside companies seeking to locate in the region etc), in interest in land (investors, occupiers), and in scale of comparison (within a neighbourhood, the region, the nation, Europe, the world)' (Healey, 1993: p. 1).

The nature of demand affects the way land and buildings are treated (for example, an investment orientation to land and property or an interest primarily in the use value of a site).

'A second dimension relates to the supply of sites and properties. This varies with the particular geography and history of places' (ibid.: p. 2).

This refers to the stock of sites and properties in a region -- their location, configuration, physical conditions and ownership. Healey concludes from this that 'a critical dimension of regional property market variation is therefore the overall state of the balances between supply and demand in all the different property market segments' (*ibid.*: p. 2). However, she mentions a third dimension of variation: the institutional relations of land and property markets.

'The significance of this institutional dimension is particularly clear in land and property development markets. In markets with weak demand and few transactions, it is these relations which become critical in bringing sites and projects forward. These in turn impact on patterns of value and transaction levels in local markets overall. These institutional relations include the mix and networks of property market interests (landowners, developers, financiers, consultants), the form of public policy towards development promotion (primarily urban policy since the 1960s), and the form of development regulation (ie: planning policy). (ibid.: p. 2).

This introduction shows that we need an approacht to real estate development processes that particularly focusses on "institutional matters". The present chapter's objective is to further explore the theoretical perspective of my study. Moreover, I will review the state of the art in real estate studies, in order to outline the current debate to which the present study aims to contribute.

The remaining part of this chapter will discuss the relation between real estate development processes and the (re-)structuring of urban areas. This relation is especially manifest when we consider supply-side constraints on urban real estate markets that obstruct the smooth functioning of the urban economy. Moreover, the neglect of these links in urban economic theory will be covered. Subsequently, I will refer to other work mentioning the neglect of the provision of the built environment (section 2.2). Then, I will briefly address the links between the urban economy and property development processes (section 2.3). In section 2.4 the missing links between urban economic theory and property development are considered in greater detail. Furthermore, clues for analysis of the supposed relations between real estate development and urban economic growth are presented. Traditional theoretical explanations for the malfunctioning of urban real estate markets, and their limited relevance for the interpretation of social problems that are related to real estate development processes are the subject of section 2.5. Finally, section 2.6 will summarise the main findings of Chapter Two and point out in which direction the study will further develop.

2.2. The Provision of the Built Environment

The field of urban studies encompasses of course more than merely the standard neo-classical models that were mentioned in the introductionary section of this chapter. Urban economic studies have in common that they analyse the urban spatial structure and the way this structure is shaped by economic processes. The urban spatial structure is, logically, the outcome of processes taking place on the urban land and property market. However -- and this is brought to attention in particular by Ball (1986) and Healey and Barrett (1990) -- the processes through which these changes in urban spatial structures have been accomplished have been almost completely neglected in the international literature on urbanisation and urban development. Ball has argued that 'the built environment in urban theories is generally treated as a passive backdrop to other social processes' (Ball, 1986, p. 447). According to Ball, the neglect of the *provision of the built environment* has arisen because urban theories usually view the built environment in functionalist terms, with emphasis placed on the *uses* to which built structures are put.[17] He considers this not only as a shortcoming in empirical urban studies, but also as a fundamental theoretical weakness as well. In his view, any urban theory ignoring the production of the built environment is unable to explain urban development properly. To fill this gap in urban theory, Ball suggests identifiying different *structures of building provision* and focussing on the social relations within these structures.[18] Empirical research should be directed to the analysis of these structures of building provision. Healey and Barrett observe the same shortcoming in urban theory:

> *'The role of landownership, the organisation of the construction industry, the nature of the finance invested in urban development and the significance of intermediaries, from developers to property consultants, lie hidden or are given little more than a passing reference in many historical accounts of urban development (...)' (Healey and Barrett, 1990, p. 89).*

Elsewhere we have argued that in traditional urban economic theory -- characterised by a search for explanations for urban dynamics -- only a one-way relationship between economic and spatial structures is recognised; urban spatial structures are explained with economic arguments (Van der Krabben and Lambooy, 1994).[19] The attention that is given in urban economic literature to the impact of economic processes on the spatial structure has resulted

---

17   Ball has defined the provision of the built environment as 'the production, exchange, distribution and use of a built structure. The actors involved may be landowners, developers, building firms, building workers, financiers, building owners and final users' (Ball, 1986, p. 455). I slightly extent this concept by adding the *maintenance of a built structure* to this definition.

18   Ball defines these structures of building provision as follows: 'the concept highlights the existence of specific sets of historically specific and country-specific social relations involved in the creation and use of particular types of buildings' (Ball, 1986: p. 448).

19   I distinguish three mainstreams in urban economic theory: neo-classical theory, Marxist approaches and institutional theory; see also Bassett and Short (1980), Lake (1983), Healey and Barrett (1990), Bovaird (1993).

in an overemphasis on the demand side of the urban system: the locational preferences of firms, institutions and households are held responsible for urban development. It seems to be commonly assumed that the supply of land and property adjusts to the demand side and that the urban property market -- in which the provision of the built environment takes place -- functions perfectly as a go-between. Consequently, the property-development process is not considered as a theoretical problem area.

As was emphasised in Chapter One, one of the starting points in this study -- similar to both Ball's and Healey and Barrett's lines of argument -- is that in many cases the dynamics of urban real estate markets either directly or indirectly influence the performance of urban economies. For that reason, we should study the role of the real estate sector in urban spatial-economic restructuring processes.

Healey and Barrett's article has been followed by a remarkable and still-growing amount of contributions to this field of research (see Section 2.4 on this point).[20] However this may be true in the British context, in an international context the property-development process has attracted less attention, especially when we consider theoretical approaches.[21] (With this statement I pass over, for the moment, numerous studies of the evolvement of property prices and rent levels. Moreover, this statement refers to *theoretical explanations* and leaves aside so-called market research.)

The motivation to undertake this research is strengthened by Healey and Barrett's call to problematise the property-development process and to theorise the relations between the groups of actors that are involved in this process. Their call has been accompanied by a research agenda, consisting of four themes of inquiry which need attention in research:

(1) The review of the changing forms of capital flow into and out of the built environment, requires an understanding of the diverse sources of capital, the different ways capital can be invested in property and the place of property in the investment strategies of different kinds of firm.

(2) The changing composition and strategies of the firms involved in the development and redevelopment of the built environment need to be explored. The emphasis would be on the way changing strategies reconstitute the interests firms have in land, property and property redevelopment and the way these interests find reflection in the negotiative practises through which action is undertaken.

(3) The various ways in which the state impinges on these changing practices, in relation to the tools of intervention employed, the way in which these affect the demand for space, the rules within which individual firms develop their strategies, and the forms

---

20   The same goes for Ball's article (Ball, 1986). Contributions to this field of research include Ball (1988), Ball and Harloe (1993), Forrest *et al.* (1990; mentioned in Ball and Harloe), Pryke (1994), Duncan (1989), Harloe *et al.* (1992), Healey and Nabarro (1990), Healey (1991a,b; 1992a; *et al.*, 1992; 1993a,b; 1994), Hooper (1992), Morgan (1990), Morrison (1992), Clark and Gullberg (1991), Harding (1992).

21   Numerous exceptions can be found, but these mainly concern the functioning of real estate markets in a few 'global cities' (London, Tokyo, New York). I referred to these studies in Chapter One. Besides, a major research project by Dieterich, Williams and Wood (eds.) (1993) that is now underway and that describes the functioning of land and property markets in six West-European countries tries to fill this gap in research.

of development processes, should be examined.
(4) Research must be directed to an assessment of the implication of the above processes for local economies in terms of capital flows, labour market demand and supply, building materials and land, the impact on land and property values, and the implications of changes for these, the resultant social, economic and environmental externality costs and benefits within local economies and the distribution of these. (Healey and Barrett, 1990: p. 98-99)

This agenda has been repeated in Healey (1992) and then is followed by a number of issues that are relevant to these themes:

(1) The significance of spatial variation: in land and property markets, development activity, in institutional relations, and the potential and actual effects of urban policy (...);
(2) The significance of temporal variation, and specifically the impact of the cyclicality of property development activity (...);
(3) The interplay between changes in land and property markets, development industry relationships, and the user and investor needs and demands of the changing city (...);
(4) The distribution of costs and benefits from development activity (...);
(5) The interplay of the specific history and geography of particular urban regions, and the efforts of locally based initiatives, the localizing forces, and the globalizing tendencies of corporate conglomerates and oligopolistic relations, international capital flows and investment patterns, and national and supranational political initiatives (Healey, 1992: p. 10,11).

These issues have already been quite extensively investigated for English cities (see particularly Healey *et al.* (eds.), 1992). In the present study, the themes and issues that are described above will serve as a guideline for research. I will refer to them both in setting up an operational theory of real estate development in Chapter Five, as well as in the case study of the Dutch housing market in Chapters Six, Seven and Eight. In short, I submit that we need more insight into how urban spatial structures are actually changed: the way the supply of land and buildings comes forward has been insufficiently explored and explained. Moreover, the way the supply-side responds to demand still seems to be a relatively unknown field of research. For that reason, I choose to concentrate on the supply side of urban land and property markets.

2.3.   Land and Property Development and the Urban Economy

The *property development process* refers to the production, exchange, distribution and maintenance of land and buildings. It may be considered as the production and consumption of the built environment. Various agents are involved -- land owners, developers, real estate agents, building construction firms, consultants, local planning authorities, municipal development companies, politicians, community groups.

The lack of academic interest in land and property development is regrettable for several reasons. Healey and Barrett (1990) argue the following:

'(...) the way in which land and property are themselves produced and consumed enters into the processes of economic production and consumption. Knowledge of the processes through which the built environment is produced and used, and in particular the processes of land and property development, is thus critical to our understanding of urban development and our attempts at managing urban development processes.' (Healey and Barrett, 1990, p. 90).

In another paper Healey holds that property development is increasingly tied into wider economic and political relations, being in part a reflection of the impact of global economic relations on the *demand* for land and property, but also as a result of changes that have taken place with respect to the supply of property, notably the increasing role of real estate as a store of capital and the globalisation of the financial sector in recent years:

'Property development is thus increasingly driven by investment criteria linked to international financial considerations. (...) There are thus two significant and related tendencies affecting property development in the contemporary period, those of globalisation of formerly highly localised relations of production and consumption, and, carried forward by this, a transformation of relations from a demand-led use-value orientation to an investment-led orientation.' (Healey, 1992, p. 1,2).[22]

These tendencies, and their impact on property development, reinforce the need to study thoroughly the institutional relations between the groups of actors involved in the property development process. Especially in Great Britain and the US the impact of globalisation processes concerning the financial sector, and the influence of investment demand by financial institutions on property market functioning has been widely recognised and empirically investigated.[23] In the Netherlands, much less attention is paid to the meaning of these tendencies in the context of Dutch cities.[24] In part, this may result from the fact that these tendencies do not occur, or, at least, are of less significance, in Dutch cities. This might be true, but it does not justify omitting the study of the possible impact of these processes. Besides, if globalisation processes are indeed missing, it would be interesting to investigate why these processes do not occur in Dutch cities.

As a result, in the Netherlands few attempts have been made to provide theoretical explanations of the results of empirical property research -- to a large extent carried out by municipalities, consultancies, and academics.[25] It is in the first place the task of academics to

---

22   See also American literature on this point: e.g. Sassen (1991), Fainstein (1993), Beauregard (1991).

23   See Harvey (1982, 1985), Fainstein *et al.* (1986), Pryke (1991), Clark and Gullberg (1991), Berry and Huxley (1992), Beauregard (1991), Berry *et al.* (1993), Corbridge *et al.* (1994).

24   See, for instance, Thrift (1994) on the significance of globalisation processes in Dutch cities.

25   See Healey and Barrett (1990) on this point; they use a similar line of argument reflecting the situation in Great Britain. Needham and Lie (1993) also argue in this direction.

provide a theoretical framework to interpret these results. However, until recently, academics have paid remarkably little attention to the processes underlying the production of land and buildings.[26]

Perhaps, the most convincing way to emphasise the significance of property development processes to urban economies is to demonstrate the interconnectedness between property development and urban economic development. Previously, we have hypothesised the links between regional economic growth and property development processes (Boekema and Van der Krabben, 1992; Van der Krabben and Boekema, 1994). These hypotheses are based on a study of economic growth and property development in 'Noordoost Brabant,' a region in the Southeast of the Netherlands (Van der Krabben, 1992). The substantial increase in the number of migrations of firms in this region between 1986 and 1991 has brought about an increase in activity on the real estate market: a growth of transactions on the market for *second-hand buildings* and an increase of new building developments (because not all remaining buildings are suitable for renewed occupancy). The latter development has strengthened by the growth of the economy. The opposite is also true: that the special characteristics of real estate markets influence urban economic growth in a number of ways. In some situations, real estate sector activity generates urban economic growth, while in other situations the real estate sector actually impedes urban economic growth.[27] Section 2.5 will refer to studies of supply-side constraints on land and property markets. Situations in which the internal dynamics of the real estate market act as a constraint to urban economic growth -- most commonly shortages of building land -- have received considerable attention in the urban-studies literature. Chapter Ten will investigate situations in which the real estate sector boosts urban economic growth. Property-led urban regeneration policies are meant to take advantage of increased real estate sector activity.

2.4. A Vacuum in Urban Economic Theory; Clues for Analysis

As mentioned in Section 2.2, urban economic theory can be divided into three mainstreams: neo-classical theory, Marxist approaches and institutional theory. This section does not intend to provide a full description of the premises and the structure of the conceptual models based on these theories (the models will be discussed in Chapter Three). Rather, I assert that in urban economic theory in general the provision of the built environment is not a part of the theory's study objective and, consequently, is not treated as a problem area; on the other hand, however, urban economic theory certainly offers clues for the analysis of property development processes.

---

26   In the Netherlands, only since the mid-1980s has the study of property markets acquired a formal status in academic research, by the establishment of the *Stichting voor Beleggings- en Vastgoedkunde*, University of Amsterdam.

27   See Chapter Ten for a more detailed discussion of the results of this research.

2.4.1. Basic premises of urban economic theories

In standard models based on neo-classical theory, land markets serve primarily an *allocative* function, in the sense that land should be used for its most profitable purpose.[28] Neo-classical urban economics focuses on decisions of consumers and producers within a given context.[29] Each person will seek an optimum situation to satisfy his needs, given a certain budget. How the context has evolved is no theoretical problem. Decisions of persons can affect spatial structures within the constraints of the given context. Neo-classical urban rent theory assumes that supply and demand relations structure land and property markets. Central to standard neo-classical models of the urban economy is the assumption that competition in cities leads to an equilibrium on the urban land market. On a micro scale, it centres on the decision-making behaviour of firms and consumers. Studies carried out in this field of research that contribute to an understanding of property development processes especially focus on supply-side constraints that affect land rent and property prices.[30]

Marxist urban theory holds two processes responsible for urban development. Traditional Marxist urban rent theory focuses on the struggle between landowners and other capitalists for a part of the surplus value that is generated in the production process.[31] Their strategies are based on acquiring development gains, and their relative power characterises the relation between spatial structure and urban economic development. More recent neo-Marxist approaches focus on how capital flows through the built environment.[32] According to Healey:

Harvey's analysis emphasizes the importance of finance capital, and the global relations which govern its flow between types of investment and locations in the contemporary period (...). His argument suggests that the dynamics of the development process in an urban region in the present period derive from general tendencies in financial investment, the role of an urban region within international patterns of economic competition, the effects of this on the economic and spatial structure within a region, and the role of public policy in creating and impeding investment opportunities' (Healey, 1991b: p. 234).

The third approach is that of institutional theory. Institutional theory concentrates on the conditioning of decisions by institutional arrangements, regulation and the influence of power on the functioning of markets. It focuses on the way in which different groups of actors and organisations that participate in urban development processes relate to each other

---

[28] See, for example, Wingo (1961), Alonso (1964), Muth (1969), Mills (1972), Richardson (1977) and Harrison (1977).

[29] The opinion of neo-classical economics expressed in this section may sound rather over-simplified. Please note, however, that it refers to the assumptions in basic neo-classical models. As I will show in Chapter Three, more advanced neo-classical models make use of more realistic assumptions.

[30] For instance: Needham (1981, 1992), Evans (1985, 1987), Kivell (1993), Needham and Lie (1993).

[31] See, particularly, Harvey (1973), Castells (1977), Massey and Catalano (1978).

[32] Most notably, from a theoretical perspective, Harvey (1978, 1982, 1985).

and to other sectors of the local economy and to regional, national and international financial and development interests.[33] Three main themes of enquiry are central to this approach (Bassett and Short, 1980):

(1) the identification of agents and institutions involved in urban development processes, their different goals, ideologies and relative power;
(2) the nature of interaction between these diverse agents and institutions and the kinds of constraints they impose on each other;
(3) the effect of this interaction on the development process.

The heterogeneity of the market -- both heterogeneous groups of individual actors and organisations operate on the market -- is the most important starting point. Institutional theory recognises the importance of relative power -- not only between labour and capital -- and the importance of cultural and institutional differences and the position of organisations.

Bovaird holds that 'the institutional economics' paradigm concentrates on making theories about the motivations of actors rather than taking them as given, as in neo-classical economics. 'In the production sphere, it theorises ways in which economic decisions have been made and co-ordinated, both within firms (...), between firms (in sub-contracting relationships and other networking approaches) and between the public and private sectors (in public-private partnerships, corporatist boosterism, etc.)' (Bovaird, 1993: p. 641). Institutional economics consists of a collection of subapproaches, of which the transaction cost approach (*new institutional economics*) is perhaps the most prominent one.[34] I will discuss this theory extensively in Chapter Four.

I expect that institutional economic theory best suits the purposes of the study. This theoretical concept explicitly provides explanations of *market conditions* -- that is, the nexus of institutions on a market. A similar argument has been put forward, for instance, by Chandler (1977; mentioned in Bovaird, 1993: p. 645). He argues that the equilibrating market mechanisms, assumed by the neo-classical paradigm, are largely irrelevant, since markets in most industrial countries are governed by the 'visible hand' of major corporations, not by the 'invisible hand' of market forces. However, we should be careful with such pronouncements: institutional-economic theory has not yet proven to be more successful with its explanations.

Until now, contributions in the field of institutional economics -- when applied to urban economies -- have paid attention almost exclusively to decisions of firms and the way this influences urban economies.[35] These studies analyse why firms move to other regions, they analyse the economic relations between firms in a specific region, and they investigate the

---

33   See, e.g., Healey (1991a), Lambooy (1980, 1985), Lambooy *et al.* (1982).

34   New institutional economics is based on Coase (1937) and is considerably elaborated by Williamson (Transaction Cost Economics, Williamson, 1985). Several authors have used institutional economics for explaining the functioning of urban economies -- notably, Scott (1988, 1990).

35   However, see Alexander (1992) on a transaction cost approach of the organisation of the public sector (the planning system).

factors underlying the success of a few regions that show larger economic growth than other urban regions. For instance, Scott (1988, 1990) has adapted some aspects of transaction cost economics -- the explanation of the emergence of different types of internal corporate organisation (vertical and horizontal integration) -- to, according to Bovaird, 'provide the basis for a major new theory of the spatial logic of modern capitalist production, the emergence of 'new industrial spaces'' (Bovaird, 1993: p. 644). Other studies with the same objective adopt alternative approaches within the field of institutional economic theory as theoretical framework.[36]

These studies have not integrated analyses of property development processes. However, as I have argued in Section 2.2, a number of studies have recently appeared that concentrate on institutional relationships within the property-development industry. These studies offer valuable information about the way the property-development industry is organised and the institutional relations between the actors involved with the provision of the built environment.

2.4.2. Clues for analysis

Even though researchers underestimate the implications of them processes underlying the provision of the built environment affect the functioning of urban economies, in each of the disciplines identified examples of studies of the property-development process are nevertheless on hand. These theoretical contributions must clearly be distinguished from the more general approaches in both neo-classical and Marxist tradition in which the demand for land (neo-classical models) and the struggle between landowners and other capital owners (Marxist models) are considered to be the explaining variables with respect to urban development. It is true that the literature in this field addresses the functioning of land markets, but it does not deal with the institutional relations underlying the *provision* of land and property.[37]

With regard to neo-classical models Healey and Barrett (1990) indicate that there have been some attempts to analyse land and property development processes using neo-classical concepts.[38] Authors who pay attention to property-development processes from a Marxist point of view include Ball (1983) and Harvey (1982, 1985).[39] Especially Harvey's work on

---

36   See, for instance, Amin and Thrift (1992, 1993, 1994).

37   Ball and Harloe (1992) use a similar argument. According to these authors 'such approaches (neo-classical Alonso-style models and Marxist-style urban rent theory -- EvdK) tried to embrace within a simple set of land-rent postulates many aspects of property development and urban structure' (Ball and Harloe, 1992: p. 9).

38   These include: Brown *et al.* (1981), Dowall (1984) and Lin Leung (1987). Moreover, Cheshire *et al.* (1985) have tried to assess the economic costs of the British planning system (all mentioned in Healey and Barrett, 1990). However, the most complete neo-classical explanation for property-market functioning can be found in Harvey (1992).

39   Ball's Structures of Housing Provision-concept is not necessarily an inherently neo-Marxist approach -- as the author argues himself in Ball and Harloe (1992) -- with the implication that it is useless outside this

the significance of finance capital for the built environment and on the circuits of capital (and the role of the production of the built environment within them) has received much attention.[40] Harvey provides a framework for analysis and, as Healey and Barrett note:

> *'(...) a way of identifying how the dynamics of the mode of production drive the processes through which the built environment is produced, while at the same time recognising the spatial and temporal specificities of these processes'* *(Healey and Barrett, 1990: p. 93).*

Ball's critique of Harvey's work is in this respect worth mentioning. He argues that 'in his work (Harvey's, EvdK) an overwhelming capital logic appears' and 'the capital logic of Harvey's work is continually expressed in the functionalism assigned to the built environment' (Ball, 1986: p. 452).[41]

In the tradition of institutional approaches, attempts to analyse the property development process are all of a recent date. Most of them follow more or less Healey and Barrett's article 'Structure and Agency in Land and Property Development Processes: Some Ideas for Research.'[42] This literature already begins to produce a much better understanding of the property-development process. Besides, Ball has made a profound study of the organisation of the building construction industry in England (see Ball, 1983, 1988). However, the larger part of these studies focus exclusively on the British context. Outside Britain, much less is known about the significance of institutional relations in property-development processes. Moreover, in these institutional analyses a convincing and powerful theoretical concept is still missing, resulting in *descriptions* of property-development processes rather than in *explanations* of these processes.[43]

One might argue that with help of institutional analysis -- in the way it has been described above -- researchers are perfectly able to describe the different situations that may occur with respect to the organisation of the property-development industry and supply and demand relations. However, without explicit assumptions with respect to human behaviour and the meaning of the institutional context, these descriptions will never possess the status of a theory.

---

theoretical corpus. However, it can be used in combination with Marxist theory, as has been done in Ball (1983).

40   Again, to mention only a few contributions in the neo-Marxist tradition: Ball *et al.* (1985), Fine (1985), Haila (1988, 1990, 1991), Checkoway (1980), King (1989a,b,c), Berry and Huxley (1992), Houghton (1993), Feagin (1987), Luithlen (1992), Krätke (1992), Logan and Molotch (1987), Logan and Swanstrom (1990), Molotch and Vicari (1988), and Vicari and Molotch (1990).

41   See also Haila (1992) for a critique on Harvey's work.

42   These include, notably: Davoudi and Usher (1990), Healey and Nabarro (eds.) (1990), Healey (1991, 1992, 1993a,b), Morgan (1992), Healey, Davoudi, O'Toole, Tavsanoglu and Usher (eds.) (1992). For alternative institutional approaches, see also Morrison (1992), Adams *et al.* (1993), Chambert (1988), McNamara (1984), Machimura (1992), Lin Leung (1987), Adams (1994), Harding (1992), and Sykora (1993)

43   Hooper (1992), in a comment on Healey's paper 'Models of the development process: a review', maintains the same argument.

In this respect I also refer to a recent discussion of the concept of *Structures of Housing Provision* (SHP) by the authors who introduced this concept (Ball and Harloe). I consider the SHP-concept as an example of the type of institutional analysis that has been discussed above - the descriptive model. Their argument is as follows:

'What is the theoretical status of the concept of SHP? It is obviously theoretical in nature as it is derived in thought. It is abstract for that reason and because it tries to encompass the principal features observed into a relatively simple organising framework. It does not of itself 'explain' any housing issue but is instead claimed to be a useful theoretical tool. To be useful however it must be combined with wider social theories, methodologies of empirical investigation and where necessary statistical analysis. As such the concept can be seen as an intermediate or operational one that has no useful life of its own but that can powerfully reveal causalities when used in the appropriate combinations' (Ball and Harloe, 1992: p. 4).[44]

The above makes clear that, so far, no agreement exists on the theoretical concept that should be used and what the necessary elements of such a concept should be. What is needed now is, as Healey argues, a theoretical model of the property development process 'which would enable the detail of agency relationships in the negotiation of development projects to be captured while at the same time allowing generalisation about how these relationships might vary under different conditions.' 'However,' she continues, 'the traditional approaches are only able to deal with market conditions, while only in some of these conditions market conditions might prevail. Nor do these models adequately address the way the interest and strategies of actors are actively constituted as circumstances change and how this relates to broader structural shifts' (Healey, 1991: p. 236).[45] An analytical framework should be developed that links the institutional organisation of the property development industry to the outcome of property-development processes and that at the same time contributes to a better understanding of temporal and spatial variation in urban development.[46]

---

44 According to Healey, Ball's approach and her own approach (an institutional model of the development process; see Healey, 1993) are in some ways similar, but they are not identical. 'However, this concept (the SHP concept; EvdK) focuses on how particular products are provided (houses, office space, etc.). The emphasis taken in this paper is on the institutional characteristics of local development *capacity*' (Healey, 1993: p. 4).

45 In this respect, an article by Gore and Nicholson (1991) is worth mentioning. They describe different models of the development process that do not seem to have any theoretical background at all. These models may be helpful in analysing property development processes, but they are certainly of little help in explaining why developments take place on certain locations and what the impact is of the strategies of the different participants in the development process.

46 Haila has also offered an approach to theorise property-development processes (Haila, 1992). She has similarly developed different models of the development process. The main difference with the present approach is that these are not in the same way based on the traditions in urban economic theory. Haila argues in favour of a special *real estate theory*, because the special characteristics of land and property markets make it impossible to compare supply/demand relations with respect to the production and consumption of land and buildings with supply/demand relations in other markets. It cannot be denied that such an approach might lead

2.4.3. Operationalisation

Chapter Three will discuss the pros and cons of the *models of the development process*, based on respectively neo-classical, Marxist and institutional theory. With respect to institutional theory, we must take notice of the following. The institutional model that will be described in Chapter Three is based mainly on Healey's work (Healey, 1992). Chapter Five will develop an alternative framework for analysis based on New Institutional Economic and Socio-Economic theory.

The latter analytical framework corresponds on the one hand with the type of institutional analyses that have been carried out in recent years in Great Britain; on the other hand, it tries to hypothesize institutional relations, institutional change, strategies of the agents and links between property development and the urban economy. To understand the complexity of urban real estate markets, we need an approach that theorises the institutional relations underlying the market's organisation. Moreover, this theoretical approach should take account of the dynamic nature of real estate markets.

The framework for analysis developed in Chapter Five will serve as a guideline for empirical research. It will be applied to interpreting the impact of the institutional organisation of the market on real estate development processes, to classifying and explaining changes in the organisational structure of the property development industry, and to analysing the malfunctioning of the market. I will now briefly pay attention to "standard" theoretical explanations of the malfunctioning of urban real estate markets.

2.5. The Malfunctioning of Urban Real Estate Markets: Theoretical Explanations

Traditionally, neo-classical economists have extensively studied market imperfections.[47] Harvey (1992), for instance, argues that the following conditions are necessary for economic efficiency through the market:

> '(...) particularly the existence of perfect competition, the absence of 'spillover' benefits and costs (often referred to as 'externalities'), and the ability of the market mechanism to supply all goods and services provided, society is able and willing to pay the necessary costs' (Harvey, 1992: p. 12)

Thus, the efficiency of a market depends, according to Harvey, on both technical and economic characteristics. With respect to the technical characteristics of real estate markets, Harvey argues that:

---

to interesting results, but I think it would be better to work with the richness of information brought forward by urban theory about urban development processes.

47 Jack Harvey has expounded neo-classical urban economics with respect to real estate development; I follow here his explanation of market imperfections in urban economies (Harvey, 1992).

'(...) physical conditions should ensure that price differences for the same commodity within the market are eliminated easily and quickly. This comes about by buyers moving to the cheaper parts and sellers moving to the dearer. This requires that both buyers and sellers must have up-to-date knowledge of price differences and base their actions solely on price. Moreover, dealing costs should be small relative to the value of the transaction' (ibid., p. 22,23).

With the real estate market, not only is it difficult to obtain *perfect knowledge*, but dealing costs are relatively high as well. 'Knowledge tends to be obtained infrequently and is limited geographically. Most occupiers (as distinct from investors) move in response to changes in family circumstances, income or business conditions. Only rarely do they move for the sole purpose of making a gain from a price or rent difference' (ibid., p. 23). Valuers and agents play a role in the property market just to provide the lacking knowledge. However, this information can never be perfect, because of the uncertainty about future gain.[48]

Not only *physical features* lead to imperfect market conditions, but also economic characteristics of property markets cause market imperfections.[49]

'We have to ask: is there freedom of entry into the market? Does the market consist of many buyers and sellers each so small that no one can exert monopoly powers? Generally speaking, there is freedom of entry into real property markets, resulting in many buyers and many sellers. But we must also recognise that certain conditions allow an owner to gain some monopolistic control' (ibid., p. 24).

According to Harvey, such conditions are:
(1) the geographical divisions of the market lead to imperfect competition between local markets;
(2) the imperfection of the capital market may prevent some would-be buyers from borrowing the large sums required for certain purchases, e.g. multi-storey office-blocks;
(3) the spatial fixity of real property puts certain site-owners in a strong position relative to buyers.

Harvey seems to consider these imperfect market conditions no threat to the smooth functioning of real estate markets. The following statement is revealing in this respect:

'We must not overemphasise the barriers in the real property market. Better knowledge can result from the increasing mobility of people and funds, and from the more sophisticated methods of calculating values. And, by and large, prices do respond, albeit somewhat sluggishly, to changes in market conditions; given sufficient time, the necessary

---

48 Uncertainty does not however, according to neo-classical theory, have to be an imperfection -- as long as the price is such that expected demand equals expected supply.

49 Other imperfect market conditions that are characteristic to land and property markets are the following: land and property are not mobile in the same way as workers or machines, land and property are relatively expensive goods, they are durable, and there are financial and institutional constraints on their supply.

adjustments to supply and demand do take place. (...) Any institution or government action which serves to make knowledge better or more readily available is likely to be beneficial' (Harvey, 1992: p. 25).

Apart from the fact that this is a rather subjective pronouncement -- how do we know that imperfect market conditions are the exception and perfect market conditions the rule? -- such an approach to markets fails to help explain, for instance, exactly why supply-side constraints do occur on urban real estate markets or why the composition of the group of actors involved in property development changes over time. In the case study of the structure of housing provision in the Netherlands (Chapters Six, Seven and Eight), I will argue, among other things, that the present insufficient supply of new dwellings is caused by various reasons related to structural features of the real estate market (i.e. structurally rising building costs, risk-avoiding strategies of property developers, traditional production methods by the building-construction industry, the close relation of the market of new dwellings to the second-hand market, structural fluctuations in house prices and development gains, etc.) These issues are obviously connected with the institutional organisation of the housing-development market.

Transaction cost economics refers to the concept of market failure in a different way. Bovaird holds, in a discussion of Williamson's work, that:

'Essentially his (Williamson's - EvdK) argument was that when the costs of writing, executing and enforcing contracts are high, markets fail and hierarchies emerge to take their place. Transaction costs are likely to be high (and therefore markets are likely to fail) when the assets required to accommodate that transaction are highly specific to it, when there is high uncertainty about the relative superiority of known alternatives or a belief that new alternatives are likely soon to become available, or when the high frequency of transactions makes it likely that the setting-up costs of a governance structure for regulating each transaction will be recouped over time' (Bovaird, 1993: p. 643, 644).

Several recent studies of property market functioning suggest that property development processes go less smoothly than is assumed in neo-classical theory. Concentrating on contributions in which the complexity of property markets has been studied, viz. the occurrence of supply-side blockages, I mention here (in what should not be seen as a complete list) the following: Barrett and Healey (1985), Evans (1985), MacGregor et al. (1985), Perry (1986) Fothergill et al. (1985, 1987), Adams et al. (1988), Henneberry (1988), Gloster and Smith (1989), Howes (1989), Morgan (1990), Adams and May (1991), Healey (1991), Adams et al. (1993), Imrie and Thomas (1993). Healey et al. (1992) provides an extensive overview of property-led regeneration policies, partially directed to take away these supply-side blockages.[50] Surprisingly, studies on this subject carried out in the Netherlands are missing.[51] The functioning of the English property market is -- probably

---

50 See also Imrie and Thomas (1993), Turok (1992), Berry, McGreal and Deddis (1993).

51 On the other hand, several studies carried out in European, Asian and American cities suggest that supply-side constraints in different forms do not solely exist in English cities, but are a wide-spread phenomenon existing in most cities. Examples can easily be found in previous footnotes.

rightly so -- considered to be more problematic, compared to the functioning of the Dutch urban property-market. However, this is not a very convincing reason not to study the influence of supply-side constraints (or the reason why they are absent) on the Dutch urban property market.[52]

Most of the English studies have sought empirical evidence with respect to the significance of supply-side blockages related to urban economic growth. The greater part of the studies concern the shortage of building land for new developments; the role of land owners, moreover, has been questioned. Other studies have analysed problems regarding the construction of new buildings and the conflicting interests of the development industry and the users of buildings (Henneberry, 1988).

So far I have discussed the malfunctioning of real estate markets. Standard neo-classical economic theory holds that we should speak of *market failure* when the market fails to achieve an optimal allocation of goods and services, given the budgets and preferences of the individual actors that are operating on the market. Normally, markets will produce an optimal allocation of resources and an optimal level of production of all outputs. Market failure exists in situations in which the operation of the market fails to produce the optimal level of output of a particular good or service. In such a situation the level of production is below or above the social optimum: the *costs* of increased provision would be exceeded by the *value* of that production, but the market fails to bring about the optimal production. However, I hold that in many cases this definition is meaningless, since we are not able to define when allocation is optimal. To be able to do this, we need to know every individual's budget and his preferences. If we do not know when allocation is optimal, then we do not know when allocation is not optimal, either.

2.6. Summary: Theoretical Explanations of Urban Economic Growth, Dynamics of Urban Change and Real Estate Development Processes

Chapter Two continued the line of argument begun in the first chapter by taking as a starting point a number of international differences with respect to property development. I have suggested that these international differences can only be understood properly by taking into consideration the institutional organisation of real estate markets and the organisational structure of the property development industry. In accordance with the arguments pointed out above, a framework for analysis should be developed that focusses (1) on the way real estate development processes are determined by the institutional organisation of the market, (2) on the organisational structure of the property development industry and its influence on production output, (3) on the strategies of the actors and on the way these strategies come forward, and (4) on the effects of institutional change on the functioning of real estate markets and its sources. I have asserted that for the purpose of this study I will employ institutional economic theory.

---

52 However, recently a shift in attention has taken place, initiated by the Ministry of Economic Affairs (see Ministry of Economic Affairs, 1994a).

Studies of property development that do take account of institutional factors -- including both empirical institutional analyses and supply-based neo-classical studies -- fail to address certain aspects of real estate market functioning that are -- in my opinion -- critical to our understanding of this market. In particular, we need more explanation regarding institutional change and how it affects property development processes, spatial variation in institutional relations and how it impacts market processes, and the influence of the nexus of institutions on how markets function. Institutional economic theory should be able to provide clues for answers, contributing to a better understanding to these issues.

Furthermore, Chapter Two's findings also show that urban economic theory has neglected the provision of the built environment. Confirming this statement are several studies of property development regarding, among other things, supply-side constraints on land and property markets, the meaning of institutional relations in local property markets, the influence of government intervention on property market functioning, and the relevance of monopoly ownership in land markets.

Finally, I have discussed the supposed imperfections of urban real estate markets and the social problems that they may cause. The theoretical explanations of the malfunctioning of urban real estate markets that have been discussed so far do not always satisfactorily explain these social problems.

PART II THEORIES OF URBAN CHANGE

INTRODUCTION

Part II deals with theoretical perspectives on real estate development processes. The main objective is to develop a framework for analysis that helps to interpret (1) the impact of the institutional organisation of real estate markets, via its influence on real estate sector activities, on urban spatial-economic restructuring processes, (2) the changes that take place through time with respect to this institutional organisation and the consequences of these changes for urban restructuring, and (3) the significance of spatial variation in this institutional organisation with respect to the outcome of development processes in different cities and/or in different countries (Chapter Five). To achieve this goal I will revert to the ideas and concepts that have been developed in the field of institutional-economic theory (Chapter Four). This chapter contains a fundamental discussion of recent literature in this theoretical field, which will set up the foundations of the analytical framework of Chapter Five. However, before I turn to institutional-economic theory, I will first discuss existing alternative theoretical approaches to the real estate development process (Chapter Three). Chapter Three aims to clarify the differences between the perspectives of the current approaches and the perspective I seek.

3 MODELS OF THE DEVELOPMENT PROCESS: EXISTING APPROACHES

3.1. Theories of Urban Change: Goals and Perspectives

One of the starting points of this book was the observation that urban economic theory has generally neglected the provision of the built environment -- the way land and property are developed. For this reason, the contributions in the field of urban economic theory -- though valuable in analysing and explaining changing patterns and trends in local economies -- fail to adequately assist the purpose of this study, namely to provide a framework for analysing urban real estate development processes. Does this imply that urban economic theory offers no clues for the analysis of urban real estate development processes? No; the previous chapter already demonstrated that within each of the recognized paradigms -- neo-classical economics, Marxism and institutional economics -- valuable theoretical analyses can be found of the functioning of urban real estate markets. Even though, according to Bovaird (1993), these contributions may fall outside the key themes of interest in the field of urban economics, they certainly deserve our attention.

This chapter will undertake a discussion of existing 'models of the development process.' Attention will be paid to the goals and perspectives of a number of development models, representing, respectively, the neo-classical, Marxist and institutional paradigm. Note that this chapter does not contain a review of the entire field of urban economic theory. Its scope is restricted to applications of urban economic theory to the real estate development process. First, section 3.2 will discuss neo-classical models of real estate development processes. Then, section 3.3 examines Marxist approaches. Section 3.4 considers institutional models of the development process. Section 3.5 criticizes descriptive non-theoretical models. Finally, section 3.6 draws a number of conclusions with respect to the explanatory power of these theoretical models and their use in the context of the present study.

3.2. A Neo-classical Model of the Real Estate Development Process

Chapter Two already briefly referred to standard neo-classical models of the real estate development process. I argued, among other things, that these models generally pay insufficient attention to just these issues that are central to the present study: the impact of the institutional organisation of the real estate market on the outcome of real estate development processes. Many neo-classical models particularly fail to take account of the dynamic character of real estate markets and the historical context in which markets evolve. Furthermore, neo-classical equilibrium models often neglect the implications of the existence of diverse forms of demand (user and investor demand), the non-economic interests of some of the actors involved in the development process (land owners) and information problems and uncertainty (see, e.g., Healey, 1991; Bovaird, 1993). The present study puts forward that the institutional organisation of the market is a significant explanatory variable with respect to, for instance, institutional change and path dependency.

This paragraph will discuss two theoretical approaches to property market functioning in the Netherlands (Needham, 1992 and Needham and Lie, 1993), that are both based on neo-classical assumptions. I will try to bring to light the value of these studies and in what sense their perspective differs from the present study.[53]

Needham (1992) attempts to explain land prices in Dutch cities. He develops a 'theory of land prices when land is supplied publicly' -- as is the case in the Netherlands. Standard neo-classical explanations for land prices assume free competition between suppliers and demanders of land. 'If there are constraints on this competition (e.g. land-use planning), this is added as a modification to the theory' (Needham, 1992: p. 669). Needham argues:

'when, however, the supply of building land is in the hands of public agencies, which determine the volume and price of supply specified by land use and location, a different theoretical approach is needed. In this situation, certain economic principles apply which determine the maximum and minimum prices at which land will be bought for development and at which serviced building land will be supplied for development. However, both the limits of this range and the actual land prices within it will depend on political choices made by the public agencies' (ibid.: p. 669).

Needham uses this supply-based neo-classical model to explain both the minimum and maximum price at which land is acquired for use as building land and the minimum and maximum price at which fully serviced land is disposed of for building upon. This explanation is based on the recognition of the influence of three sorts of market constraints on a single municipality acting as land developer. 'Even though the municipality dominates the land market within its own boundaries, it is strongly constrained by prices set elsewhere. These are:
- the existing-use value of land to be acquired for development (the municipality cannot acquire land below existing-use value);
- the price at which other municipalities in the region dispose of building land (the municipality cannot dispose of land above the prices charged by other municipalities in the region);
- the residual value of land for marketable uses (the municipality cannot dispose of land above residual value) (see Needham, 1992: p. 673).

Then, the political decisions are summed up that are assumed to have an important effect on land prices. These decisions include the following: 'the content of the law on compulsory purchase and the way it is interpreted, the possibility of subsidising the land-development process, the chosen mix of land uses in the plan area, the quality of the land servicing, the amount of land supplied, and the possibility of setting disposal prices below the maximum' (*ibid.*: p. 675-6). Needham argues that political choices affect land prices in two ways:
'- the political choices of other municipalities in the region affect the maximum disposal prices which can be realised by a single municipality in the region;
- the single municipality is fairly free about how it sets prices within the market constraints. How it decides to use that freedom is a matter of political choice' (*ibid.*:

---

53 The choice of these studies has been made more or less arbitrarily. However, these represent the few attempts to develop a theory of the functioning of the Dutch real estate market.

p. 683).

Since in the Netherlands most municipalities consider it their task always to provide sufficient building land, the prices paid for serviced land disposed of by municipalities for marketable uses are relatively low (because there is no scarcity of building land).

The paper by Needham and Lie (1993) elaborates partially on Needham (1992). Needham and Lie analyse the way in which the public regulation of property supply affects property prices, risks and returns. They study two aspects of this supposed relation in particular. Does public regulation stimulate supply or restrict it? Is that regulation steady and predictable, or unpredictable? Needham and Lie suggest an analytical framework suitable for studying these issues. The framework includes the following aspects (see Needham and Lie, 1993: p. 3-5):

- the three markets (development, investment, and user); regulation of supply is different on each of these markets;
- the effects of public regulation not just on prices but on risks and returns also (e.g. binding land-use plans reduce risks). In an efficiently working market, it is to be expected that the higher the risk that the supplier faces, the higher the returns will be that he requires on his capital);
- the difference between the short term and the long term: changes in the public regulation of property supply will have a marginal effect on prices in the short term, but possibly a much larger effect in the long term (because the property market is a stock market);
- the difference between "the firm" and "the industry": a demand for the product produced exists for the whole industry, but the demand facing the individual firm depends on the competition between the firms in that industry;
- the difference between a micro- and a macro-analysis: any study of the effects of the public regulation of property supply must not be limited to looking only at the direct effects on the property regulated (micro-analysis). Indirect effects, i.e. on risks and returns, on long-term price development, should also be involved in the study;
- an "institutional approach": property prices cannot be understood simply by applying theories from neo-classical economics and then adding the "institutional factors" to see how they modify the market outcomes. This method is incorrect because it omits the indirect and long-term effects of institutional factors on property prices.

The analytical framework serves as a basis for the development of a theory of the effect of the public regulation of property supply on property prices, risks and returns. By dividing the influence of public regulation of property supply into two components -- whether property supply is stimulated or restricted and whether the regulation is steady or changeable -- it is possible to distinguish four varieties of public regulation of property supply. Furthermore, the effects on prices, risks and returns can be deduced from this. Needham and Lie describe the effect of the regulation as follows:

'- a stimulating regulation will reduce prices, a restricting regulation will increase prices, but without necessarily affecting risks/returns;
- a steady regulation will reduce risks/returns, a changeable regulation will increase them, but without necessarily affecting the level of prices' (Needham and Lie, 1993: p. 11).

I have discussed these two papers rather extensively, but not to criticize the line of argument that has been developed in them or the assumptions that underlie the theory. Instead, my purpose is, as I pointed out above, to clarify the differences between Needham's and Needham and Lie's approach and the approach that is being developed in the present study.

What then are these differences? First, I have referred to the theories developed in Needham (1992) and Needham and Lie (1993) as supply-based neo-classical models, because they are primarily concerned with the supply side of the real estate market. As such, they problematise the property development process. On the other hand, they pay no attention to the demand side. As a result, the motives and strategies of the diverse groups of actors that buy and/or invest in land and property are not identified. Second, in Needham's and Needham and Lie's models the 'institutional context' is reduced to direct government intervention on the land and property market. From the perspective of institutional-economic theory a much broader meaning is assigned to 'the institutional organisation of the market.' It includes, next to government intervention, the organisational structure of the property development industry, the rules that regulate the market, property rights and institutional (non-market) relations between different groups of actors. Third, the assumptions regarding human behaviour and economic processes in both models are apparently -- though not explicitly mentioned -- still neo-classical. It is important to notice that in institutional economic theory these assumptions are fundamentally different (human agents act boundedly rational, the meaning of uncertainty and the influence of non-economic factors, the significance of institutional change and path dependency; see Chapters Four and Five), with -- in my opinion -- important analytical implications.

Finally, and most significantly, the perspective of Needham's and Needham and Lie's models is in fact completely different from that of the present study. The supply-based neo-classical models are primarily concerned with explaining land and property prices (and risks and returns). In doing so, they problematise the property development process and take account of institutional factors. The goal of my study, however, is to develop an analytical framework that enables us to interpret the institutional organisation of the real estate market itself and its impact on real estate development processes. At the roots of this intention is the assumption that institutional organisation is responsible for differences in time and place (with respect to real estate development). Therefore, I must conclude this section by saying that the neo-classical models of the development process cannot be used for the purpose of this study, but that both analytical models can in principle perfectly complement each other.

3.3. Marxist Approaches: Circuits of Capital

David Harvey's work has shaped numerous studies that have been carried out in the tradition of Marxist urban economics (Harvey, 1978, 1982, 1985). Harvey builds his analysis of *the urban process under capitalism* upon the definition of three circuits of capital. The primary circuit concerns the production process, the secondary circuit refers to the capital flows into fixed assets and consumption-fund formation, and the tertiary circuit of capital comprises, first, investment in science and technology and second, a wide range of social expenditures (Harvey, 1982: pp. 200-4). The production of the built environment can be understood in the context of these three circuits. Building production takes place in the secondary circuit. The capital flows into fixed assets can be distinguished in fixed capital enclosed within the production process and fixed capital which functions as a physical framework for production. The latter Harvey refers to as the *built environment for production*. With respect to the consumption fund, some items are directly enclosed within the production process, while others act as a physical framework for consumption (houses, etc.). Harvey calls the latter the *built environment for consumption*. Over-accumulation in the primary circuit of capital leads to capital flows into fixed assets, including the built environment. The dynamic underlying the production of the built environment is indissolubly linked to the constant interplay between different circuits of capital, to a larger or lesser extent modified by the state. In a discussion of Harvey's work, Healey points out:

'Harvey's analysis emphasizes the importance of finance capital, and the global relations which govern its flow between types of investment and locations in the contemporary period. He persistently stresses temporal and spatial variation in the way capital flows into and out of property. His argument suggests that the dynamics of the development process in an urban region in the present period derive from general tendencies in financial investment, the role of an urban region within international patterns of economic competition, the effects of this on the economic and spatial structure within a region, and the role of public policy in creating and impeding investment opportunities' (Healey, 1991b: p. 234).

In the 1980s and 1990s many authors applied the circuits of capital-concept to the analysis of real estate development.[54] Jointly, these studies have clearly enlarged our knowledge of the role of finance capital with respect to real estate development. They help us to understand where the money comes from in the property-development process and what the dynamics are behind the fluctuations in the amount of capital that flows into the built environment. However, when we again regard both Harvey's circuits of capital-concept and the results of the studies that are based on this concept in the light of the present study's perspective, we must conclude that the theoretical models based on Harvey's concept hardly focus attention on the property-development process itself. For instance, they do not provide any information about the profitability of property development, the division of profit margins, trends in prices and costs, etc.

Healey makes a similar remark: 'Yet they (Marxist models, EvdK) barely penetrate into the detail of the events of the development process and the nexus of agency relationships which might surround each' (Healey, 1991: p. 235). Harvey's explanation of the production of the built environment gives us no explicit clues with respect to the way the institutional organisation of the real estate market influences the outcome of property-development processes. For, an investigation of this relation demands the analysis of the strategies of the actors involved in the property development-industry and of the institutional relations between them.

The conclusion of this section is more or less identical to the conclusion of the previous

---

54 See Chapter Two.

one. I will not make use of the circuits-of-capital concept in my study. However, analyses carried out in the tradition of Marxist economics do provide important insights into the real estate game -- notably, the role of finance capital in the development process -- that need our attention.

3.4. Institutional Models of the Development Process

Healey (1992) presents an institutional model of the real estate development process that takes account of the complexity of the events and agencies involved in the process and the diversity of forms the process may take under different conditions. Structure and agency are linked to each other through the concepts of material resources -- land rights, labour, finance, information and expertise -- institutional rules, which govern how resources are used, and ideas, which represent the role of ideology in shaping the development process. The analysis of the development process could proceed through four levels, including (1) a description of the development process in operation, (2) an analysis of the agencies involved in the process -- identifying roles and power relations, (3) the assessment of the strategies and interests of actors involved in the development process, and (4) theorisation and description of the particular societal circumstances. The latter level of analysis involves theorisation of the nature of modes of production and regulation, of ideology and of the relations between them. As Healey argues, with respect to the theoretical level, 'the critical issue here is to make the connection with the social relations expressed in the prevailing mode of production, mode of regulation and ideology of the society within which development is being undertaken (Healey, 1992: p. 37).

In Healey's model the social relations 'which constitute the strategies and interests of actors, and the resources, rules and ideas available to them' (*ibid.*: p. 37) are theorised. This theoretical framework makes it possible to explain why in an international context development processes differ in form and why there is temporal variation with respect to property development. However, it essentially leaves unrevealed the economic and non-economic reasons underlying the actor's strategies. Economic action is, moreover, deeply influenced by information problems that should therefore be allotted a central place in the theoretical framework. Finally, it does not theorise the dynamics behind institutional change -- why does institutional change takes place? -- though it certainly recognizes the temporal variation with respect to the institutional context. In essence, Healey's institutional model of the development process theorises *the relation* between the institutional context and the property development process. However, it does not enter into the institutional context itself -- (the emergence of) the particular institutional organisation of a local or national real estate market is not explicitly theorised -- and, furthermore, it does not theorise human behaviour -- the strategies of the agents involved in the property development process. Note that the perspective of Healey's institutional model is different from the perspective that has been chosen in the present study. Healey's model provides a framework for an *institutional* analysis of property-development processes. My aim is to develop a framework for an *institutional-economic* analysis of property-development processes. Economic theory can then be used to make explicit the assumptions underlying the model and to theorise the institutional dynamics of the local or national economy and the economic actions of the individual agents.

3.5. The Blind Alley of Descriptive Models

Finally, I will pay brief attention to a number of descriptive non-theoretical models of the development process. Gore and Nicholson (1991) discuss a number of sequential or descriptive approaches to the property-development process. These models consider the development process as a chronological sequence of stages, during each of which certain events occur. Next to these sequential models, Gore and Nicholson also distinguish so-called behavioural or decisionmaking approaches. They point out that 'these emphasise the roles of different actors in the process and the importance of the decisions they make in ensuring its smooth operation' (Gore and Nicholson, 1991: p. 706). In these approaches the development process is often represented as a flow diagram, either in a linear form or in a cyclical form. Since both type of approaches have in common that they lack any theoretical basis, I group them together.

A large variety of this kind of model has been developed. They are useful in some respects because they make explicit both the events that are part of the development process, as well as the roles of the agents and agencies that are involved in the development process and the decisions that are taken by these agents and agencies. The challenge, in this respect, is to design a model that, on the one hand, must be detailed in form in order to embrace all actors, events, decisions, and relations that are significant to the property-development process, while, on the other hand, must be generalistic to be applicable in all different sorts of situations. In my opinion, however, these descriptive models are, neither from an academic, nor from a policy viewpoint, of great use. They do not try to theorise the property-development process. We can, therefore, endlessly go on designing new, more sophisticated examples of these models, but it will bring us nowhere. Gore and Nicholson make a similar remark:

'Indeed, in many respects it is unreasonable to think that a diagrammatic representation can provide anything other than a convenient starting point for further explorations of the process. (...) In itself, this is a useful attribute, but it also signifies a lack of progress. This suggests that further attempts to derive a universally applicable model of the development process should be discouraged' (Gore and Nicholson, 1991: p. 728-9).

Without a theoretical basis, these descriptive models will do little to enlarge our understanding of the development process. As such they may be considered blind alleys.

3.6. Conclusions: Explanations of Urban Dynamics

The primary objective of this chapter was to place the theoretical perspective of the present study in the context of alternative (theoretical) approaches to the property-development process. I have consciously restricted the discussion to a comparison of the theoretical perspective -- the theoretical 'goals' -- of each of the models. A more fundamental critique of neo-classical and/or Marxist urban theory falls outside the scope of this book, but can easily be found elsewhere. Neo-classical and Marxist urban theory, even when leaving aside their respective assumptions of human behaviour and economic action, can be criticised on the way they deal with the institutional context. They do not provide the tools to analyse the meaning of the institutional organisation of the real estate market to real estate development, neither do they aim to analyse (changes in) the institutional organisation itself. I have attempted to make clear that the specific objective of my study calls for an alternative analytical framework. This framework must add to a better understanding of the meaning of the institutional organisation of the market to urban real estate development. Furthermore, it must make it possible to explain in what sense variations in this institutional organisation are responsible for spatial variation in real estate development. Finally, this theory will help us to understand the dynamics underlying institutional change and related changes in real estate development.

4 INSTITUTIONAL ECONOMIC THEORY: A REALISTIC APPROACH

4.1. Introduction

Chapter Four and Five aim to build a framework for analysis: a set of theoretical tools suitable for the analysis of urban real estate development processes. For this purpose I will turn to institutional economic theory. In order to clarify the objective of developing this framework, I will restate the aim of the study.

The study intends to investigate the processes that underlie the functioning of urban real estate markets and to explain why these property-development processes are changing over time, why they are often different in distinctive sectors of the urban property market, why they vary between locations both within a city and between different cities, and why -- in an international context -- urban property market functioning shows such large divergences. I have suggested that, apart from the nature of demand and supply in a local real estate market, the institutional organisation of that market plays a significant role with respect to the outcome of real estate market processes. The influence of the institutional organisation of the market on real estate development forms the prime focus of the study. The framework for analysis of the urban development process based on institutional economic theory, which will be deveioped in Chapter Five, should supply us the tools to address the issues that are relevant to the study of the impact of institutional factors on real estate development processes -- particularly in the Dutch context.

How I will develop this framework for analysis is as follows. The present chapter will review the state of the art in institutional economic theory. The theoretical tradition of New Institutional Economics will be taken as the starting point. However, this tradition will then be criticised from a socio-economic point of view. Thus, the chapter provides an (out of necessity relatively short) outline of current thinking in institutional economic theory. It sets forth the assumptions of institutional economics, the notion and meaning of institutions and institutional relations, the role of government intervention, the interpretation of the evolutionary character of economies, and the explanation of international differences in economic processes. Note, however, that the discussion of institutional economic theory in this study is limited. It is a means to an end. For, the final objective of this chapter is to derive from institutional economics the tools that are needed for the analytical framework that will be developed in Chapter Five. For this purpose, I will conclude Chapter Four by listing what should be the basic elements of the analytical framework that is based on institutional economic theory. As I already stated in the general introduction, the reason for turning to the institutional-economics literature is to find out in what sense institutional economic theory can contribute to a better understanding of real estate development processes. It is expected that it will focuss our attention on certain aspects of these processes that are hardly or not addressed in alternative approaches.

This chapter will now discuss successively the current state of the art in institutional economic theory in relation to its origins (section 4.2), and the significance that is given to markets and the interpretation of the market as an institution, related to problems of coordination (section 4.3). Then, I present the basic premises of new institutional economics and, simultaneously, go over the criticism levied by other disciplines within the field of institutional economics (section 4.4). Section 4.5 deals with the institutional-economic interpretations of the evolution of economies (sources of institutional change) and the historical path of a national economy that determines institutional change (path dependency). Finally, section 4.6 I will bundle the vital elements of institutional economic theory into a framework and argue how they can be used as 'tools for analysis' of real estate development processes.

4.2.   Institutional Economic Theory: Rejecting Neo-classical Assumptions

Contributions to institutional economics have in common that they acknowledge the influence of institutions, social practices and history on our ideas, perceptions and actions. However, the impact of these institutions on economic performance can be judged in different ways.

In recent years, a number of interesting books and articles have appeared dealing with the significance of institutions in the economy, of which I mention Hodgson (1988), Zukin and DiMaggio (*eds.*) (1990), Thompson, Frances, Levacic and Mitchell (*eds.*) (1991), Granovetter (1992), Granovetter and Swedberg (*eds.*) (1992).

This enumeration is, most certainly, no exhaustive list of contributions in the field of institutional economic theory. However, I have deliberately selected this work, because the authors all present clear overviews of the current state of the art in institutional economic theory.[55] Moreover, they have in common the aim of integrating the insights of economic and social sciences -- or, using Swedberg and Granovetter's words, *'the opening up of the academic debate about the economy to include a genuinely social perspective'* (1992: p.1). I regard this process of integration as a potentially promising and fruitful development and will therefore use these books as the basis of my line of argument in the present chapter.

Next to the progress that has been made in the field of, particularly, New Economic Sociology and Socio-Economics, the work of Coase (1937) and Williamson (1975, 1985) has inspired many scholars to contribute to the field of Transaction Cost Economics or New

---

[55] At this place I will not give a complete overview of the state of the art in institutional economics, because it falls outside the scope of this book. Therefore, I confine myself to a reproduction of Swedberg and Granovetter's classification of the field of research concerned (Swedberg and Granovetter, 1992: p. 2). They distinguish *Rational Choice Sociology* (the neo-classical model should be extended to topics that by tradition only sociologists have dealt with), *New Economic Sociology* (the key notion is that many economic problems that by tradition belong to the economists' camp can be fruitfully analysed with the help of sociology), *Socio-Economics* (neo-classical economics is not enough to solve economic problems; a much broader perspective must be used), *Psycho-, Socio-, Anthropo-Economics* (certain findings from psychology, sociology, and anthropology should be directly integrated into the economist's model), *Transaction Cost Economics* (many problems at the intersection of law, economics, and organisation can be solved by assuming that institutions gravitate to forms that efficiently reduce transaction costs).

Although the boundaries between these approaches are not always clear, I will concentrate mainly on the field of Socio-Economics and Transaction Cost Economics.

Institutional Economics.[56] One of the most prominent authors in New Institutional Economics is 1993 Noble Prize winner Douglas North.[57] However, in my view, North's notion of the meaning and creation of institutions deviates on important points from Williamson's transaction-cost approach (although they still belong to the same discipline, because they judge institutions solely on their efficiency). I will argue right away that North's concept of institutional change and path dependency offers better starting points for my analysis than does Williamson's approach, which is still close to neo-classical economic theory. I will try to integrate valuable insights of New Economic Sociology and Socio-Economics -- mainly following Hodgson's *Economics and Institutions, a manifesto for a modern institutional economics* (1988) -- with North's theory that has been developed in *Institutions, Institutional Change and economic performance* (North, 1990).

Institutional economic theory originates from a growing dissatisfaction with the explanatory power and the lack of reality in neo-classical economic theory. During the present century orthodox economic theory has continuously been attacked from various sides. Unfortunately, these attacks -- although often rightly brought forward -- were normally not accompanied by solid alternative models of economic activity. It is indeed a difficult task to replace the 'logic' of neo-classical models by an alternative set of explanatory variables. However, most academics seem to agree now on the existence of anomalies in the economy: empirical results that do not fit in mainstream neo-classical theory.[58] Some authors try to solve thes anomalies within the boundaries of neo-classical economics; others try to solve them by developing an alternative theoretical framework. Institutional economic theory belongs to the latter group. At this moment it can not yet be concluded which of these attempts is most fruitful.[59]

Neo-classical theory emphasises one function of the market: allocation. Decisions are made within a set of limiting conditions, such as given preferences, given budgets, and a given period of time. For individual producers and consumers, the efficient allocation of given means (of production and of income) over given goals depends on relative prices and the relative positions of the demand and supply curves. This is related to the character of a theory as a framework for decisionmaking, under severe restrictions. In a perfect market, allocation through the market mechanism is sufficient to achieve an optimal solution of the coordination problem. Markets failing to meet this condition need a different mechanism. In a 'pure market', coordination between individual decisionmakers is smooth because of the basic assumptions of full information, full mobility, full divisibility and correct prices. As soon as these assumptions are not dropped, an answer must be found to the question of whether economic theory has developed a body of knowledge related to the coordination of

---

56   For a recent overview of contributions to the field of Transaction Cost Economics see, for instance, Williamson (1992).

57   See, for instance, North (1981, 1990).

58   See, for instance, Pen (1995), Klamer (1995), Van Dalen (1995), Barkema (1995), Wakker (1995), Van Damme (1995), Fase (1995), and Theeuwes (1995).

59   Note that this debate falls outside the scope of this book.

decisions in markets that are not perfect.

The *problem of coordination* is also referred to by Frances et al. (1991), who suggest that coordination implies the act of bringing into relationship otherwise disparate activities or events. 'Tasks and efforts can be made compatible by coordinating them. Bottlenecks and disjunctures can be eliminated, so coordination is usually discussed under a sign of *efficiency*. By coordinating a set of items something can be achieved which otherwise would not be. It is the positive performative consequence of coordination that makes it such an attractive social practice and objective. Various agents and agencies can be 'ordered,' 'balanced,' 'brought into equilibrium,' and the like, by the act of coordination' (Frances et al., 1991: p. 3). The problem of coordination is then related to the question how social coordination is achieved.[60] Real economic life compels us continually to ask ourselves what the best way would be to coordinate the activities of various agents and agencies. Solutions to coordination problems can be distinguished in three 'models.' Either coordination is left to the market, or it is consciously organized in the form of a hierarchy, or social networks come into existence to solve coordination problems. These *models of coordination* -- the term is taken from Frances et al. (1991) -- will receive more attention below.

The theoretical problem that arises because neo-classical theory confines itself to pure market situations is not a 'new' issue in economic theory. It has already received attention in the debate between the Austrian School and the Anglo-Saxon neo-classical and Keynesian theorists in the first half of the twentieth century.[61] In Robbin's classical definition, the conception of economics was based on scarcity, preferences and limited means. Economics was considered to be a science, that emphasised the decisionmaking process taking place under well-defined conditions. Robbins defined economics as follows:

'the science which studies human behaviour as a relationship between ends and scarce means which have alternative uses. (...) When the time and the means for achieving ends are limited and capable of alternative application, and the ends are capable of being distinguished in order of importance, then behaviour necessarily takes the form of choice (...) It has an economic aspect' (Robbins, 1935: p. 14-16).

The Dutch economist Hennipman (1945) also stressed this approach towards a closed definition, setting apart economics as a separate science based on a formal approach rather than on a certain sector of social life. Hennipman (1945: p. 5) emphasises that economics is a science of man and of human behaviour.

The Austrian School similarly stresses human behaviour as the focus of economic theory, but differs in its definition of economics. This School emphasises that humans not only

---

60 Examples of social coordination are agreements that are based on trust or family relations. Democracy and dictatorship are also forms of social coordination. All types of coordination that do not involve *market relations* can be defined as social coordination.

61 See also the line of argument in Van der Krabben and Lambooy, 1994.

choose between given ends but that human behaviour is 'purposeful.'[62] Kirzner, one of the Austrian theorists, criticises Robbins' definition:

'Robbins' structure of ends and means (...) ignores the fact that ends are never presented to the actor coincidentally with the means (...) Ends can be conceived as observable states of affairs only after their achievement. At the time of the contemplation of action, ends are to the actor only anticipations of future hoped-for states of affairs' (Kirzner, 1976: p. 125).

His second critique is related to the fact that 'ends' are not objective -- as Robbins assumes, but subjective. Kirzner holds that 'ends' are explicitly defined by the individual agent itself (so they are subjective). Hennipman (1962) also argues that 'ends' contain a subjective element. Kirzner adds a third point, namely that the ends-means dichotomy is an oversimplification: 'Ends may be considered as means to further ends, and (...) means may be equally well considered as the ends of earlier actions' (*ibid.*: p. 125). He identifies instead two insights as basic to economics: 'First there is the insight that *human action is purposeful*, and second that there is *an indeterminacy and unpredictability* inherent in human preferences, human expectationism, and human knowledge' (*ibid.*: p. 42,43).[63]

The conclusion is that Robbins' definition can only be considered as a special case within a broader framework, valid *only when ends and means are given beforehand.*[64] Most so-called 'general theories' are in fact special cases and not general at all. In section 4.3 I shall refer to Hodgson's work with respect to this point; he takes the means-end conception one step further than the Austrians do.

The theoretical discussion, focusing on coordination problems, was distorted by the fact that it was restricted to the distinction between central planning and the perfect market. A later approach -- by Keynes -- accepted the need for government guidelines, and even the need for active government participation in investment and consumption. Keynes accepted

---

62   Hodgson considers the difference between purposeful and goal-directed behaviour as follows. 'The difference lies in the set of possible responses to the structured environment faced by the individual. (...) In both these cases (goal-directed behaviour, EvdK) the goals are still themselves determined or fixed. The purposeful agent is essentially different in that it can change its goals, and furthermore it may actually do this without any stimulus from outside. Human beings are regarded purposeful systems of this type. The capacity to change both behaviour and goals without external stimulus means that humans have a *will*, and that some of our choices are real ones (Hodgson, 1988: p. 11).

63   However, note that the Austrian School goes too far in its defence of 'purposeful human behaviour'. According to Hodgson: 'they seem to argue that action bears no significant influence of the environment, or that it is beyond the scope of economic theory to enquire as to how purposes and actions may be determined' (Hodgson, 1988: p. 11). Austrian theorists wrongly suggest that 'institutions and collectives in themselves are not purposeful, except as the aggregate of the various purposes of the numbers, furthermore, according to this view, individual action alone is regarded as the prime explanation or cause' (ibid.: p. 60).

64   Hennipman (1962) provides an interesting overview of the discussion of the basic elements of economic science (until 1962). He argues that it is essential for economic science to contribute to the solution of important issues in economic policy. In this task economic science must keep its (social) neutrality, but at the same time should be careful with providing unconditional answers to *social* problems (p. 106).

the need for *institutional arrangements* (as we now call them), to compensate for 'market failures,' in order to acquire a socially optimal allocation and distribution and volume of production. Neo-classical theory offers no good solution to the coordination problem, because this theory has no satisfactory solution of 'collective action.' Collectivities are assumed to be a mere identity of the 'representative person', without differences of interest, information and power. In other words, standard neo-classical economic theory ignores the fact that, next to markets, also hierarchies and social networks act as coordinative mechanisms.

In institutional economics, the basic premises of neo-classical theory have come under severe attack. According to Hodgson, at the core of neo-classical economic theory is a set of ideas concerning rationality, knowledge, the economic process and the human agents. Economic agents are assumed to show rational, maximizing behaviour, whereby their preferences are exogenously given. Furthermore, chronic information problems are believed to be absent. And finally, the theory focuses on movements towards or attained equilibrium states of rests, rather than on the continuous processes of transformation through historical time (Hodgson, 1988: p. XIV). Hodgson then criticises neo-classical theory on these three main points. First, the assumption of maximizing rationality is no longer tenable. In neo-classical theory the agent is not endowed with choice. That is, neo-classical theory unjustly ignores the fact that the preferences of agents may change and that, consequently, their goals may change as well. The capacity to change both behaviour and goals without an external stimulus means that humans have a will. Second, the neo-classical conceptions of time and equilibrium are incorrect. Economic phenomena are increasingly being seen as both evolutionary and dynamic. Neo-classical theory has failed to make any significant advance in understanding long-run technological progress and transformation. Third, neo-classical theory pays insufficient attention to the growing recognition of the conceptual significance of institutions in economic life (see Hodgson, 1988: p. 5).

Fig. 4.1 clarifies the differences between neo-classical economic theory and institutional economic theory. In neo-classical economic theory both the tastes and preferences of individuals, and the technological possibilities and constraints that impinge upon the economy, are regarded as exogenous or given. Instead, in institutional economic theory both technology and individual tastes and preferences are regarded as part of the economic system.

Institutional economics itself has extensively investigated the problem of coordination. According to institutional economists, this problem of coordination has to be considered in two different ways. First, organisations are created to improve the smooth functioning of the market. This assumption is often based on the ideology of (methodological) individualism; second, organisations (and/or institutions) are created to encompass 'non-monetary values,' such as moral values, trust and emotions, which in neoclassical theory are assumed to be part of the utility function.[65] Both organisations and institutions are needed to take up the

---

65 The distinction between institutions and organizations is crucial in institutional economic theory. North argues that 'like institutions, organizations provide a structure to human interaction. Indeed when we examine the costs that arise as a consequence of the institutional framework, we see they are a result not only of that

coordination of market decisions. They can be seen as mechanisms to solve the problem of transaction costs, as an improvement of the imperfect markets, or as a means to improve the social effects of the market, for instance to achieve a just distribution of income.

FIGURE 4.1
The scope and boundaries of, respectively, orthodox economic theory and institutional economic theory

Boundaries of orthodox economic analysis

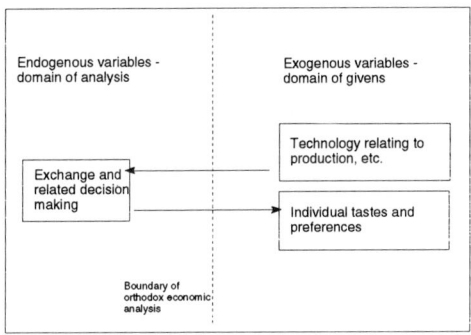

Boundaries of institutional economic analysis

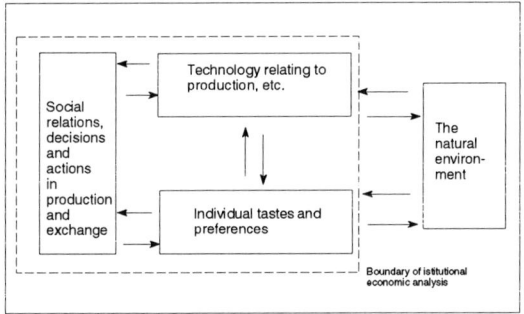

source: Hodgson, 1988: p. 13, p. 16

Coordination of economic actions,[66] thus, occurs via three mechanisms: that of *markets*, of

---

framework, but also of the organizations that have developed in consequence of that framework. Conceptually, what must be clearly differentiated are the rules (the institutions / EvdK) from the players (the organizations / EvdK). The purpose of the rules is to define the way the game is played. But the objective of the team within that set of rules is to win that game (...)' (North, 1990: p. 5).

66 Swedberg and Granovetter define 'economic action' as 'a type of behaviour that has to do with choosing among scarce means that have alternative uses' (1992: p. 6). Furthermore, 'economic action is

organisations, and of *social networks*. With respect to organisations, two dimensions must be considered. First, the dimension of society-wide coordination, through institutional structures like laws, regulations, fiscal policy and by structured bargaining, and second, the dimension of coordination between private parties, or between the government and (parts of) the market parties. The theories of Coase and Williamson (Transaction Cost Economics) deal with coordination between private parties; Socio-Economic theory deals with the first problem.

The concept of 'social network' refers to 'a regular set of contacts or similar social connections among individuals or groups. An action by a member of a network is *embedded*, because it is expressed in interaction with other people' (Swedberg and Granovetter, 1992: p. 9). The recognition of social networks is important, since it helps to explain the emergence and maintenance of a social institution. What remains unclear until now is what should be understood by the term 'institution.' I distinguish both social institutions and economic institutions. Hodgson defines a social institution as 'a social organization which, through the operation of tradition, custom or legal constraint, tends to create durable and routinized patterns of behaviour' (Hodgson, 1988: p. 10). An economic institution can then be defined as an economic organization that is primarily meant to reduce uncertainty and to increase economic efficiency. New Economic Sociology (or Socio-Economics) takes the former conception as a starting point, while New Institutional Economics (NIE) interprets institutions in the first place from an efficiency point of view. I consider the definition of social institutions, which may include economic institutions, as the most appropriate one. The meaning that is given in NIE to economic institutions is too limited. Economic institutions are limited to, for instance, contracts, property rights and government intervention. Social institutions, however, also involve habits, norms and contracts.

4.3. Markets and Coordination

To work under the aegis of the emphasis on (optimal) allocation requires the knowledge of explicit preferences and of the available means. For many situations these requirements can be met, even when the goals and the means are not fully 'given.' However, difficulties arise in situations where these conditions cannot be met. This especially holds true when real time is decisive. For example, property development may be problematic because of the relatively long period of time between the start and the completion of a development project. Information constitutes another problem. Think only of the considerable uncertainty in assessing future gain in developing a new office building, due to the limited number of transactions in local office markets (particularly in small towns) and the fact that there are only a few 'buyers.' Information can be complex for those involved in decisionmaking. Consequently, decisionmakers can adjust their goals depending on the available means in different situations or time-paths. Besides, in real life the choice of the goals is interrelated with the availability of means. Hodgson remarks with respect to this point 'that the

---

socially situated and cannot be explained by reference to individual motives alone. It is embedded in ongoing networks of personal relationships rather than being carried out by atomized actors' (ibid.: p. 9).

possibility of the ends being altered or affected by the chosen means is ignored. A simple, one-way causality from one to the other is assumed. Thus, in orthodox theory, the end justifies the means (Hodgson, 1988: p. 93). In contrast, Hodgson speaks of 'adaptive ends.'

Conventional theories assume that these two variables -- 'ends' and 'means' -- are independent of each other. In fact the variables are often interrelated. Hence, the mathematical optimum of a choice is difficult to find in a dynamic context. Moreover, theories and theoretical constructs are being used as normative devices (the concept of the Pareto-optimum!). In a complex world with incomplete knowledge, there is no such thing as one Pareto-optimum; there are many of them. Even a world with complete knowledge would have many Pareto optima. But the concept has no meaning in an uncertain world since it cannot be established whether or not such an optimum has been reached. Of course, if loosely defined, the concept of Pareto optimum can be used as a norm for acquiring a 'better' situation for the majority concerned, but in that case mathematical precision is lacking. The use of such a concept in choosing policy instruments for any problem, including issues related to property market functioning, could be misleading if it were to be used as an exact standard.

Markets are necessary to coordinate individual decisions. Two other possibilities -- apart from markets -- for meeting this goal are (central) planning and cooperation, although it would also be possible to define these alternatives as quasi-markets. To perform this coordination function, markets need some additional attributes. First, a set of rules with which market parties should comply, in order to smooth the bargaining and to further the conclusion of contracts and the transfer of property or user rights; and, second, information about the nature of the property rights, the quality of the goods or services and the possibility of delivering within a certain time.

The institutional setting of markets is important. Markets are structures for exchanging products and services, or for transferring property or user rights. At the same time, a market is an information-transmitting structure, relating persons and firms. Property and user rights are defined socially and their transfer is a social act. Institutions, or systems of rules, relate the structures of the determination of rights and those of the transfer. In other words, the institution and the market function inseparably together. Markets must thus be seen as a special type of institution. Hodgson's definition is in this respect illuminating. He defines the market as 'a set of social institutions in which a large number of commodity exchanges of a specific type regularly take place, and to some extent are facilitated and structured by those institutions. Markets, in short, are organised and institutionalised exchange' (Hodgson, 1988: p. 174).

A theoretical problem is how institutions come about. There are two options: first, institutions are designed consciously by the participants in the market, or, second, institutions are inherited from the past. New Institutional Economics focuses on the first one, and emphasises the possibility of acquiring an appropriate organisation for a firm in a given market.[67] Many institutions and organisations are inherited, however, and are imposing

---

67 The New Institutional Economics concept of the emergence of institutions is, however, much too simplified. Economic institutions do not emerge automatically in response to economic needs, as New Institutional Economics seems to assume. 'Rather, they are constructed by individuals whose action is both facilitated and constrained by the structure and resources available in social networks in which they are

conditions on the behaviour of men. The latter issue is studied in New Economic Sociology.

The fact that economies function within a set of inherited institutions and are strongly influenced by past decisions on infrastructure, built environment, technologies, education, etc., results in many irreversibilities and in the so-called 'path-dependency': the economic system is affected by the path it has taken in the past. The automatically developing equilibria of neo-classical theory are 'disturbed' by this phenomenon and by various 'feedback mechanisms.' Two of the more important feedback relations are those of technology and organisation within the economy. Heertje (1973) has shown that technology cannot be taken as 'given' for the functioning of the economic system, but is inherently part of it.[68] The same goes for organisation. Economic development affects organisation, but organisation impacts economics as well. Equilibria are disturbed by many kinds of feedback; the price-mechanism is thus not the only mechanism affecting the functioning of the markets.

4.4.   Basic Premises of New Institutional Economics; problems of coordination

What are the basic premises of new institutional economic theory? The previous two paragraphs have shed some light on this, but I will summarise now the theoretical starting points and point out the main fields of interest in institutional economic theory. For this purpose, I will use Douglas North's book *Institutions, Institutional Change and Economic Performance* (1990), as a representative of the New Institutional Economics perspective, and Geoffrey Hodgson's book, *Economics and Institutions, a manifesto for a modern institutional economics* (1988), more or less representing the socio-economics perspective. I intend to integrate the arguments in these books into one framework for analysis.

New Institutional Economics has adopted Coase's argument that 'when it is costly to transact, institutions matter' (Coase, 1937). Transaction costs arise because of the complexity and dynamism of environments and the costliness of information. Questions of information and knowledge are vital to institutional economics. In Williamson's transaction-cost approach (= New Institutional Economics), the fundamental unit of analysis is the transaction. 'Transactions can take place across markets or within organizations. Whether a particular transaction is allocated to the market or to an organization is a matter of cost minimizations' (Douma and Schreuder, 1992: p. 102). Transaction-cost economics is based on two assumptions about human behaviour. First, human beings are boundedly rational; the knowledge of the decisionmaker is severely limited. This will pose a problem in an environment that is characterised by uncertainty and complexity. Second, human beings sometimes display opportunistic behaviour. Not everybody behaves opportunistically, but

---

embedded' (Granovetter, 1992: p. 7).

68   New technologies will lead to innovations that, in turn, lower transaction costs. According to North, these innovations consist of organisational innovations, instruments, and specific techniques and enforcement characteristics. 'These innovations occurred at three cost margins: (1) those that increased the mobility of capital, (2) those that lowered information costs, and (3) those that spread risk' (North, 1990: p. 125).

some people do, and it is difficult or costly to tell *ex ante* whether they will or not. The following example makes this clear. When someone tries to sell his house to a certain person, he can never be sure *ex ante* if this person will actually buy the house. For this reason, he wants him to sign a contract. On the other side, the person who wants to buy the house doesn't know if the seller tells the truth about the quality of the house. Therefore, he will ask an expert to inspect the house before he decides to buy it. Opportunistic behaviour is problematic only if it occurs in conjunction with small numbers of trading partners. 'If there is only one seller he does not have to worry about his reputation, because you do not have an alternative. In this case you want to have (the product) inspected, so you have to pay transaction costs' (Douma and Schreuder, 1992: p. 106).

These two particular aspects of human behaviour point out the significance of uncertainty in explaining human actions. 'These uncertainties arise as a consequence of both the complexity of the problems to be solved and the problem-solving software (...) possessed by the individual' (North, 1990: p. 25). In this context we must consider the role of institutions; they reduce the uncertainties involved in human interaction.

'Institutions provide the structure for exchange that (together with the technology employed) determines the cost of transacting and the cost of transformation. How well institutions solve the problems of coordination and production is determined by the motivation of the players (their utility function), the complexity of the environment, and the ability of the players to decipher and order the environment (measurement and enforcement)' (North, 1990: p. 34).

The institutions that are necessary to accomplish economic exchange vary in their complexity. North distinguishes informal constraints, formal rules and third-party enforcement. Informal constraints (like taboos, customs, and traditions) are part of the culture that underlies society. Formal rules include political (and judicial) rules, economic rules, and contracts. Political rules 'define the hierarchical structure of the polity, its basic decision structure, and the explicit characteristics of agenda control' (*ibid.*: p. 47). Economic rules 'define property rights, that is the bundle of rights over the use and the income to be derived from property and the ability to alienate an asset or a resource.' Contracts 'contain the provisions specific to a particular agreement in exchange' (*ibid.*: p. 47).

Finally, third-party enforcement would involve, in principle, 'a neutral party with the ability, costlessly, to enforce agreements such that the offending party always had to compensate the injured party to a degree that made it costly to violate the contracts' (*ibid.*: p. 58).

Furthermore, it is important to recognise the distinction between transaction- and information costs. Eggertsson defines transaction costs as 'the costs that arise when individuals exchange ownership rights to economic assets and enforce their exclusive rights' (Eggertsson, 1990: p. 14). The concepts of information costs and transaction costs are not identical. As Eggertsson argues, 'a lonely person on a desert island will encounter information costs as he goes about his "home production," but an isolated individual does not engage in exchange and therefore will have no transaction costs. (...) When information is costly, various activities related to the exchange of property rights between individuals give rise to transaction costs' (Eggertsson, 1990: p. 14).

Socio-economic theorists have criticised new institutional economics on various points, of which I consider the following issues as most significant. First, authors in the field of new institutional economics commonly seem to hold the idea that an institution exists because it is efficient. This approach of institutions is too narrow in its scope. The meaning of institutions involves much more than just stimulating efficiency. Second, institutions are generally considered as constraints to individual economic action. However, as will be shown below, institutions certainly play an enabling role as well. Third, the new institutional economics concept of dynamics in markets is problematic; among other things, because it ignores the social networks that condition institutional change. And fourth, the way new institutional economic theory deals with information problems is unconvincing. It still assumes that information problems can eventually be solved, while socio-economic theory more realistically argues that uncertainty is something we have to live with. It follows from these points of criticism that the assumptions underlying each of both theories -- of which I consider the socio-economic assumptions clearly more realistic -- differ substantially. These assumptions have already been mentioned above. Section 4.6 will use the socio-economic assumptions in its framework for analysis.

Hodgson develops his institutional theory on the basis of a number of different themes, including (1) the meaning of contracts and property rights, (2) the role of markets, prices and norms, (3) the relationship between uncertainty, institutions and the firm, and, finally, (4) the relationship between expectations and economic activity. Jointly, they form the foundation of his conceptual framework.

Contracts and property rights are fundamental to economic exchange on markets. Problems of information -- i.e. related to the possibility of opportunistic behaviour of one of the agents -- make it necessary to draw up contracts and define property rights. Non-contractual arrangements -- most notably, trust -- play a significant role in the way agents deal with information problems. Although trust and other associated non-contractual values are ultimately unprovable and incalculable, they are essential for market systems to work, due to the uncertainty and complexity of these markets. The recognition of contractual and non-contractual arrangements and property rights is fundamental to an understanding of international differences in market functioning and of the way market systems evolve through time.

Markets, prices and norms play important roles. As shown above, the market is just one of the mechanisms through which commodity exchange can take place. Moreover, the market includes a generalised mechanism to establish and publicise prices, and to promote goods and services. In contrast, there are many cases when exchange is established other than through the market. Finally, norms are essential to understand the working of markets and how prices come about. This is related to the fact that decisions to buy or sell at a given price depend in part on expected prices in the future. But future prices may themselves fluctuate; norms are then necessary to form judgements about these fluctuations.

The relationship between uncertainty, institutions and the firm; uncertainty and information problems are characteristic to markets. Rules, norms and institutions play then a functional role in providing a basis for decisionmaking, expectations, and belief. The institutional 'solution' to uncertainty can either be realised on 'the market' -- market institutions create and legitimate norms through the interaction of relatively autonomous traders typically without long-term commitments to each other -- or within the firm -- the firm is a social institution which generates other conventions and rules (e.g. loyalty) on a more permanent basis. The main difference between Hodgson's view and the transaction-cost view of the nature of the firm is that Hodgson argues that the rationale of firms is not simply a matter of transaction costs (as the transaction-cost approach argues). 'The function of the firm is, therefore, not simply to minimise transaction costs, but to provide an institutional framework within which, to some extent, the very calculus of costs is superseded' (Hodgson, 1988: p. 207). The choice between the market and the firm also depends on the possibility of 'quantification': 'the norms and conventions of the market relate, most crucially, to the matter of price. Within the firm, however, there is no single, clear quantitative expression of a price norm of convention to which actors can relate' (*ibid.*: p. 206).

The relationship between expectations and economic activity; expectations are important to economic activity and should be endogenous variables in the theoretical model. Central to institutional economic theory should, therefore, be a study of the way expectations are shaped and how they transform. Hodgson stresses that 'culture, habits and institutions colour perception and judgement and play a very important part in the formation of expectations' (*ibid.*: p. 225).

I regard Hodgson's interpretation of the functioning of markets and the role of institutions as being more realistic than the New Institutional Economics conceptions -- this is in line with the criticism that has been expressed above. Nevertheless, I do believe that especially North's explanation of institutional change and the significance of path dependency -- jointly responsible for the way economies evolve through time -- offers valuable insights into economic action.

4.5. Institutional change

Economies evolve through time. It is important to recognise the mechanisms underlying the dynamics of an economy. North has aimed at developing a theory of institutional change. His primary objective in his book is to achieve an understanding of the differential performances of economies through time. He argues that 'separating the analysis of the underlying rules from the strategy of the players is a necessary prerequisite to building a theory of institutions' (North, 1990: p. 5). The difference between institutions and organisations and the interaction between them shape the direction of institutional change.

'Institutions, together with the standard constraints of economic theory, determine the opportunities in a society. Organizations are created to take advantage of those opportunities, and, as the organizations evolve, they alter the institutions' (ibid.: p. 7).

This institutional change is incremental in form and 'comes from the perceptions of the entrepreneurs in political and economic organisations that they could do better by altering the existing institutional framework at some margin. But the perceptions crucially depend on both the information that the entrepreneurs receive and the way they process that information' (*ibid.*: p. 8). Because the act of acquiring information entails costs, these perceptions do not always result in efficient choices. To understand the processes underlying institutional change we must take into account the way institutional constraints shape organisations and their objectives *and* the kinds of knowledge and skills that will be acquired by the organisation to further its objectives -- as this plays a major role in the way the stock of knowledge evolves and is used.

How organisations and institutions interact has implications for the performance of economies over time. In exploring this interaction, North introduces the term *adaptive efficiency* (as opposed to neo-classical *allocative efficiency*):

'Adaptive efficiency (...) is concerned with the kinds of rules that shape the way an economy evolves through time (...). It is also concerned with the willingness of a society to acquire knowledge and learning, to induce innovation, to undertake risk and creative activity of all sorts, as well as to resolve problems and bottlenecks of the society through time' (ibid.: p. 80).

Adaptive efficiency thus refers to the effective organisation of markets. As mentioned above, in North's theoretical concept institutional change is believed to take place only incrementally; the institutional framework is stable. The most important source of institutional change is fundamental change in relative prices, such as changes in the ratio of factor prices (i.e., changes in the ratio of capital to land), changes in the cost of information (i.e., the process by which the entrepreneur acquires skills and knowledge changes perceived costs of measurement and enforcement), and changes in technology. Moreover, changes in preferences of individuals may cause institutional change.

Little is known about the sources of changing preferences or tastes. Nevertheless, essential to North's argument is that these cultural changes take place at a different rate than that characterising the changing of formal rules. '(A) major role of informal constraints is to modify, supplement, or extend formal rules' (*ibid.*: p. 87). Therefore, changes in formal rules will in general be modified by the norms and values underlying a society. Another source of institutional change may thus be changing ideas, norms and values.

Path dependency
According to North, two forces shape the path of institutional change: increasing returns to scale and imperfect markets characterized by significant transaction costs. Increasing returns may arise because of various reasons. For instance, costs will be reduced once the institutions are functioning smoothly, or coordination effects occur because other institutions are positively influenced as well.

Moreover, the long-run path of economies is shaped by the fact that markets are imperfect and therefore give rise to significant transaction costs. In an imperfect market the information feedback is fragmentary: 'then the subjective models of actors modified both by very imperfect feedback and by ideology will shape the path' (North, 1990: p. 95). This allows for an explanation as to why economies have evolved along different lines. Economic growth depends on the extent to which these 'increasing returns' mechanisms take place in the institutional context. Thus, a fundamental change in relative prices (see above) affects two societies differently, because:

> *'in each society the change will result in adaptations at the margins, and the margins affected will be those where the immediate issues require solution and the solution will be determined by the relative bargaining power of the participants -- that is, the organizations that have evolved in the specific overall institutional context. (...) Because the bargaining power of groups in one society will clearly differ from that in another, the marginal adjustments in each society will typically be different as well. Moreover, with different past histories and incomplete feedback on the consequences, the actors will have different subjective models and therefore make different policy choices'* (North, 1990: p. 101).

The term 'path dependency' is not exclusively used by North. For instance, according to Swedberg and Granovetter, the idea of path-dependent development has been generalised to organisational and institutional forms by Granovetter, 'arguing that economic institutions are constructed by mobilization of resources through social networks, conducted, of course, against a background of constraints given by the previous historical development of society, polity, market, and technology' (Swedberg and Granovetter, 1992: p. 18). Path dependency is, according to North, the key to an analytical understanding of long-run economic change. 'The source of incremental change is the gains to be obtained by organizations and their entrepreneurs from acquiring skills, knowledge, and information that will enhance their objectives. Path dependence comes from the increasing returns mechanisms that reinforce the direction once given a path' (North, 1990: p. 112).

The path-dependency concept makes it possible to interpret variations in economic performance, not only between nations but between regional and urban economies as well. It focuses the attention on differences between economies, replacing the neo-classical emphasis on uniformity. It is explicitly this *variation* I am interested in, in the context of the present study.

4.6. A Framework for analysis: basic elements

The above discussion of new institutional economics and socio-economics has provided us tools necessary to build up a framework for analysis. Of course, the reproduction of a theoretical debate that has attracted attention of countless scholars can hardly take place within one chapter of a book. Out of necessity many interesting aspects of this debate have therefore been left unmentioned. Nevertheless, it is now possible to derive from the above the basic elements of my framework. These basic elements are still rather abstract. They will be operationalised in Chapter Five.

First, turn to the *objective of the theory*. Central to institutional economic theory are problems of information, which determine economic action and the working of markets. The theoretical objective is, in the first place, to explain what kind of informational problems exists, what the consequences are and how problems of information are solved. The specific role of institutions, related to these information problems, is the key subject of study. In this respect, explanations are sought regarding (1) the meaning of contracts, property rights and non-contractual arrangements, (2) the role of markets, prices and norms, (3) the rationale of the firms as opposed to the market, and (4) the relationship between expectations and economic activity. Institutional theory focuses our attention on the strategies of market parties and the way uncertainty determines these strategies. Second, and related to the former, the behaviour of individuals -- the strategies of firms -- can be determined by different rationalities (human behaviour is purposeful). Some actors strive for maximum profits, while others are satisfied with sufficient income; the rationality of public-sector strategies is based on public welfare. Different kinds of rules and norms play a role: monopoly power of land may guarantee a maximum income to the landowner, but generally it is not 'accepted' (norms) as market strategy. Third, institutional economic theory explicitly aims to contribute to a better understanding of the dynamics of economies. How do economies evolve through time? What are the mechanisms underlying institutional change? How do institutions come about? What is the significance of long-run technological progress? Why do economies evolve along different lines and, related to this, why do different economies function separately? Finally, institutional economic theory emphasises the path dependency of economies: the way markets function at present is shaped by decisions that have been made in the past. Fig. 4.2 presents the subjects of study in institutional-economic theory.

FIGURE 4.2
Institutional economic theory: Subjects of Study

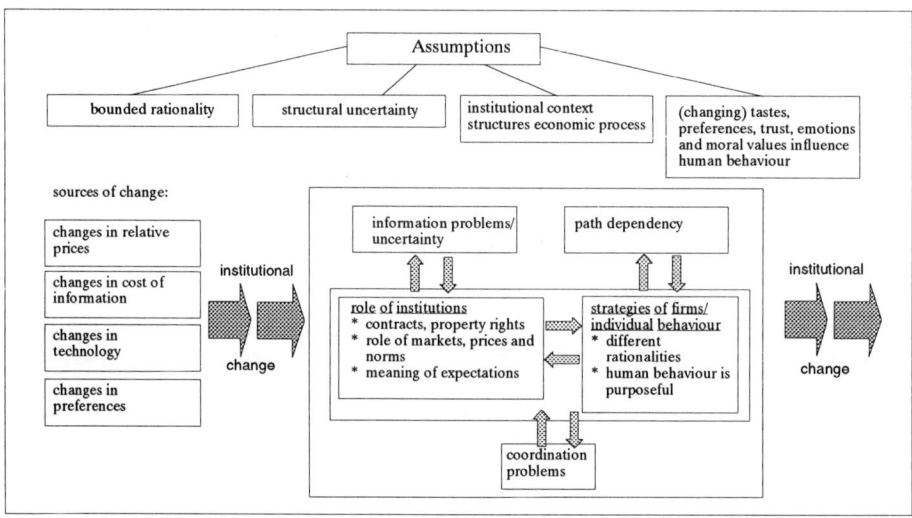

Summarised, the framework for analysis aims to contribute to a better understanding of (the significance of) informational problems, of different rationalities behind human behaviour, of institutional change, of path dependency, and of the impact of these issues on the functioning of markets.

Next, turn to the *assumptions* included in the theoretical framework. Institutional economic theory is based on assumptions concerning rationality, knowledge, the economic process and the human agent. First, it is assumed that human agents act boundedly rational; information problems are characteristic to human behaviour. In some situations humans do not even aim to act rationally; they show, for instance, habitual behaviour. Second, uncertainty is structural to economic activity. As a result, transaction and information costs appear. Uncertainty is particularly connected to future development; this frequently causes problems to market parties, since economic decisions often require information about the future. Institutions, like rules, norms, trust, habit, etc. are 'created' to reduce the lack of information. Third, the economic process is structured by the institutional context, consisting of norms, rules and social networks. Institutional factors, like price norms and expectations about future developments are relevant to explaining economic action. Fourth, human behaviour is supposed to be purposeful; agents can choose between different goals. Tastes and preferences characteristically change, while trust, emotions and moral values affect the decisions of economic agents and agencies. In turn, institutions influence, together with social practices and history, our ideas, perceptions and actions, thus shaping the path an economy takes through time.

Next, turn to the *indicators* included in the theoretical framework. Institutional economic theory can be used to analyse economic processes (i.e. real estate market processes). Empirical analysis based on institutional economic theory may be complicated, because we have to study the meaning and relevance to economic processes of qualitative parameters such as norms, expectations, trust, habits and non-contractual arrangements, the significance of different types of coordinative mechanisms such as social networks, the influence of path dependency and the factors that determine the degree of uncertainty in a market related to the development of costs, market prices and profit margins. However, it is important to analyse these aspects of the institutional context because it becomes possible then to examine the impact of the institutional organisation of the market on the functioning of this market. This calls for analysis of certain aspects of 'economic action,' i.e. the strategies of market parties, the profitability of the production of certain goods, development gains related to a particular market strategy, the way market prices evolve, etc. On the other hand, account must be taken of the variations in the institutional context, between different countries, different regions or different cities. From a theoretical perspective, the challenge should then be to link institutional variation and different outcomes of market processes to each other. Furthermore, we can study institutional change. Institutional change, in turn, should then be related to the 'sources' of institutional change. In this respect, the challenge is to analyse the relation between institutional change and the way the outcome of market processes evolves through time.

5 THE INSTITUTIONAL ORGANISATION OF THE REAL ESTATE MARKET: FRAMEWORK FOR ANALYSIS

5.1. Analysing the institutional context

In the previous chapters I have argued why the institutional context of urban real estate markets should be studied explicitly. First, it has been argued that property development processes often vary between places and through time. Among other things, the scale on which new building developments take place, market values of land and property and rent levels, the number of transactions, the type and quality of new buildings, the location of new development projects, returns on real estate investments, the type and quality of new property developments, the age of the existing building stock, etc., substantially deviate between one urban region and another. The same goes for temporal variation. For example, property prices continually fluctuate, new building technologies are introduced, investments in real estate often show an capricious tendency, the quality of new buildings mutates through time, the group of actors involved with property development changes through time, and so on. Second, it has been suggested that this diversity -- both in spatial and in temporal terms -- is linked with, successively, the nature of demand in an urban region, the supply of sites and properties (both the stock of land and buildings and new building developments), and the institutional organisation of land and property markets. Furthermore, I have made clear that the influence of the institutional organisation of land and property markets on the outcome of urban development and redevelopment processes will receive most attention in this study. Third, the decision to develop my study in this direction, viz. the analysis of the institutional organisation of the market and its influence on the outcome of market processes, has been based on several arguments, among them the role of 'institutional factors' with respect to social problems related to real estate development, with respect to international variations in the outcome of development processes, and with respect to changes that take place on real estate markets. Fourth, the institutional models of the development process in Chapter Three have demonstrated both the significance of institutional variation with respect to market organisation and the relevance of this institutional variation for the functioning of real estate markets. To understand the functioning of real estate markets correctly, we must take account of the role of information problems, different rationalities in human behaviour, the meaning of institutional change and path dependency. Fifth, institutional economic theory is needed because it makes it possible to analyse the institutional organisation of the market and its relevance to urban real estate development. The institutional organisation of the market refers here to the composition of the group of agents and agencies involved in real estate development and the institutional economic relations between them (e.g. the distribution of costs and benefits from development activity), the financing of real estate investments (changing forms of capital flow), the role of the public sector, the status of property ownership and property rights and the set of rules that regulate the market.

This chapter aims to apply the framework for analysis to a study of real estate development processes. This framework should contribute, particularly, to a better understanding of the role of information problems, the significance of different rationalities in human behaviour, the meaning of institutional change and path dependency, with respect to real estate development processes. Research will branch out in two directions. First, I will investigate spatial variation in the institutional organisation of real estate markets. Variations in the institutional context will then be related to real estate development processes. Second, I will analyse changes through time in the institutional organisation of the real estate market and the way this institutional change is shaped by the path dependency of urban real estate markets. Again, this institutional change will then be linked to changes in real estate development processes.

Fig. 5.1 shows the elements of the institutional organisation of the real estate market

FIGURE 5.1
An institutional approach to real estate development processes: subjects of study

I The institutional organisation of the real estate market	II Spatial and temporal variation in the organisational structure	III Impact of institutional organisation on real estate market processes
* composition of the group of actors taking part in the development industry * rationalities behind the strategies of market parties * institutional-economic relations between agents involved in the development industry * public sector interventions in land and property markets * legal and normative rules regulating the market * status of property ownership and property rights	A. Spatial variation * degree of uncertainty * information costs * path dependency * wider institutional and political context B. Temporal variation * sources of change: changes in relative prices, changes in information costs, changes in technology, changes in preferences * path dependency	* building construction costs * real estate market prices * development gains and profit margins * the volume of new building development * the number of transactions * the scale of new development areas * the type and quality of real estate * the ageing of the existing building stock * the location of new buildings

The chapter is drawn up as follows. The first part (sections 5.2 and 5.3) will analyse spatial variation in the institutional organisation of real estate markets. Section 5.2 identifies various aspects of this spatial variation and then interprets these aspects with help of the framework. Section 5.3 analyses the relation between market organisation and the outcome of development processes. The second part (sections 5.4, 5.5 and 5.6) is devoted to institutional change. Section 5.4 analyses, successively, the sources of institutional changes and the path dependency of these changes. Section 5.5 pays attention to the strategies of the agents and agencies involved in the development industry, particularly focusing on the changes that have taken place with respect to these strategies. Section 5.6 lists the resulting changes in the outcome of property development processes. Finally, section 5.7 concludes.

5.2. Spatial Variations with respect to the Organisation of the Real Estate Market

The way property-development processes take place in different cities may vary greatly. It has been assumed that this cannot fully be understood by merely analysing the demand for and supply of land and buildings, leaving unnoticed the institutional organisation of the market. This section focuses on variations in this institutional organisation. Institutional aspects of real estate markets that can be generalized to any real estate market are examined.

First, I will discuss variations in market organisation. Subsequently, section 5.2.2 will try to explain this institutional diversity.

5.2.1.   Variations in market organisation

Variations in market organisation are distinguished into variations in the composition of the group of agents and agencies involved in real estate development and the institutional economic relations between them; the financing of real estate developments; the role of the public sector; the status of property ownership and property rights; and the set of rules that regulate the market.

With respect to *the composition of the group of actors* taking part in the development industry, the following points are noteworthy. Real estate is developed by various agents and agencies. Commercial-property developers, for instance, are sometimes linked to banks or to real estate investment companies. They may originally have been local building contractors, but it could also be a foreign company operating on an international scale. New dwellings are not only built by professional developers, but also by private persons, building for their own use as well. Housing associations are another group of specialised real estate developers. Real estate investors as a group are similarly heterogeneous: pension funds, insurance companies, real estate investment companies, private investors, foreign investors. Moreover, in each sector of the real estate market, the group of agents and agencies involved in real estate development is different. For instance, some developers concentrate their activities fully on constructing housing, others on developing commercial property; sometimes they are active in both sectors.

The strategies of the actors vary both in different sectors of the real estate market and between different cities. In a small and fragile local real estate market, developers are probably more cautious with respect to new development projects than they would be in a large and healthy market. Moreover, large internationally operating developers and investors are likely to operate more professionally than are small local developers (or the private persons that act as one-off housebuilders: different rationalities form the strategies of the groups of actors). This implies, for instance, that each of the two groups manage market uncertainties in a different way. The large companies are, on the one hand, able to conduct more research in order to reduce risk and they can better spot changes in demand and/or prices, while on the other hand they can more easily bear the risks of developments with an uncertain future. Small local developers and private persons face, to a larger extent, information problems. Related to the former, some developers build commercial property speculatively, while others do not. In some urban regions they develop industrial property for the market (in England, but not in the Netherlands). In addition, a significant diversity exists with respect to the scale on which developments are carried out by the developers.[69] Furthermore, land development, the development of new dwellings, and sometimes also industrial property development are carried out both by market parties and the public sector; this varies not only in an international context, but also between cities within one country as well. In these cases, public development strategies are certainly different from market

---

69   See Dreimuller (1980) on the strategies of Dutch property developers.

parties' strategies. However, note that numerous government bodies operate on the real estate market: development corporations, public investment companies, municipal land departments, specialised corporations acting as administrators of public private partnerships, etc.

With respect to renovation and redevelopment projects, the strategies of owner-users are, most likely, different from the strategies of investors who own real estate because of a pure commercial interest. For instance, the latter group of financial institutions will respond to a fall of property values by selling their real estate assets (and buying, instead, more shares), while owner-users in the same situation probably will not sell their property (for them, only the use-value counts; see further discussion below).

Now turn to *the institutional economic relations* between the agents involved in the development industry. A broad distinction can be made between market and non-market relations. Examples of the latter include the following: building contractors that develop new projects in a joint venture, development companies as daughter companies of financial institutions, public private partnerships, etc. Relations between agents in the development process often go smoothly via regularised patterns and standard procedures -- for example, land sale from land department to developers, the sale of a dwelling by one owner-occupier to another. However, in some cases unique institutional relations have to be created -- for example, when risky large inner-city redevelopment projects are initiated. Then, standard procedures and contracts may not be available. Public-private partnerships, managed by a corporation that has especially been established for this purpose, are examples of such unique relationships. These relations are all more or less the result of rational decisions by the agents. More difficulties arise when taking into consideration economic relations that are based on moral values like habits, trusts and routines. This helps to explain how localised networks of human agents come into existence.[70]

The *financing of real estate development* is another aspect of the institutional organisation of the market. Several authors have analysed the influence of international capital flows on real estate development in 'world cities.'[71] In smaller cities, capital flows come mainly from national finance capital and are restricted to only a few projects. It is important to recognize the origins of the capital flows into real estate. Foreign investors, for instance, may hold different opinions with respect to market conditions than do domestic investors.[72]

The various ways in which the public sector intervenes in land and property markets also result in differences in the institutional organisation of real estate markets. The variety of public sector agencies that actively intervene in real estate markets has already been mentioned above. The active role of Dutch municipalities as developers on urban land

---

70   See, for instance, Amin and Thrift (1993, 1994) on the meaning of localised institutionalised patterns.

71   See numerous authors on the 'global city concept', like Sassen (1991), Fainstein (1993, 1994), Pryke (1994). See Thrift (1994) on applying the globalisation-thesis on the Dutch Randstad.

72   See, for more information on Dutch financial institutions' investment strategies, for instance, Blankenstein-Bouwmeesters and Lukkes (1984), Conijn and Papa (1987), Van Gool *et al.* (1993).

markets has been extensively studied.[73] Public-sector involvement with real estate development encompasses much more than only active government interventions. Via, *inter alia*, its spatial policy, housing sector policy and regional-economic policy, the public sector sets, either consciously or unintentionally, the conditions for economic action. Public-sector policy, and in some situations the absence of public-sector policy, affects the degree of uncertainty and risk in a local real estate market; it influences the expectations of markets parties and the profitability of development projects, and, ultimately, the strategies of market parties.

The impact of government intervention is closely related to *the rules* that regulate the market. The current set of rules leaves Dutch municipalities relatively free to operate on urban real estate markets. They are, for instance, free to choose between active and passive land policy. The fact that almost all of them have deliberately chosen for active intervention in the land market -- that is, they purchase the land for new building schemes -- significantly influences the functioning of the land market (see Needham, 1992). Moreover, the planning system, zoning plans, the policy with respect to building permits, quality demands with respect to new building developments, the legislation with respect to financial institutions' investment strategies, the influence of the political system, etc., jointly determine the availability of new building schemes, the development of building costs, the possibility of capturing development gains, profit margins, etc.

Another example can be derived from the housing market study that will be described in the subsequent chapters of this book. On the Dutch housing market, as will be argued in Chapter Eight, the national government's spatial policy actually constrains the implementation of the national government's housing policy, since it increases housing development costs and reduces at the same time the availability of building land for housing.

Finally, *the status of property ownership and property rights* is part of the institutional organisation of the real estate market. Several points are relevant to our discussion. Property rights are partially determined by the government's right to purchase land and buildings compulsory and by the extent to which government bodies make use of this right. Norms also affect legal ownership rights. For example, land speculation is a perfectly legal act.[74] From an economic point of view, it can be a rational strategy to buy land, keep it until its value has risen and sell it subsequently. However, from a moral point of view, land speculation is often disapproved of. This may prevent many actors from so behaving. Another example concerns the moral status given in many countries to home ownership. This probably motivates many households to buy a house, even if they can hardly afford it.

I have now examined a number of issues that are related to the institutional organisation of the real estate market. The subject has, however, certainly not exhaustively been treated.[75] Before turning to the analysis of the impact of the institutional organisation on the

---

73   See, for instance, Giebels *et al.* (1985), Kortenoever (1989), and Kruijt *et al.* (1990) on the role of municipal land departments on land markets in Dutch cities.

74   Land speculation is defined here as the purchase of land with the sole purpose to sell it as soon as the value has increased.

75   See Chapter Six for a detailed treatment of the institutional organisation of the Dutch housing market.

functioning and outcome of real estate markets, I will now first try to interpret spatial variation in the institutional organisation of the real estate market with help of institutional economic theory.

5.2.2.   Interpretations of Spatial Variation

Variations in the institutional organisation of the real estate market are, according to this theory, connected with the composition of the group of actors involved in the development process, the institutional-economic relations between them, the role of the public sector in local real estate markets, the set of rules and the status of property ownership. Important to these institutional aspects are the degree of uncertainty in a local market, the path dependency of local real estate markets and institutional change. This section will pay particular attention to the degree of uncertainty. Institutional change and path dependency will be discussed in sections 5.4 and 5.5.

The *degree of uncertainty* brings into play the complexity of a local economy. The complexity, in turn, may be caused by the heterogeneity of real estate as a product, the different natures of both buyers and sellers on this market, the problematic accessibility of local markets, the geographical division of markets, the incomplete information about price levels, the influence of a large diversity of intermediaries, the large size of development projects, the considerable length in time of both preparation and production of new buildings, etc. The strategies of agents in the development process may be influenced by the problems that are caused by the incompleteness of information. For instance, weak local economies feature more uncertainty with respect to the implementation of large-scale redevelopment projects than do prosperous urban regions. In a weak local economy, developers/investors require, therefore, solid conditions from the municipality to secure their profit margins/returns. Information problems are partly due to technical characteristics of real estate markets.[76] However, they can also be caused by the structural uncertainty about future market developments, i.e. market values, production costs, future demand, investment yields -- especially because the life span of buildings is relatively long, while the life span of land is even endless.

The attractiveness of land and buildings as an investment object is closely related to the issue of uncertainty. In the Netherlands, it is generally assumed that pension funds, insurance companies and other investors invest mainly in real estate to spread risk. They content themselves with relatively low returns, as long as these are higher than the *rekenrente* -- this is the minimum return, calculated on an actuarial base, that they must make to cover their obligations (for instance, paying pensions). Real estate is generally considered to be a safe investment because of government influence on this market. Public-sector policy especially reduces the uncertainty with respect to future urban developments.[77]

---

[76] See Chapter Six for technical characteristics of the real estate market, in general, and their influence on the Dutch housing market, in particular.

[77] This seems to be the general opinion; however, no convincing empirical evidence exists with respect to financial institutions' investment strategies on urban property markets. Investors are not exactly open-handed

The low returns go together with relatively low rents on the Dutch commercial-property market.[78] This situation is in sharp contrast with the conditions in other West-European countries, especially in Great Britain and France, but also in Spain and Germany. In these countries financial institutions invest in commercial property because high returns are feasible.[79]

Financial institutions' participation in real estate projects can, *de facto*, be entirely ascribed to the element of risk, which is characteristic to all property development, and the possibility of acquiring sufficient returns on their investment. Investing in real estate is risky because of the uncertainty with respect to future gains.[80] Risk is thus linked to uncertainty and incomplete information. Crucial to the functioning of modern markets, and certainly also to the functioning of urban property markets, is the market's ability to turn *uncertainty* into *risk*. Risk is a measurable concept -- although I realise that this pronouncement is in itself risky -- and can therefore be linked to a *rate of return*. Financial institutions argue that the higher the risk, the higher the rate of return on investments has to be.[81] The optimal investment opportunity shows a minimal risk and a maximum return. However, the high level of uncertainty on the real estate investment market has not only disadvantages. Imperfect market conditions will make it possible for some investors to build up an information lead with respect to other investors. Moreover, they will be able to keep this lead during a longer period than would be possible under perfect market conditions. Investors can thus realise exceptional returns.[82]

---

with providing information.

78   See Van der Krabben (1993), and Lie (1994) on this point.

79   This does not necessarily mean that returns on real estate investment in these countries are indeed higher. For a detailed study of financial institutions' investment strategies with respect to real estate in various West-European countries, see Lie (1994).

80   Compared to, for instance, the market for government bonds, real estate investments are considered more risky because of the higher uncertainty on real estate markets. This relative uncertainty of real estate investments is the result of, among other things, the heterogeneity of real estate, the fact that the real estate market is divided in several submarkets, and, in general, the imperfect market conditions that are characteristic to real estate markets.

81   See Goslings (1990) on this point; he makes a similar distinction between risk and uncertainty. According to Goslings, risk can be defined by a calculation of probability, while uncertainty indicates a series of single events in random succession. The distinction between uncertainty and risk has been introduced by Knight (1921) and was later reproduced by Keynes (referred to in Hodgson, 1988: p. 188). Hodgson recites Keynes when he writes: 'Uncertainty (...) applies to a situation where there is no scientific basis to form any calculable probability whatever' (Hodgson, p. 188). In contrast, to risk a definite probability can be attributed.

82   It follows from this that the concept of uncertainty is apparently more complicated than it is assumed to be in new institutional economic theory. For, the line of argument in new institutional economic theory is that uncertainty is typical to all human behaviour and that institutions and organisations are created to reduce this uncertainty (in order to create perfect market conditions). In a perfect market there should be optimal information; imperfect markets are, among other things, characterised by non-optimal and/or asymmetric information. This is all true. We can indeed consider the concept of risk as an *institutional solution* (or a tool for strategic behaviour) for the existence of uncertainty in markets. However, this explanation covers only part of the reality. Financial institutions' strategies are based on the existence of risk in a market and their interests

Financial institutions can freely choose to invest in risky projects, speculating on high returns on their investments. It is, however, remarkable that in some countries financial institutions are prepared to accept higher risks than are their colleagues in other countries. The latter depends on their motivations to invest in, for instance, real estate, and on the alternative investment opportunities that are open to them. Do they accept high risks, in order to realise high returns, or do they minimise risks, being satisfied with relatively low returns?

Note that the existence of variations in risk is an essential element in the way modern markets, including urban property markets, function. It has been emphasised that (1) financial institutions pursue various investment strategies (which may all be rational) and (2) a more differentiated approach to the meaning of uncertainty in markets is needed -- especially in markets where investors play an important role. Asymmetric information will sometimes lead to market failure, but it is at the same time a necessary market condition for financial institutions to invest in real estate. Investors that are prepared to accept high risks will judge institutions that mean to reduce market risk as inefficient, when the interference results in lower returns.

Since uncertainty is structural to real estate markets, the actors most likely have to rely on expectations that are usually partially based on norms, trust and habits. Above, the discussion centred on the meaning of norms (i.e. with respect to land speculation) and expectations (i.e. regarding future returns). In the study of the Dutch housing market, I will analyse the consequences of the price fluctuations on the owner-occupied housing market. I will argue that these fluctuations have led to a behaviour by private developers that is (too) strictly based on risk reduction: as a result, they may miss new development opportunities (they are not prepared to accept high risks). On the other hand, these fluctuations have resulted in alternative strategies by existing owners regarding the sale of their property, primarily based on the possibility of cashing in extra money gains -- a move-up market has come into existence. The "risk-reduction" behaviour of private developers on the housing market is, probably, partly based on expectations regarding house-price fluctuations, on mistrust in the stability of the owner-occupied housing market and on habits (developers have 'always' been careful with respect to the development of new owner-occupied dwellings).[83] The existing owners' decision to sell their house and to use the money gains -- house prices in the Netherlands have been rising for some years now -- to buy another dwelling clearly depends on their expectations about future price development. If they expect

---

are not in all respects served by absolute risk reduction. A distinction should be made here between two types of risk. On the one hand, we can easily assume that all individual actors, including financial institutions, try to reduce their 'individual' risk in order to maximise profits. If financial institutions consider investing in real estate, then they will certainly investigate market
conditions to minimise the chance of bad results with respect to their investments. However, the reduction of *market risk* -- this is, in fact, the general expectation of risk -- does not serve their interests because the returns would decline then as well. Actually, all financial institutions strive for asymmetric risk reduction.

83 Note that many speculative developers -- but this point concerns other branches as well -- have built up their current market position over a long period of time based on a certain strategy. Some of them will change their strategy when market conditions alter. Others won't be prepared to do so: they hold on to their traditional strategy. 'Traditional behaviour' is, in fact, an example of habitual behaviour.

that house prices will continue to rise, they will likely postpone this decision. Otherwise, they will decide to sell their house. Again, moral values are involved. The fact that the market value of owner-occupied dwellings apparently begins to gain in importance compared to the use value, indicates a change of norms and/or habits.

5.3.   Consequences for the Outcome of Market Processes

The next step in the analysis is to investigate the (potential) impact of the institutional organisation of the real estate market on the outcome of real estate development processes. It is assumed that the institutional organisation of the market may influence at least (1) building construction costs, (2) market prices of real estate, (3) development gains and profit margins, (4) the volume of new building developments, (5) the number of transactions, (6) the scale of new development areas, (7) the type and quality of real estate, (8) the ageing of the existing building stock, and (9) the location of new buildings. To demonstrate the supposed relations between the institutional organisation of the real estate market and these issues, I will refer, in various cases, to the findings of the study of the Dutch housing market, which is the subject of Chapters Six, Seven and Eight.

(1) building construction costs
Building construction costs vary both interregionally (see Van der Krabben, 1993) and in an international context (see Ball, 1988). This may be due to differences with respect to the quality of new buildings (as I suggested in Van der Krabben, 1993), or to a different market efficiency, related to the organisational structure of the development industry.[84] These differences in building costs are relevant to our discussion, since, for instance, the level of these costs directly affects the profit margins of real estate development and, consequently, the strategies of the development industry. Other reasons may be responsible for differences in building costs as well. In the study of the Dutch housing market, I will argue that the continual increase of building costs (in real prices) during the last twenty-five years is connected with technical characteristics of building construction, on the one hand, and the traditional behaviour of the construction industry, on the other hand. Furthermore, the construction of large-scale building development is, generally speaking, relatively cheaper than small-scale development. The costs of both land and building development are considerably reduced, when carried out on a large scale. It seems plausible that this prevents developers from shifting from large-scale housing development to small-scale housing development. It is suggested in the case study that this is one of the reasons for the present shortages in housing production.

(2) market values and rent levels
It has been widely recognised that commercial-property rents in the Netherlands are low

---

84   For instance, it is a well-known fact that building construction costs of new dwellings in Germany exceed the costs of similar dwellings in the Netherlands, due to tighter regulation of building quality in Germany.

and hardly rising, and yet, that there is only minor variation in office rents throughout the country. This is caused, so it has been suggested, by the lack of scarcity in urban land markets, the relative uniformity of the Dutch urban landscape, and the historically defined fact that some of the larger cities, particularly Amsterdam and The Hague, have deliberately decided to spread office development over various locations within the city.[85] The lack of scarcity in urban land markets is the obvious result of the active land policy by municipalities. They see it as their task always to provide sufficient building sites and they do not necessarily need to maximise their profits from land development (see Needham, 1992). The motivation behind the municipalities' role on urban land markets forms a different question: is this "historically" determined or does it follow from a lack of interest in land development by market parties (because land-development costs exceed the market value of land)?

Municipal land policy, together with the existing urban spatial structure, seriously affects the profitability of both land and property development. As a result, the motivations of financial institutions to invest in real estate in the Netherlands hardly stems from the expectation that office rents will rise in the future. It is more likely that just the stability of office rents forms the motivation for them to invest in real estate. On the housing market other mechanisms are at work. In the housing market study I will examine the close relation between the fluctuations of market prices on the second-hand owner-occupied housing market and the profitability of new housing development.

(3) development gains[86] and profit margins

The level and division of development gains determines the strategies of the real estate developers. Development gains may occur, for instance, as a result of the implementation of new land-use plans. They may also result from a sudden increase of the attractiveness of a certain location, because of developments that take place on a location nearby. It is important to recognise that the strategies of some developers are actually directed to acquiring these development gains, while other developers do not especially build their strategies on the possibility of realising development gains. In the former case, developers often hold land banks, while in the latter case they usually do not. The choice for one these strategies may have important consequences -- in different directions -- for the functioning of real estate markets. The relevance of this issue to the Dutch housing market, again, will be investigated in the following chapters.

(4) urban economic growth; the volume of new building developments

In what sense is the level and direction of urban economic growth determined by the special characteristics of (urban) real estate markets? The availability of business sites, differences with respect to the driving forces underlying development processes between various sectors of the real estate market, and technical characteristics of real estate development (impeding, for instance, a quick response to increases in demand) may be of

---

85 See Brouwer (1994) for a geographical analysis of real estate development in Dutch cities (also Louw, 1994), and Bateman (1985) for a comparable analysis, but then in an international context.

86 Healey defines 'development gains' as follows: 'The concept of 'development gain' refers to the land value generated by location. As urban areas expand or are transformed, the value of location may increase or change' (Healey, 1994: p. 177; taken from Ball, 1983).

influence. Chapter Ten is entirely devoted to this issue.

(5) the number of transactions, the size of the groups of, respectively, buyers and sellers

Commercial real estate owners respond to changes in real estate market values; for owner-users, the use-value of their property usually forms the point of reference. This means that competition may seriously vary between a local real estate market that is dominated by commercial owners (the financial institutions) and markets that contain a majority of owner-users. For instance, in the Netherlands it used to be common practise that municipalities, as land owners, negotiated with only one developer for the development of a new housing scheme.[87] In case of large-scale commercial property development, only a few investors and developers have, respectively, the money and the capacity to participate in such a project (oligopolistic market). Moreover, these projects are now often developed in public-private partnership constructions; as a result, the way competition takes place has changed. Monopoly ownership occurs in markets that are characterised by scarcity and poor accessibility (access to the market for 'outsiders' is constrained). Two issues that are related to monopoly ownership are relevant to our discussion. First, the group of monopolists is heterogeneous in its composition. Some of them have unintentionally become monopolists (for instance, an owner of farming land that is intended for commercial use in a new zoning plan). Others deliberately try to obtain a monopoly position on the land market, by speculating on future developments. The occurrence of the second type of monopoly ownership depends, among other things, on the development gains that can be made on local land markets. In the housing market study I will argue that in the Netherlands the situation is changing. The allocation of the VINEX locations has increased the attractiveness of monopoly ownership on these locations.

Second, for the latter type of monopoly ownership to exist, market parties must exist, whose intentions are to speculate on monopoly ownership. This type of developer probably does not operate on every local market, despite the fact that the opportunities may be available. This brings into play the path dependency of a local economy. The organisational structure of a local development industry, including the strategies of the agents that are involved in this industry, is partially historically determined.

(6) the scale of new development areas; large- versus small-scale building projects

It has been argued above that the organisational structure of the development industry influences the scale on which new developments take place. Generally speaking, large real estate developers prefer to develop new dwellings in large quantities, while the one-off-building owner-occupiers build their dwellings on a single plot. This not only affects the costs of development, but, of course, the "sight" of newly developed areas is shaped as well. A large-scale development approach often results in a monotonous -- but probably high-quality -- urban landscape, while small-scale developments bring with them a more differentiated urban landscape. Furthermore, the relative price of land -- compared to

---

87 Only recently this seems to have changed. Traditionally, in many municipalities land departments usually negotiated with only one private developer about the development of, for instance, an owner-occupied housing scheme. Now, increasingly a competitive element seems to be introduced. Land departments ask several private developers to make a bid for the building land and to calculate the development costs; opposed to the former, this may result in higher land prices.

building construction costs -- determines building densities. Note that in an international context, the ratio of the price of land to building construction costs varies widely.[88] As a result a different locational pattern of building developments may be expected in these countries: not only the development of buildings in higher densities, but also a stronger competition for land on the most attractive locations.

(7) the type and quality of real estate
When local development activity is dominated by investment demand, another outcome may be expected -- standardised buildings, a dichotomy in the 'status' of business parks (toplocations versus peripheral locations), higher density developments on top locations, more "booms" and "slumps" in development activity -- than would come out in a city that is dominated by user demand. In business sectors (manufacturing industry, the service sector), commercially developed real estate (business buildings for rental) is likely to be of a better quality than is real estate built by the owner-users. This follows from the expectation that for owner-users, primarily the use-value of the building plays a role and not the market value -- they have no intention of selling their property in the near future. Quality is then only functional (from the point of view of production). The result of this can easily be seen in many -- irrefutably -- unattractive industrial areas, to be found in almost every city. The attractiveness of office buildings -- in commercial terms -- is closely related to location, but when 'location' does not matter -- for example many, more or less identical locations are available (within one specific business park), the 'quality' of the building itself comes into play. It is typical of real estate markets that prices (e.g. office rents) are determined in a market including both second hand and new buildings and high-quality and poor-quality buildings. On the Dutch office market, the 'price' of office space varies between locations -- office rents on top locations in the four large cities are about twice as high as rents on office locations in small and medium-sized cities -- but only minor price differences can be recorded both between second-hand and new buildings, and between high-quality and poor-quality buildings.[89]

(8) the ageing of the existing building stock and the pace of replacement of obsolete buildings
Why is it that some areas become run-down and others are revitalised? The ageing of the existing building stock, together with the pace of replacement of obsolete buildings, depends not only on the changing demands of the users (both households and companies; in this case we should call it *functional* ageing), but also on the development of real estate prices, on developments with respect to building construction and demolition costs, on the possibility of making profits out of redevelopment projects, on institutional constraints to redevelopment, and, finally, on the ownership situation (then we should call it *economic* ageing). First, we must distinguish two groups of owner-investors: small private investors and large institutio-

---

88 For example, in Amsterdam this ratio is about 20:80 -- that is, the value of the land in real estate projects is about 20% of the total value of the projects (land and buildings), while in cities like Paris and London an opposite relation (80-20) can be found.

89 This is in contrast with the situation on the housing market in the Netherlands; remarkably, price differentiations on this market seem to be much more profound (see chapter Seven and Eight).

nal investors. The first group used to operate as landlords in the large cities. The property was mainly used as sort of a provision for old age, with the result that renovations often were not carried out (unprofessional management, gains after renovation would not exceed the costs). Financial institutions, on the contrary, may be expected to act as 'economic agents' and, for instance, respond to changes in market prices. In principle, they are able to define the point in time at which either renovation or demolishment must take place (as soon as the gain from a renovated or a new building, minus the costs from, respectively, renovation or demolishment, exceeds the gain from the present use). In this case, the building's use-value plays only an indirect role. Real estate market mechanisms determine then the pace of urban redevelopment.

Second, and related to the former, the renovation and/or replacement of buildings that are owned by the final users (in business sectors) sometimes turns out to be problematic because the resale value is relatively low (buildings are only for specialised use) and redevelopment is often not profitable, particularly when the building is located in a run-down industrial area.[90] As a result, the owners of industrial buildings may face a dilemma. From a production point of view -- concerning the functional quality of the building and/of the location -- they should rebuild or relocate; however, this is prohibitive because of the loss that they would make on their present property.

(9) the location of newly developed property

Again, we should distinguish between commercially developed real estate and real estate that is commissioned by the final user. Commercial-property developers are likely to show most interest in 'top locations,' wanting to be sure of sufficient revenues from their investments.[91] Companies building for their own use can then choose only from the "left-over areas." In countries with a hierarchical land rent structure, this more or less automatically results in a dichotomy of business parks. High land rents on top locations exclude the companies building for their own use from these locations. In countries, such as the Netherlands, in which this hierarchical structure is missing, this selection does not take place. The (possibility of) mixing of functions/uses on top locations in Dutch cities reduces the attractiveness of these locations for commercial developers. For this reason, municipalities have developed so-called theme parks which are only accessible to a beforehand-determined group of companies (a specific sector, a certain 'size' of the company).

I have now discussed spatial variation with respect to the institutional organisation of the real estate market, interpretations of this variation with help of institutional economic theory, and the spatial-economic consequences. Examples of real estate market functioning have been presented in order to provide evidence of the relevance of the institutional organisation of the market to urban development and redevelopment processes. Now, I will turn to the dynamics of urban real estate markets, investigating the consequences of temporal variation

---

90   Fothergill *et al.* (1987) have investigated the problem of locational inertia in Great Britain.

91   A distinction should be made between companies building for their own use out of necessity, because commercial property developers consider letting commercial properties to them as too risky, and companies who choose themselves to build their own buildings, because their property must *radiate* their corporate identity. The latter group is also established on top locations.

in the institutional organisation of the real estate market (institutional change) for the outcome of market processes.

5.4.   Temporal variation with respect to the organisation of the development industry

What kind of changes take place with respect to the institutional organisation of the market, what are the sources of this institutional change, and what are the consequences for urban development and redevelopment processes? Shifts in urban development, or *urban development cycles*, have been for long a popular subject of study. For instance, the Dutch 'Rotterdam School' has studied urban development by using a model of successive stages in urban development.[92] These studies, however, pay no attention to the impact of real estate development processes on urban change. Alternatively, Barras has extensively investigated the real estate mechanisms underlying urban development cycles (Barras, 1983, 1984, 1985, 1987). He focused mainly on the role of technical change with respect to office development. My perspective is somewhat different.[93] I consider technological innovation as just one, though an important one, of the potential sources of institutional change. Moreover, I aim to investigate the way institutional changes, as far as they are relevant for real estate development, are historically determined. Successively, I will now analyse the diverse sources of institutional change and the path dependency of this change (fig. 5.3).

5.4.1.   Sources of institutional change

Fundamental changes in relative prices -- i.e. changes in the ratio of factor prices, changes in technology, and changes in the cost of information -- are considered to be vital sources of institutional change. Furthermore, changes in ideas, norms and values influence the strategies of agents and agencies involved in real estate development and thus, potentially, the institutional organisation of the market.

The first change is that of *the ratio of factor prices*: changes with respect to the ratio of labour costs to capital costs, the ratio of building construction costs to land development costs, the ratio of land values to real estate values, the revenues from commercial real estate development to industrial property or housing development, the ratio of real estate investment returns to other investment opportunities' returns, and the ratio of renovation costs to the costs of demolishment. When the costs of land development increase (because of environemental demands), relative to the construction costs of a new dwelling, this may shift

---

92   See Berg (1985), Van der Meer (1989).

93   Note that Barras concentrates mainly on the influence of technological change on the demand for office buildings. My concern is primarily with the supply side: the production of real estate. I focus, therefore, on the influence of technological innovation on building production.

cause institutional change. As a result, for instance, land prices will rise (they must at least exceed the costs of land development), and private developers may choose to change their strategies. They may start to hold land banks, and/or they are only prepared to build relatively expensive dwellings, to be able to cover the land costs.

A sharp increase of, for instance, housing prices is not an institutional change in itself. Such an increase may, however, be the source of institutional change when the increase in prices leads to a fundamental shift in the behaviour of existing owner-occupiers. Institutional changes may include, for example, that house owners become more alert to price alterations. The significance of the market value of their property becomes more important to them than it used to be, leading to increased activity on the housing market. The sudden turmoil with respect to a supposed scarcity of building land in many Dutch cities in the 1990s may lead to changing strategies of land owners, based on their expectations of future land prices. Possibly, they expect now that land prices will rise in the near future. Therefore, they do not sell land at this moment, speculating on higher gains in the future. In the housing market study in subsequent chapters I will show that mutations of building construction costs and fluctuations in house prices lead to important institutional changes on the housing market, particularly when we take the relationship between the housing development market and the second-hand housing market into consideration. As will be shown below, changes in the ratio of factor prices can affect both the institutional relations between the agents that are involved in the development industry and the strategies of these agents. Some of the changes in factor prices are structural (for instance, changes in the costs of building construction, because of new building techniques), while others are conjunctural (e.g., changing housing prices). As a result, institutional changes may either be structural or temporal themselves.

The second fundamental element stimulating institutional change is *changes in technology*: technological innovations that are relevant to property development processes include new building techniques (i.e. mass production of buildings, high-rise buildings), new valuation methods, new cost-calculation methods, innovations on financial markets, innovations that directly affect the demand for office space and industrial buildings (new telecommunication techniques, new transportation techniques). These innovations influence, among other things, the costs of production, the profitability of new developments, the degree of uncertainty in a market (i.e. the introduction of new cost calculation methods), the size of user demand for specific types of property, and the size of investment demand for property. Yet, the most remarkable aspect of technological innovation on real estate markets is probably the low content in which it appears. I will argue in the case study that a very important consequence is that, in contrast to other branches of industry, sales trends in building construction have not been determined by technological innovations (see Chapter Eight).

The Third element stimulating institutional change is *changes with respect to the costs of information*: changes in information costs depend on changes in uncertainty. The degree of uncertainty affects, via the strategies of the agents, the institutional organisation of the market. For instance, I recall my argument with respect to risk and uncertainty, in section 5.2.2. The strategies of financial institutions with respect to real estate investments depend on the distinction between calculable and incalculable uncertainty. Changes in information costs may occur, for example, as a result of technological innovations, new formal rules, shifts in government policy, etc. The implementation of a new development plan by the local government makes clear the opportunities for private developers to start new development projects. As a result the risks for developers may be considerably reduced. Important to keep in mind -- and I will explain this in greater detail in the case study -- is that a link exists between the degree of uncertainty and (fluctuations in) the profitability of real estate development. Below, this will be further discussed on the basis of the path-dependency concept.

Changing ideas, norms and values is the fourth area stimulating institutional change; one of the most profound shifts that have taken place in our norms in the last decade concerns the environmental consciousness that has become essential to almost every urban economic development issue (and, of course, other issues as well). This phenomenon, for example, leads to extra costs related to the cleaning of soil pollution, it results in stronger protests against all kinds of new proposed developments (especially when areas of natural beauty are damaged; e.g. airport expansions, new motorways or railways), it means that costs of demolishments have increased (waste reduction), and that new ecologically sound building techniques have been introduced (even complete ecologically sound residential areas are developed); noreover, companies that cause inconveniences in inner-city areas have been forced to move to other areas, a more rigid environmental legislation has come about, new business parks must preferably be built near public transport junctions (to reduce private transport), renovations and even demolishments of complete housing blocks need to be carried out because of threats to public health, new development areas are becoming scarce, since more and more areas are dropped as appropriate expansion areas because of environmental considerations, etc. These developments directly affect real estate development -- they change the profitability of real estate development; new formal rules are added, new investment opportunities are created, and so on.

Meanwhile, the government has introduced -- partly out of financial necessity -- a new style of policy making that can be considered to be a more entrepreneurial style of managing and yet can be seen as a shift towards a policy that costs of public sector policy must provide at least equal returns. This affects urban spatial-economic development in several ways. First, the internal organisation of municipalities has changed. Municipal departments act now as financially independent business units that are sometimes competing against each other (i.e., house building associations are privatised, municipal land departments charge now market prices for building land, while they used to charge only the cost price of land). Second, a competitive element has been introduced in negotiations between municipalities and market parties (e.g. municipalities negotiate with more than one developer, while formerly they did not). Third, regional governmental collaborations have been started (Amsterdam and surrounding municipalities, for example, and the cities of Arnhem and Nijmegen, Enschede and Hengelo). Fourth, policies aiming to create an artificial scarcity of urban land markets have been implemented (in order to raise land prices). Fifth, all kinds of arrangements between public and private parties have come about (i.e., with respect to inner-city redevelopment projects, the management of car parks, administrative corporations). Sixth, more advanced methods are now used to calculate the costs of proposed building developments (residual valuation techniques). And finally, the scale of many commercial-development projects seems to have been enlarged (business parks are developed as a whole).

Jointly, these changes in the ratio of factor prices, costs of information, technology, and ideas, norms and values, cause a variety of institutional changes on real estate markets. A detailed examination of institutional changes that underlie the functioning of the Dutch housing market will be provided in Chapter Eight. The pace and direction of institutional change is 'path dependent'; the meaning of 'path dependency' to real estate market functioning will further be discussed in the subsequent paragraph.

5.4.2.   Path dependency of institutional change

In order to understand why a similar development in, e.g., costs results in distinct changes with respect to the institutional organisation of real estate markets in different countries and in different patterns of urban change, we need to take account of the way the organisational structure of a particular market and the economy of a particular spatial entity (city, region or nation) are historically determined. For instance, in the Netherlands land development has traditionally been carried out by the municipalities. Above, was outlined the consequences of this strategy for scarcity and price developments on land markets and spatial restructuring processes in Dutch cities. Increasing market prices for land -- related to an artificial scarcity of land -- would probably increase the profitability of land development, and thus the attractiveness to private developers as well. However, a shift from public to private land development has not yet taken place, perhaps because private developers lack the know-how and the capacity to do so. Moreover, because developers have no experience with land development, the risks may be too high (because risk can be reduced by investigating market performances in the past; with respect to land development such information is not available). Another example concerns the limits to the capacity of the development industry in an urban region. In a traditionally weak local economy, in which mainly small firms operate, the development industry may lack the capacity or the capability (to "measure" the risk, for example) to respond to a rising demand for property.[94] Path dependency is also determined by a nexus of moral values, such as norms, habits and trust. In particular, habitual behaviour often leads to path dependency. Traditional building construction firms, for instance, may be used to operate on the housing market exclusively. If the relative profitability of the construction of dwellings drops, compared to the profitability of, for example, office buildings, the construction firms may lack the market information -- due to their habitual behaviour -- so that they will not change their strategies. The concept of path dependency demonstrates that the degree to which institutional changes in a national or international context take place and the degree in which institutional changes are succeeded by changing strategies of market parties depend on the specific characteristics of the national or urban economy -- in terms of institutional efficiency, government intervention, market imperfections and the incentives behind individual behaviour.

---

94   See also various publications by Healey on real estate developments in Newcastle-upon-Tyne in North-East England, as an example of such a 'weak' local economy (Healey, 1994).

5.5. Changing strategies

As seen in the examples of institutional change on the Dutch real estate market in the previous section, the processes of change often involve changing strategies of the agents and agencies that are involved in the property-development industry. The next section will examine the dynamics of the strategies of these agents and agencies.

the property development industry
In the last decade, property developers and financial institutions have, on several points, drastically modified their strategies, as they were confronted with rising costs in some situations and larger profit margins in other situations. For financial institutions, 'new' opportunities for real estate investment have come about, such as infrastructural works, recreational projects, and hotels. From the mid-1980s foreign investors have bought real estate in the Netherlands. Dutch financial institutions and real estate investment companies are now increasingly investing in foreign real estate themselves (partly because of a change in formal rules). During the last few years, the property of the real estate investment companies has substantially increased, mainly due to changing investment strategies by the financial institutions and positive financial results from these investment companies. Apparently, the financial institutions are unsatisfied with the performance of their own assets. The real estate investment companies are, in principle, able to carry out more professional research on the real estate market, since that is their prime interest. This trend has been accompanied by a succession of mergers between investment companies; they can thus better manage their funds and spread risks (among other things, because they are able to invest in different sectors of the real estate market).

Finally, it seems that financial institutions, as owners of existing office buildings and as investors in new commercial real estate, face a dilemma, as a result of the hausse in office development in the 1980s and the present economic recession. On the one hand, they need to invest in new office development: if they do not, their competitors will do it; on the other hand, the high vacancy rates in their older assets saddle firms with considerable losses, as demonstrated by the fact that vacancy rates are rising -- and it is expected that they will keep rising for some years -- while the total amount of office space still expands. In part, this dilemma is related to the special characteristics of the Dutch commercial property market: only minor differences can be found between office rents in the existing building stock and rents of recently-developed office space. Therefore, companies (the 'final users') can relatively easily move to new buildings, while the buildings they have left are difficult to relet. Furthermore, the high vacancy rates are caused by the present economic recession and changing locational preferences of office users.

Property developers, in their turn, are challenged with a declining demand for office space, forcing them, among other things, to change their strategies: they stop building speculatively. However, economic recession is usually not immediately followed by a decline in building activities, since projects that are in the pipeline are still being developed.[95] The strategies of property developers are, in principle, aimed at producing as many buildings as possible; thus, in a declining office market they are continuously seeking

---

95 This explains why the amount of office space has still increased in the 1990s.

for an expansion of building production in new directions.[96] The present recession on the office market and, simultaneously, the sharp increase in both house prices and the demand for dwellings may drive some developers to shift from office development to house building and the development of shopping centers. In the case study I will argue, however, that developers just do not sufficiently take account of the fluctuations in the profitability of speculative house building, which are structural to the housing market. Moreover, the creation of an (artificial) scarcity on urban land markets may possibly lead to fundamental changes in the strategies of property developers, assuming that the scarcity is accompanied by rising land prices and office rents on 'top locations,' on the one hand, and sharper price differences between top locations and peripheral locations, on the other hand (however, see also the discussion in the previous paragraph). Another consequence of this scarcity on the land market may be that developers will increasingly diversify their strategies with respect to the development of real estate on top locations and on peripheral locations. On top locations they will be able to develop more prestigious office buildings, they will build in higher densities, and they will accept higher risks, while on peripheral locations developers will only participate in projects that are commissioned by the final user.

Finally, note that cost increases for property developers are often passed on for the government, especially with respect to environmental costs and redevelopment costs. It follows from this that changing costs do not necessarily cause changes in market values. Because developers usually do not own property they do not suffer from (institutional) changes that lower the value of real estate. As we will see below, municipalities *do* suffer.

municipalities

With respect to the position of municipalities and other government bodies on real estate markets, substantial changes have taken place. First, land-development costs have, probably quite drastically, escalated.[97] New developments are now with increasing frequency carried out on locations that are already in use; as a result, the existing buildings must first be demolished and, sometimes, compulsory purchase costs must be paid (an extreme example: the relocation of market gardens, for instance in Amsterdam, The Hague and Nijmegen). The costs of the development of new house-building locations are probably continually rising, since only 'second-best' locations are left over (for instance, the municipality of Amsterdam intends to impolder the IJ lake to use the new land for a large housing project; the costs of impoldering are incorporated in the total land development costs). Moreover, cleaning costs because of soil pollution are becoming a burden to municipalities.[98] The gains from land sale have increased as a result of the shift to a market-oriented policy with respect to determining land prices.

With respect to the (administrative) relationships among cities, at least two important changes have taken place. On the one hand, in connection with a more entrepreneurial

---

96 Note that this may conflict with the interests of real estate *owners*.

97 This can logically be expected, following the argument in the previous paragraphs, and is due to tighter environmental legislation. However, there is no empirical evidence that supports this pronouncement.

98 Recently, the provincial government of Groningen -- probably a relatively "unpolluted" province -- has calculated that cleaning costs of polluted land in the future, in the province of Groningen, will amount to a total sum of three billion guilders.

management style, cities are now increasingly competing against each other in attracting companies and institutions to their regions, both in an international context (for instance, the establishment of European Community institutions in one of the EC countries) and in a national context. The main reason for this is that the municipalities try to expand local employment opportunities, but such a competition affects, as a side effect, real estate market values as well.

On the other hand, municipalities have started to cooperate on a regional level in various policy fields. The most important development with respect to the functioning of real estate markets is that in some regions, now, a regional land policy will be implemented. This means, for instance, that municipal land departments within a certain region make agreements with respect to the development of business parks and/or the level of land prices. This affects not only real estate market values, but also the spatial-economic structure of these regions (i.e. regional building sites for the manufacturing industry are developed, a regional top location for commercial development can be developed in one of the involved cities).

the final users

Institutional and technological changes have altered both locational preferences of firms and the demands of firms with respect to production space. Locational choices have especially been influenced by reorganisations in production processes (both externally and internally) and by an unmistakable internationalisation tendency. In general, the mobility of companies has increased.[99] This has resulted in a a number of economically successful regions, although less attractive regions are increasingly characterised by obsolete run-down business areas. With respect to production space two, more or less contradicting, developments have taken place. On the one hand, a continuous tendency toward the standardisation of production space can be noted, especially on the office market; on the other hand, both office and manufacturing space are used to express the companies' 'corporate identity' (i.e., an electronics company that builds a factory in the form of a chip). The former trend enlarges the trade on real estate market; the latter trend diminishes market activity.[100]

5.6. Changes in the outcome of development processes

The final step in this analysis is now to examine the resulting changes with respect to urban development and redevelopment. Some of these changes have already come up in the preceding sections. This section will list some further examples of changes in the outcome of real estate development processes. First, related to changing government strategies, locations

---

99 See, for empirical evidence, e.g. Kemper and Pellenbarg (1991), Van der Krabben and Boekema (1994).

100 A negative side effect of the poor "negotiability" of real estate can be that companies are tied to certain locations because their properties are unsaleable.

are more and more occupied by the most profitable use.[101] This causes not only a segregation between *uses* but also a different spatial structure. Furthermore, the intended creation of scarcity on urban land markets (which is also related to the regionalisation tendency) may result in an enlarged diversification of locations and real estate projects, assuming that price differences (land prices and office rents) between top locations and peripheral locations will increase.

Second, municipalities have, in recent years, taken up urban redevelopment mainly on a large scale and integrally (as opposed to a fragmented restructuring of cities). This probably leads to a well-balanced urban structure. However, the complexity of these large-scale development projects brings into question the *manageability* of this type of urban redevelopment.

Third, on the office market, professional real estate owners have partially replaced the previous owner-users -- causing an evolution of the property-development market: the share of professional real estate owners' property in the total office building stock has increased. Professional real estate owners are expected to respond more rapidly to real estate price changes. This implies, among other things, that the technical ageing of commercial properties gradually becomes subsidiary to economic ageing. As soon as an alternative use of the location gives better revenues, the present use will be replaced. Thus, the built environment increasingly gets a temporary character; in that case, capital destruction is an inevitable side effect. On the other hand, it is likely that the pace of revitalisation of the built environment will increase -- being a positive effect of the shift in ownership relations -- although costs of demolishment and land cleaning costs may act as a constraint to redevelopment. As long as redevelopment costs exceed the revenues from both the existing use and the alternative use, structural vacancy in office buildings seems to be inevitable. Furthermore, in a development market that is dominated by professional real estate companies we may expect a trend towards a standardisation of commercial properties, because for this category of owners the resale value of property is decisive (it is expected that it is easier to relet a standard type of building). These buildings are likely to be of a relatively high quality. Finally, and related to the former argument, professional real estate companies make different and probably stronger demands on the (quality of) location than owner-users do, mainly because they want to reduce the risk of vacancy after the first user has left. Consequently, we may expect them to buy property preferably on top locations, characterised by high and rising office rents and a large demand for office space.

Fourth, on peripheral locations mainly "functional" buildings that are owned by the users are developed. With respect to these buildings, functional ageing, as distinguished from economic ageing, determines the life of buildings. This may result for some areas in monotonous urban landscapes, dominated by low-quality functional buildings, which take up a constantly growing part of urban regions, as well as run down areas, characterised by obsolete buildings and neglected public spaces.

Fifth, the plausible implication of the developments listed above is that a segregation arises between the top locations and the peripheral locations. A negative side effect of this is that a breeding ground is created for monopolistic and speculative behaviour (on top

---

101 Municipalities have increasingly become aware of the fact that the use of the land determines the market price of land. Previously, they were satisfied with prices that only covered their costs of land development.

locations). The tendency towards locational segregation is even strengthened by the changing accommodation demands of large internationally operating companies. They prefer prestigious head offices on top locations, and buildings for the manufacturing industry (production activities) on the cheaper peripheral locations, being able in that way to "radiate" their corporate identity on an attractive top location and to reduce their accommodation costs on the peripheral location.

Finally, the housing market is subject to important organisational shifts as well. The percentage of home ownership is rising; the larger part of the present housing production concerns owner-occupied dwellings. The housing associations, which own a considerable part of the housing stock, have been transformed from government bodies that were financed by the state to financially independent-operating social entrepreneurs. As a result, the market mechanism will put its stamp to a larger extent on housing development processes, intensifying the segregation tendency that has been discussed above. For instance, housing associations try to obtain lucrative locations and negotiate with private developers to develop these locations jointly (social housing combined with retail development or owner-occupied housing). Simultaneously, the small private investors on the housing market -- consisting of people who owned houses to be ensured of an 'old age income,' and of private landlords, who often used to hinder the implementation of urban renewal plans, seem to have disappeared now. Jointly, these developments indicate that, in general, a better maintenance of the housing stock may be expected.

5.7.   Conclusions

Chapter Five has attempted to point out the *institutional aspects* that should be studied in relation to real estate development. Most relevant to the analysis of real estate development processes are the following: (1) The impact of uncertainty and information problems on economic action. In many situations the decisions of market parties and the public sector are clearly affected by uncertainty, for example about future development or about decisions of other actors; (2) The assumption that different actors may hold different strategies, each with its own rationality -- this helps to understand why the specific composition of the group of actors involved in the development industry in a locality may influence the outcome of development processes in that locality; (3) Individual behaviour, moreover, is shaped by various kinds of 'informal rules,' like habits, trust and norms -- for instance, the decisions of owner-occupiers to sell or not; (4) The significance of institutional changes on real estate markets to development processes -- changes in the institutional organisation of real estate markets result in new relations on real estate markets, alternative strategies of market parties, new perspectives for public sector policy and changes in development costs and market prices, all potentially resulting in changes in the development process; (5) The path dependency -- the way present economic action and public-sector policy is shaped by decisions that have been made in the past -- of the real estate sectors' development activities; to be able to understand correctly development processes we must take into consideration the way the real estate market has evolved through time.

I have analysed the way these issues determine the observed spatial and temporal variation in the institutional organisation of the real estate market and the related variation in urban-development processes. This analysis demonstrates the important influence of institutions on real estate markets. The examples of real estate market functioning in the Netherlands, which have been presented throughout this chapter, have demonstrated that, to understand real estate development properly we must take account of institutional aspects of the real estate market and of institutional change. In the next chapters the framework for analysis will be applied to a study of the Dutch housebuilding market. This study concentrates on the impact of the institutional organisation of the housebuilding market on the performance of this market.

PART III **THE HOUSING MARKET: A CASE STUDY OF ORGANISATIONAL STRUCTURE, INSTITUTIONAL CHANGE AND PATH DEPENDENCY**

INTRODUCTION

Chapters Six, Seven and Eight present the results of a case study concerning, respectively, the institutional organisation of the housing market in the Netherlands, trends in housing production and market parties' strategies, and the institutional changes that took place with respect to the institutional organisation of the housing market and the production of housing in the Netherlands. This case study will attempt to show how the institutional organisation of the real estate market has impacted the way (re-)development processes -- in this case the development of new dwellings -- take place in Dutch cities and, ultimately, the spatial form of these cities. Following the line of argument that has been developed in Chapter Five, I intend to show that, apart from the nature of demand and supply in a local real estate market, the institutional organisation of the housing market plays a significant role with respect to the outcome of real estate market processes. I will pay particular attention to the impact of information problems on the housing market, the strategies of the actors involved in the property-development industry, institutional changes that are relevant to housing development, and the path dependency of the housing market.

The case study analyses some important issues that are characteristic to housing development in Dutch cities. Moreover, it focuses on institutional changes that took place on the housing market and their impact on housing development processes. In accordance with my argument in the previous chapters, I claim that the present approach reveals some vital aspects of these issues that are left unnoticed in other studies of property development.

The organisational structure and functioning of the housing development industry in the Netherlands will be studied in a historical perspective. An overview of the changes that took place in about twenty five years of housing construction, concerning the organisational structure of this branch of industry, the strategies of the actors involved in the development industry, the meaning of all kinds of norms (habits, trust), the functioning of the housing market in general (i.e. costs, market prices) and the "output" of the market, show the relation between changes with respect to the institutional organisation of the housing market, on the one hand, and the development of new dwellings, on the other hand.[102]

The topicality of housing development in the Netherlands is irrefutable, since at present the level of new housing construction appears to be insufficient, leading to a serious shortage in the housing stock of several Dutch cities, notably in the Randstad (Amsterdam, Rotterdam, The Hague, and Utrecht). Both the Ministry of Housing and the National Council for Housing have raised the alarm. They warn that for years the production of new dwellings will lag behind the need for new dwellings. Most commentaries argue that the functioning of the land market (a shortage of building land), the unexpected growth of the number of households, and a failing national government policy are to be blamed for these shortages.

The Cultureel Planbureau (CPB) expects that in 1995 the shortage of dwellings will amount to at least 3.5% of the total housing stock. In a historical perspective, this figure appears to be very high (see CPB, 1994). This figure is supported by the results of a study by Kolpron Consultants, commissioned by the Ministry of Economic Affairs (Ministry of

---

102 The period of twenty-five years has been used mainly because of pragmatic reasons. For this period, it was possible to collect sufficient data.

Economic Affairs, 1994e). This study estimated that between 1995 and 2005 the need for new dwellings amounts to maximal 665,000 dwellings (yet to be built).[103] At the time the Kolpron-study was carried out (the beginning of 1994), the total number of dwellings that will be built in already planned housing schemes in the same period came to 467,380 dwellings -- only 72% of the assigned number.[104] However, there is more at ussue here: the shortage of dwellings is not only caused by the above-mentioned reasons. Also the 'property system' -- the term is taken from Badcock (1994) -- affects development processes.

Related to this 'crisis in housing production' -- should we speak of a crisis? -- is the massive reorganisation of the housing sector, including the privatisation of the housing associations and the withdrawal of the government from this sector. At present many publications appear that are concerned with the structural changes that take place at the housing market. The implementation of the housebuilding schemes on the VINEX locations attracts most attention. In the VINEX Report (Ministry of Housing, Physical Planning and the Environment, 1990), the national government has allocated a number of locations where in the next ten years a substantial part of the total amount of new dwellings in the Netherlands must be built. The implementation of these plans is often complicated and not without problems (especially in the Randstad). One of the reasons I have attempted this case study is my feeling that, *inter alia* with respect to the development of the VINEX locations, we need more information about the functioning of the housing market and the role and strategies of the housing development industry. For instance, the apparent impotence of private developers to produce enough non-subsidised owner-occupied dwellings (to meet household demands), despite the recent substantial rise of house prices and the correlated undeniable increase of development profits, seems at least surprising. We find ourselves in a paradoxical situation: an overcharged housing market characterised by a rapid increase of house prices, and at the same time a stagnating production of new dwellings.

A special role is granted to the housing construction industry. Its traditional way of building, partly due to the special characteristics of the housing market (I will explain this in Chapter Six), influences the production of new dwellings as well. Chapter Six will argue that we should not only focus on this supposed housing production crisis; other issues deserve attention as well. Generally speaking, the case study aims to provide better knowledge of the way the institutional organisation of a national property market affects the spatial restructuring of cities.

The case study focuses on housing development, with a brief analysis of the recent restructuring of the social housing sector in the Netherlands. Most attention, however, will be paid to the speculative development of owner-occupied dwellings, both subsidised and non-subsidised. The analysis is exclusively focused on the Dutch context. At certain points, the results of this research will be interpreted from an international point of view. It will be argued that some aspects related to the institutional organisation of housing development

---

103 The figure of 665,000 dwellings has been presented in the Trendrapport (Ministry of Housing, 1992). The Trendrapport contains the most recent calculations by the national government of future housing need.

104 Between 50,000 and 100,000 dwellings will be developed in existing urban areas (mainly urban renewal). The remaining part of the planned new dwellings (367,000 to 417,000 dwellings) will be built in new expansion areas. The location of these expansion areas is mainly in the direct proximity of existing urban areas.

markets are typical of just the Dutch case, while in other respects explanations for certain developments are based on more universal characteristics of housing markets.

Research method
Price changes and changes with respect to the quantity of production output are taken as indicators of institutional-economic developments. The strategies of the actors in housing-development processes and the way they respond to price changes are analysed by focussing on their actual participation in speculative house building: for example, the number of new dwellings they build every year, their production output, and the amount of money they invest in house building.[105] This analysis makes it possible to investigate what kind of institutional changes take place, what the 'sources' of these institutional changes might be and how market parties respond to these changes. With respect to the latter we can also 'judge' the rationality of their decisions.[106]

The set-up of the case study is as follows. After a more detailed discussion of the aims of the case study in section 6.1 and drawing up a number of hypotheses in section 6.2, I will describe in the remaining part of Chapter Six the institutional organisation of the Dutch housing market: the agents involved in house building, their strategies, the way the government intervenes in this market, the status of property ownership and property rights, the set of rules that regulate the housing market and the institutional-economic relations between the actors and the path dependency of this market. Then, Chapter Seven analyses on the one hand the changes that took place with respect to housing production during the research period and on the other hand the resulting changes that took place with respect to the housing stock and the spatial structure of Dutch cities. Moreover, the chapter examines the functioning of the owner-occupied housing market, mainly focussing on fluctuations in house prices (related to the development of, among other things, building costs). Finally, the chapter discusses what the implications of these developments are for the consumption of housing.

Chapter Eight aims to interpret the changes that took place with respect to housing development and why these changes took place. Subsequently, the sources of the institutional economic changes, the changes with respect to the institutional organisation of the housing market and the way market parties respond to institutional economic changes are analysed. With respect to the latter, the profitability of both speculative land and house-building development are brought into question. Chapter Eight will explicitly refer to the significance of the institutional factors that follow from Chapter Five's framework for analysis.

Much of the (quantitative) information about housing development has been collected from national statistics on housing, building construction, prices and investments. Additional quantitative information is based on sources of the Economic Institute of Building

---

105 Note that putting real production figures at the centre of analysis is a conscious choice. It implies that with help of this method the motives behind the strategies of market parties cannot be revealed in this study (among other things, because it would be very hard to do so). In other words, the way that market parties respond to institutional-economic changes is analysed, but the reasons for them to make a certain decision remain unknown -- thus empirical evidence is lacking

106 See Chapter Seven and Eight; I distinguish different kinds of rationalities.

Construction and the Dutch Society of real estate brokers. Other information has been gathered from a large number of research reports, newspaper articles and (academic) journals.

6 THE HOUSING DEVELOPMENT INDUSTRY: ORGANISATIONAL STRUCTURE AND INSTITUTIONAL CHANGE

6.1. The Aims of the Case Study

This chapter will apply the framework for analysis to the field of housing studies in order to examine the specific institutional organisation of the housing development market in the Netherlands and its impact on housing development; in other words, an analysis of the way the supply of new dwellings takes place. The study aims to contribute to a better understanding of the functioning of the housing market. The way the production and development of housing is organised is explicitly related to the outcome of market processes: the dwellings that are built (amount, type, quality, location, etc.) and the restructuring of urban patterns.

Chapter Six and the two subsequent chapters will analyse post-war house building construction in the Netherlands. I will analyse, successively, the institutional organisation of the housing market in general and the organisational structure of the housing development industry in particular, the reorganisations that took place during about twenty-five years of house building, the changing strategies of the agents that are involved in house building, the institutional changes that took place in this branch of industry, the (technological) innovations that are relevant to housing construction and development, and the resulting continuous restructuring of the outcome of the housing market. After discussing the aims of the case study, I will present the framework for analysis in section 6.2. Sections 6.3, 6.4, 6.5 and 6.6 will discuss the characteristics of the institutional organisation of the Dutch housing market, with particular attention to, successively, the composition of the group of agents involved in house building (section 6.3), to government intervention with respect to housing development (section 6.4), to the strategies of the agents involved in house building (section 6.5) and, finally, to the institutional economic relations between the different group of actors, especially focusing on the financing of new housing developments (section 6.6). I will now discuss the objectives of the case study. The study aims at the following:

(1) to demonstrate and interpret the organisational structure of the Dutch housing development industry, regarding the agents involved in house building, their strategies, the way the government intervenes in this market, the status of property ownership and property rights, the set of rules that regulate the market and the typical nexus of institutional economic relations;
(2) to analyse the (institutional economic) changes that took place with respect to this organisational structure, as determined by both the institutional and technological innovations and the path dependency of the performance of an economy;
(3) to track the sources of institutional changes and to examine the pace at which these changes took place;
(4) to analyse the changes that took place with respect to the housing stock in Dutch cities (the number, type and quality of dwellings, new development locations, renovations and demolishments, etc.) and the spatial structure of Dutch cities;

The analysis focuses on the characteristics of the development industry in relation to the present shortages of housebuilding production. However, a variety of other themes is also covered by the case study, such as the relation between new housing construction and the functioning of the second-hand housing market, as well as production methods and the development of building costs, the rationality of the decisions of professional 'builders,' versus the rationality of home owners' strategies, the profitability of speculative housing and land development, the influential role of the national government and the municipalities on land and housing markets and the large amount of public money with which this role is accompanied, the consequences for households, and, finally, the consequences for (the quality of) the built environment and urban spatial structures.

Housing development is an interesting research topic, since the housing market features several typical aspects that make this market complicated: many diverse groups are involved in investment, development, production, mediation and consumption, both market and non-market relations exist between these groups, and changing government policy significantly influences market functioning. The analysis of the shortages of housing production brings into question why (and by which processes) the level of production output changes through time. And, moreover, what might be the consequences of these changes? Should only the shortage of (on a short term) available building locations and an unforeseen growth of demand for housing (both population and household growth) be blamed for the present low level of housing production? This study argues that the municipal land department's inability to supply land in time and the housing industry's failure to respond quickly to a changing demand for housing are just as much responsible for the present shortage in housing production. Concerning the latter point, on which I will elaborate in Chapter Eight, I partially follow Ball's explanation for the housing production crisis in Great Britain at the the beginning of the 1980s (see Ball, 1983). Certainly, the way new dwellings are produced -- the strategies of the developers -- is a significant factor as well. The profitability of speculative housing development -- and, related to this, of speculative land development -- seems to be the decisive factor in this case. I readily support Needham's surprise of the fact that 'the land development process in the Netherlands is hardly ever discussed or analysed in terms of development gains' (Needham, 1992: p. 684). I would like to add to this that a similar point can be made with respect to speculative housing development. The development gains of speculative housing development have similarly never been subject of academic debates in the Netherlands. More interesting than the exact level of profitability of speculative housing development itself, are the considerable fluctuations that occur with respect to the degree of profitability. How can (fluctuations in) returns on housing development be explained and which factors determine (fluctuations in) the costs of new house building construction? Moreover, how do market parties respond to fluctuations in costs and returns?

Related to the 'profitability issue' is the issue of government involvement, and, more especially, financial involvement in housing development. I aim to bring into the discussion whether the considerable amount of public money that is involved in housing development is wellspent. For instance, who or what benefits from housing development subsidies: the developers, the 'consumers' of housing, the housing associations, the built environment? Furthermore, the traditionally active involvement of Dutch local governments on urban land markets needs more research. What are the resulting consequences for the profitability of housing development and for urban spatial structures? Moreover, what are the financial risks for local governments (and the society as a whole) that accompany their active role on land markets? Likewise relevant for research and debate are a number of political issues concerning the wide range of possible negative side-effects of the present way of house building: high housing expenses for (certain groups of) households, 'undeserved' development gains for speculative developers and profits for owner-occupiers, a low quality of new dwellings and/or the insufficient maintenance of existing dwellings, a sub-optimal location of new or existing dwellings, and a sub-optimal spatial restructuring of cities.

The housing market contains, as a specific type of market, certain typical aspects that make it a special case. In the first place, the housing market is a stock market, which means that the existing stock of dwellings takes the largest share in the total supply of dwellings each year.[107] One implication is that the development of the price of new owner-occupied dwellings is determined by price fluctuations on the second-hand housing market. This is related to the fact that dwellings are stable in value for a relatively long time.[108] Another implication is that the profitability of speculative housing development is, among other things, subject to price developments on the second-hand market. For my argument in the next chapters, it is important to gather from this that -- within certain limits -- trends in selling prices and in building costs of new dwellings are autonomous (see Chapter Eight and also Topalov, 1985).

A second characteristic of housing markets is the large diversity of the group of 'suppliers' of owner-occupied dwellings. On the one hand, are the professional private developers who offer new dwellings; on the other hand, are the households as non-professional one-off sellers who put their property up for sale. Moreover, the housing associations sometimes offer dwellings from their property for sale. It can be expected that each of these groups of actors responds differently to price fluctuations and changes in interest rates and inflation.

Third, the possibilities of mass production of dwellings are limited, mainly because of technological restrictions. As a consequence, production costs are relatively high and they do not tend to decrease.[109] The composition of the building construction industry must be linked to the way new dwellings are produced. The larger part of this branch of industry consists of small, traditionally operating firms that operate only on local or regional levels; multinatio-

---

107   Goodchild argues that about 85 to 90 percent of the dwellings sold in any year in Great Britain are existing dwellings (Goodchild, 1991: p.47; cited in Badcock, 1994). In the Netherlands this percentage is lower. From a report by the Nederlandse Vereniging van Bouwondernemers (NVB, 1994) we know that on the second-hand owner-occupied housing market in 1993 about 75,000 transactions (new dwellings not included) took place. In 1993, 48,115 new owner-occupied dwellings were completed. This means that of the total number of dwellings sold in 1993 (about 125,000 dwellings) approximately only 60% are existing dwellings! This percentage is probably subject to considerable fluctuation.

108   Compare, for instance, the housing market with the market for cars. Since the 'value stability' of cars is considerably less than the stability of the value of dwellings, the share of second-hand cars in the total supply of cars is also considerably less than the share of second-hand dwellings in total supply. This implies that the price of new cars is to a much smaller degree determined by the price for second-hand cars.

109   Compare the production of new dwellings with, for instance, the production of a video recorder. After the introduction of video recorders on the market th,ey have shown a constant tendency to become cheaper. This is probably partly due to a sharper competition between producers, but, more importantly, it has also to do with the growing demand for video recorders, which has been accompanied by the introduction of new and cheaper (mass) production methods. Such mechanisms have only to a small degree appeared for the housing development market.

nals are missing on this market, and the degree of innovation is very low.[110]

Fourth, because of the relatively high production costs per dwelling and the fluctuation in demand, developers consider it generally too risky to keep a large store of new dwellings. Furthermore, it takes a relatively long time to produce a new dwelling. As a result, the market responses to changes in price and/or demand are often delayed.

Fifth, the production of new dwellings always involves the development of land on a specific location. The functioning of the land market has its own characteristics and may complicate the development process. A typical aspect of the owner-occupied housing market are the considerable regional variations in price levels.[111] Note that this variation might lead to regional variations in the profitability of new housing development as well. On the other hand, dwellings are always bound to their location. This may be of influence on the value of the property, since the attractiveness of the location may change.

Sixth, a considerable amount of money is involved with the purchase of a house. For many households, buying a house is a once-in-a-lifetime investment. Sometimes, this may influence their behaviour -- for instance, they pay more than they can afford. In most cases households need to finance their new property with a mortgage. This brings in both the involvement of financiers, like banks and insurance companies, and the significant influence of fluctuations in the interest rate.

Finally, just as the group of 'suppliers' of dwellings, the group of owners of dwellings is also of a diverse composition (owner-occupiers, housing associations, private landlords). The way they maintain their property and the way they respond to price changes is likewise diverse.

Surprisingly, and not in accordance with the above sketch of the complexity of this market, in the Netherlands economic-theoretical approaches to housing development are rather exceptional in the extensive literature on housing issues. As far as I know, the relation between the organisational structure of the housing development industry, institutional and technological changes, and the outcome of housing market processes has never been investigated in the Dutch context. In Great Britain, however, these topics have been studied more extensively. In this respect Ball's book on the political economy of owner occupation can be considered as trendsetting (Ball, 1983).[112] Ball argues that the typical organisational structure of the housebuilding industry in Great Britain is responsible for the crisis in housing construction in the early 1980s.[113]

In the field of housing studies other issues have attracted more attention in the Nether-

---

110   In the 1950s and 1960s the degree of innovations in housebuilding construction was much higher than in more recent years (see De Vreeze, 1993). However, and this is also true for the innovations that took place in the 1950s and 1960s, this has not resulted in substantial reductions of building construction costs.

111   See Chapter Seven and also Sociaal Planbureau (1994) and Rouwendal (1994).

112   Ball's work has been followed by subsequent studies on this subject. See Harloe and Martens (1985), Ball (1985), Topalov (1985), Folin (1985), Ball, Harloe and Martens (1988), Ball and Harloe (1993). See also Dunleavy (1981).

113   I will expound on this work in Chapter Eight.

lands. First, many studies have dealt with issues related to the consumption of housing, particularly dealing with the future need for housing.[114] Second, the ups and downs of the building industry as a branch of industry has extensively been studied.[115] Third, a number of studies on the functioning of the housing market, especially the owner-occupied housing market, has appeared.[116] And fourth, in relation to the other issues, public sector housing policy has always been subject of study.[117]

As I already mentioned in the introduction to Part III, the need to improve our knowledge of house building construction has gained in importance, all the more since housing shortages in Dutch cities have suddenly become a topical subject again, while it was commonly believed that post-war housing shortages were finally solved and that the attention could now be directed to qualitative aspects of housing. Moreover, and related to the former, at this moment a rigorous reorganisation of the public-housing sector is taking place, implying, evidently, an irreversible break with the traditional involvement of the national government in public housing. Housing associations, which own a large part of the housing stock, have recently found a new role on the housing market, as social entrepreneurs. They act now financially independent of the public sector. This means, among other things, that their market strategies may structurally change -- with, possibly, important implications for house-building production.

It should be clear now that this case study follows a different path of analysis than do most of the traditional housing studies. In summary, the chapter will first relate the particular institutional organisation of the housing development market in the Netherlands to the 'outcome' of market processes. This relation will further be investigated in the case study with help of empirical evidence. Second, the way in which the spatial structure of Dutch cities influences housing production will be studied (for example, regarding the availability of building locations, production costs, market prices for houses). Third, the relevance of institutional changes and technological innovations with respect to both the organisational structure of the construction industry and the output of housing production will be analysed. And finally, I will try to explain the relevance of these institutional changes. I will demonstrate that institutional economic theory contributes to a better understanding of market mechanisms, of institutional economic changes *and* of the way in which the agents respond to these changes. The case study will show that the path

---

114   See, for instance, a large number of publications by Priemus (e.g. 1983, 1984) and by Dieleman (e.g. 1985); and also Van Kempen (1992), Floor and Van Kempen (1994), Nationale Woningraad (1994), Van den Broek and Schellevis (1994).

115   See especially the series of publications by the Economic Institute for the Building Industry (e.g. EIB, 1980 a,b; 1991a,b; 1992a,b) and the annual reports on expectations for production and employment by the same organisation (e.g. EIB, 1994).

116   See the research reports by the OTB, including Conijn and Papa (1987) and Boelhouwer and Van der Heijden (1989); and also RIGO (1987, 1991), Janssen (1992), Ministry of Housing (1992).

117   See, for instance, Van der Schaar (1987, 1991), Boelhouwer and Priemus (1990), Boelhouwer and Van der Heijden (1992), Helderman (1993), NIROV (1994), SPB (1994), Dieleman (1994).

dependency of economic systems is clearly visible in the case of housing development.

6.2. Propositions: guidelines for study

A number of propositions are drawn up concerning the functioning of the Dutch housing market. These propositions set the direction for further research -- as I will attempt to examine the validity of the propositions.

First, the present low level of housing production is not only connected with a shortage of building locations, but should also be related to the strategies of private developers, the interventions of local governments on urban land markets, the national government's spatial policy, and typical characteristics of housing construction (increase of building costs).[118]

Second, both public-sector agencies and market parties that are operating on the housing market may respond to different rationalities. In some situations the behaviour of those actors results in sub-optimal outcomes of development processes, either from an allocative point of view, or from a productive point of view.[119] For instance, from a *productive efficiency* point of view, I will question the way private developers respond to fluctuations in market prices, accompanied by fluctuations in the profitability of speculative housing development. They fail to respond quickly. With respect to this point, keep in mind that price fluctuations seem to be just characteristic to housing markets.

Third, I will argue that in some situations the public sector's aim to improve the spatial structure of Dutch cities contradicts unintentionally the productive efficiency of the Dutch housing market. The present national government's urbanisation policy and the early designation of new house-building locations hampers the smooth functioning of the housing market, because the development of housing construction costs -- and more specifically of land development costs -- are influenced in a negative sense.

Fourth, in the Netherlands private developers hardly make use of the possibility to make profits out of speculative land development. The development of building land in Dutch cities is still left to the municipalities. This is in sharp contrast with the situation in most other West-European countries. For instance, according to Ball (1983), speculative developers in Great Britain make the larger part of their profits out of 'land banking,' while profits on speculative house building are only small. With respect to the situation in the Netherlands, there are two possibilities: either speculative land development in Dutch cities

---

118   With respect to the latter point, see also Topalov (1985); according to this author, construction costs show a long-term tendency to grow relative to general price levels but to fall relative both to the total costs of development and to selling prices. However, Topalov adds to this that these tendencies are not steady: the evolution depends on changes in the production system within the sector and on the relations between the agents.

119   The issue of allocative efficacy versus productive efficiency is discussed in Chapter Nine. Allocative efficacy refers to the allocation of the output of housing development processes, regardless of the input (e.g. with respect to the number and location of new dwellings). Productive efficiency refers to the output in relation to the input in housing development processes, irrespective of the allocation of the newly built dwellings (e.g. with respect to the production process of new dwellings).

is not profitable, or private developers miss profits that are feasible out of land banking. Related to this issue is the question how development profits are divided amongst the various agents: who appropriates the gains on speculative house building?

Fifth, just as question marks can be put to private developers' lack of interest in land development, another question that remains is whether the municipal land departments should bear the (financial) risks that are inextricably bound up with land development.

Sixth, a doubt should be cast on the necessity of all government subsidies on housing development. A more flexible use of housing subsidies -- for instance by taking account of regional variations in profit margins -- might lead to better results. With respect to this point, note that the large government expenditures on housing relate to decisions about the organisation of the housing market that are taken in the past. This especially concerns the role that was appointed to housing associations and the active participation of municipalities on urban land markets; two aspects that are typical to the Dutch situation.

Seventh, it can be expected that in the future, if house prices should collapse, a new and more severe crisis in housing production may occur. This is the inevitable consequence of the government's (financial) withdrawal from the housing sector.

Finally, spatial restructuring processes usually initiated by the public sector in Dutch cities have hardly been determined by financial-economic motives. However, this has somewhat changed in recent years. Many municipalities have become aware of the possibility of making profits out of land development at attractive locations. This has possibly intensified the coming into existence of a scarcity of building locations for housing, particularly on attractive locations. The case study aims to find empirical evidence that supports these hypotheses. I will make use of institutional-economic theory to interpret the results of the empirical research.

6.3. The Agents involved in House Building

In 1993, a total number of 83,689 dwellings was completed in the Netherlands (tab. 6.1). More than half of the total number of new dwellings concerned non-subsidised owner-occupied (or rental) dwellings;[120] the development of the remaining part was subsidised. Almost two-thirds of all new dwellings were developed in the owner-occupied sector, including non-subsidised dwellings, premium-assisted dwellings and owner-occupied dwellings with one-time allocation.[121] The larger part of the completed dwellings in the owner-occupied sector, approximately 40,000 dwellings in 1993, was built by private developers. They developed almost half of all new dwellings. Unfortunately, no specific data with respect to the composition of this group of agents are available. In the Netherlands, private developers are a diverse group of agents. A part of them operates on this market indepen-

---

120   The share of rental dwellings in the category of non-subsidised dwellings is small.

121   Premium-assisted dwellings and owner-occupied dwellings with one-time allocation both belong to the category of subsidised owner-occupied dwellings. The category of premium-assisted dwellings is to a higher degree subsidised than the owner-occupied dwellings with one-time allocation.

dently. Usually they do not build the dwellings themselves -- this is contracted out to building construction firms. Some of the private developers can be classified as *building entrepreneurs*: building construction firms that act as speculative developers (they do build the new dwellings themselves). The *Society of Building Entrepreneurs* estimates that about 10% of all building construction firms can be relegated to the category of building entrepreneurs (Society of Building Entrepreneurs, 1993; EIB, 1992).[122] Private developers may also be linked to financial institutions and develop those projects that are financed by the mother company.

Private developers can be considered as the 'organizers' of the development process: they bring in the land, take care of financing the project, contract the building construction firms and sell the completed dwellings to the new owner-occupiers. Note that in the Netherlands municipalities generally bring in the building land; thus, private developers do not take care of land development (servicing the land, infrastructural works) themselves. The profits they derive from the development process depend on their specific role as risk takers in the development process. Therefore they are also referred to as *speculative developers*. Speculative land development, as well as the sale of completed dwellings to owner-occupiers, can bring in development gains. The latter is related to the fact that the market value of new dwellings is determined by the price-making process in the market for second-hand owner-occupied dwellings.[123]

A not inconsiderable number of non-subsidised owner-occupied dwellings is built by private persons: 14,679 dwellings in 1993. Usually this concerns a non-recurring activity by private persons who decide to build a house for their own use. Section 6.5 discusses their role in the development process. Financial institutions commission in only a few cases new housing developments (3,152 dwellings in 1993). However, as will be discussed in section 6.6, they are also involved in the development process in their role as financiers.

In the social rental sector, 22,360 dwellings were completed in 1993, mainly built by housing associations. Municipalities built the remaining part of the social rented dwellings. However, their role as commissioners of new dwellings has been largely diminished in recent years. Due to the drastic reorganisation of the social housing sector, the strategies of both the housing associations and the municipalities have undergone a radical transformation (see section 6.5).

Table 6.2 focuses on the owner-occupied sector. Both the number of owner-occupied dwellings completed as well as the share of non-subsidised dwellings in the total substantially increased in the last three years. In absolute figures, the number of subsidised owner-occupied dwellings that has been completed in the 1990s decreased, being symbolic for the current reorganisation of the housing sector in the Netherlands. The increase of house building in the owner-occupied sector is indicative not only of a growing demand for dwellings in this sector, but also of a growing confidence of private developers in the

---

[122] Apparently, the small number of building entrepreneurs within the branch of the building construction industry is connected with the typical organisation of this sector. I will discuss this below.

[123] I will discuss both the strategies of private developers and the mechanisms that determine housing prices further in section 6.5

profitability of housing development.[124]

TABLE 6.1
Dwellings completed, by type of financing and by principal in 1993
(in absolute figures)

	state govern municipa-lities	housing associati-ons	financial institutions	speculati-ve deve-lopers	private principals	TOTAL dwel-lings
social rental sector	2 289	19 274	39	383	375	22 360
premium rental sector	78	863	877	272	129	3 219
premium assisted owner-occupied dwellings	56	815	205	8 561	358	9 995
owner-occupied dwellings with one-time allocation	13	365	336	4 971	156	5 841
non-subsidised owner-occupied or rental dwellings	83	604	1 695	25 213	14 679	42 274
TOTAL	2 519	21 921	3 152	40 400	15 697	83 689

Note: Social rental sector comprises public sector subsidised dwellings mainly built by housing associations. Sector of subsidised dwellings comprises subsidised rental or owner-occupied dwellings built by order of institutional investors or housing associations. Sector of non-subsidised dwellings comprises non-subsidised owner-occupied or rental dwellings mainly built by speculative developers and private persons.
Source: CBS Statistics

---

[124] Despite the increase in housebuilding in the owner-occupied sector, still a shortage exists in building production. The annual number of social sector dwellings that was completed had dropped in the same period.

TABLE 6.2
Newly built owner-occupied dwellings, by type of financing 1991-1993 (in absolute figures)

	1991	1992	1993
premium-assisted owner-occupied dwellings	15 676	13 313	9 995
owner-occupied dwellings with one-time allocation	8 357	7 025	5 841
non-subsidised owner-occupied dwellings	29 815	34 236	42 274
TOTAL	53 848	54 574	58 110
(percentage of owner-occupied dwellings in newly built dwellings total)	65%	63%	69%

Source: CBS Statistics

Table 6.3 shows the composition and number of firms involved in the building construction industry. In 1991, 10,264 firms were involved in the building construction industry (the construction of both residential and non-residential buildings). Characteristic to this branch of industry is that most of these firms are small, both with respect to the number of employees and with respect to production output. More than two-third of these firms employed less than ten workers. Only 188 firms employed more than 100 workers -- 1.8% of the total number of firms; jointly they are responsible for one-third of total production in 1991. The firms with less than ten workers employed have on average a turnover of one million guilders a year, while the average turnover of firms with more than 100 workers employed amounted to 70 million guilders a year per firm.

TABLE 6.3
Composition and number of firms involved in the buildingconstruction industry in 1991 (residential and non-residential building)

number of workers	number of firms	production mln gld)
< 10	6 933	6 983
10-100	3 143	19 485
> 100	188	13 145
TOTAL	10 264	39 613

Source: CBS Statistics

Having introduced the main actors on the housing market in the right context, I will now give a detailed analysis of government intervention on this market.

6.4. Government Intervention

Dutch housing policy is now undergoing drastic reorganisation. These restructuring processes have mainly been initiated by the national government.[125] This section will cover the public sector's present position on the housing market. Chapter Eight will place policy developments in a historical and international perspective. Then, I will also bring up possible sources for the shifts in government intervention.

The reorganisation of the housing sector that is now underway can best be characterised as a shift from a centralised housing policy to a policy in which the national government withdraws itself from the market and leaves more space for market parties.[126] The National Report on Housing in the 1990s (*Nota Volkshuisvesting in de jaren negentig*, Ministry of Housing, 1989) provides the framework for the present national government housing policy. This report is aimed at (1) stimulating owner occupation in housing, (2) decentralisating housing policy, (3) privatising housing associations and municipal housing departments, and (4) deregulating the housing sector. Though the political view that underlies this report is still valid, several reports have already appeared that have adjusted the content of the National Report on Housing to actual trends: notably the *Tussenbalans 1991* and the *Trendrapport* on Housing. The most important adjustments in these reports concern the estimation of both the quantitative and the qualitative future need for new dwellings until 2015 and the house-building program for the same period. These adjustments have become necessary because of the faster growth of the number of households than was anticipated; until 2000 the estimated number of dwellings that must be built must be extended by 165,000 dwellings. The larger part of the newly built dwellings must be owner-occupied dwellings. Note that the house building program, which has been drawn up by the national government, is only indicative; the realisation of the program has been left to market parties.

Until 1989 the Ministry of Housing financed all social housing development via long-term loans to the housing associations. From 1989 on the financial involvement of the national government with the social housing sector has been limited to regulation, provision of guarantees, and the distribution of subsidies. Housing associations now depend on the willingness of financial institutions to lend money for social housing. However, most of them have been able to build up a considerable financial reserve. The privatisation of the housing associations and the municipal housing departments (their becoming financially independent) has been accompanied by the foundation of the Special Fund for Housing (*Centraal Fonds Volkshuisvesting*) and the Guarantee Fund for Social Housing (*Waarborgfonds Sociale Woningbouw*). The first fund is meant to attract financial institutions to invest in social housing -- the fund serves as a guarantee; the second fund is a solidarity fund. All housing associations (and the national government) have obliged themselves to contribute to this fund; housing associations in financial trouble can make an appeal to it.

Moreover, the Ministry of Housing has announced a large-scale financial operation, called the *bruteringsoperatie*. This operation will be implemented in 1995 and will lead to a

---

125   See also par. 6.1.

126   See Helderman (1993), Boelhouwer and Van der Heijden (1993), Cultureel Planbureau (1994).

considerable reduction of capital flows on the housing market. It implies that the reimbursements of government loans by housing associations that the Ministry of Housing still has put out will be cancelled by the government subsidies that the Ministry of Housing still owes the housing associations. In total this amounts to the considerable sum of Dfl. 37 billion.

Finally, the subsidy system is being reorganised: subsidies on operating costs will expire as of 1995. The system will then be confined to household subsidies and specific building subsidies, mostly bound to particular locations. The reorganisation of the system will imply that about 90% of newly built dwellings in the social rented sector will receive a one-off incentive building subsidy of Dfl. 5,000. A supplementary subsidy will be granted on the VINEX locations of Dfl, 8,500 per dwelling. For the development of subsidised owner-occupied dwellings (formerly called the premium-assisted owner-occupied sector), comparable incentive and supplementary subsidies are also available.[127] To complete this picture, renovation subsidies are also being reduced: subsidies are granted to housing associations only for renovations of dwellings that were formerly owned by private landlords and that are purchased by housing associations. Through these reorganisation processes, the individual household subsidies seem to have remained the national government's main regulation instrument with respect to the social housing sector. In the owner-occupied housing sector a number of fiscal capital flows are relevant, notably the deprivation of national government's tax income because of the tax deductibility of interest on mortgages, and the extra tax incomes of the rateable value and tax on selling prices.[128] Local governments can influence the development of new dwellings via its land policy, combined with the provision of land subsidies for housing development on specific locations.

The implications of the present reorganisation of the housing sector can be summarised as follows:
(1) the national government's involvement in house building has been substantially reduced;
(2) the realisation of the house building program is questionable, since it is left to the market parties (and their willingness to build new dwellings);
(3) the number of new non-subsidised owner-occupied dwellings that is going to be developed will exceed the number of new social-sector dwellings;
(4) all future new social housing development must be financed with the housing associations own-capital reserves or with long-term loans provided by financial institutions;
(5) the position of housing associations on the housing market has been changed into a financially independent role as social entrepreneurs;
(6) (low-income) households are confronted with a sharp increase of social-sector housing rents, as a result of the national government's objective to bring social sector rents more in line with real market value.

---

127   Strangely enough, the supplementary subsidies on VINEX locations for owner-occupied dwellings exceed the supplementary subsidies for rented dwellings: Dfl. 12,000 per dwelling against Dfl. 8,500 per dwelling.

128   Boelhouwer and Van der Heijden (1993) estimate that the deprivation of tax income in 1987 amounts to about Dfl. 5.85 billion, while extra tax incomes because of rateable value and tax on selling prices amount to, respectively, Dfl. 720 million and Dfl. 850 million.

Table 6.4 shows the gross expenditures by the Ministry of Housing with respect to housing in 1993 and 1994. Gross government expenditures in 1993 still amounted to almost Dfl. 15 billion; in 1994 this figure has dropped to Dfl. 13.3 billion. Cutbacks concern especially the contributions to the housing associations and renovation subsidies. In the meantime, the share of the expenditures on individual household subsidies has increased.[129]

TABLE 6.4
Gross expenditures by the Ministry of Housing with respect to housing, 1993 and 1994

		1993	1994
		(x 1000 gld)	
1. urban renewal		1 068 650	1 035 250
2. loans social rental sector		523 322	417 355
3. household subsidies		2 219 500	2 251 700
4. building and exploitation subsidies including:			
a.	contributions to social rental sector	1 248 600	1 129 729
b.	contributions to housing association (liquidity shortage)	4 694 069	3 978 084
c.	renovations social rental sector	656 237	329 687
d.	contributions to sector of owner-occupied dwellings	813 137	676 107
5. remaining		876 511	847 761
6. TOTAL GROSS EXPENDITURES		12 100 026	10 662 670
7. remaining Ministry of Housing		2 698 658	2 671 094
(TOTAL MINISTRY OF HOUSING		14 798 684	13 333 764)

Source: Ministry of Housing

The national government can steer developing house building by providing subsidies on building developments and by means of its location policy. The latter is the subject of the national government's urbanisation policy, which has been laid down in the VINEX - the Fourth National Report on Physical Planning Extra (Ministry of Housing, Physical Planning, and the Environment, 1990). Recently (1994), the national government has made contracts with a number of municipalities (the four large cities and a number of others) with respect to the supply of new locations for house building -- the VINEX locations. These municipalities have committed themselves to develop these locations in order to make them available for the construction of new dwellings. Together, the locations should provide sufficient space for realisation of the national house building programme (if they will be developed in time). However, the national government's *spatial policy* may obstruct the national government's

---

[129] The long-term trend of government expenditures on housing will be discussed in Chapter Seven.

housing policy; several difficulties are expected to arise.

First, the municipalities do not yet own all the land in the VINEX locations. Private developers have already acquired land that might hinder the implementation of municipal land-use plans or, at least, make implementation more expensive. Land speculation never caused many problems in the Netherlands; this may change now, however, as one of the consequences of the national government's decision to designate certain areas as future house building locations is that these designations create an artificial scarcity of building locations.

Second, the national government's spatial policy is directed at promoting the development of new dwellings mainly in expansion areas in the direct proximity of existing urban areas. About 70% of the new dwellings must be built in the Randstad. This sets preconditions to house building: land acquisition costs on areas near the Randstad cities are expected to be relatively high. The issue is further discussed in Chapter Eight.[130]

Thus far I have mainly discussed the role of the national government on the housing market. In what way are local governments engaged in housing development? Even though their influence on this market is partially indirect, the significance of their influence may be substantial. Roughly, local governments influence housing development processes via four different policy instruments: (1) via land policy and their active role on local land markets, (2) via spatial policy, (3) via the strategies they follow with respect to the implementation of land-use plans, and (4) via informal structures of consultation of housing associations and private developers. Local governments in the Netherlands usually play an active role on local land markets: they acquire land, develop the land, sometimes manage vacant building plots, and sell land to both public and private agencies. Their active role enables them to determine -- be it consciously or not -- the degree of scarcity on a local land market and, related to this, the price of land. In turn, the degree of scarcity may affect the profitability of land development -- by its effect on land prices -- and the strategies of property developers.

Furthermore, local governments designate via their spatial policy instruments areas for housing development. As such they not only (partly) determine the attractiveness of available building locations, but they affect the costs of plan development as well. For instance, the development of new dwellings in an area that first must be impoldered is usually more expensive than a similar development in an area that is already opened up.[131]

Local governments are also able to affect the quality of plan development. Municipalities determine, for instance, the *plan density* (the number of dwellings per acre), the mix of different types of dwellings and the level of services (infrastructure, etc.). Finally, municipalities usually consult housing associations and private developers informally, before they start developing new projects. Note that such informal consultations are used primarily to ease the decision-making processes. However, they may also affect competition and price-

---

130 See also Dieleman and Van Engelsdorp Gastelaars (1993) for a discussion of the relation between housing policy and urbanisation policy.

131 For non-Dutch readers, such plans are currently being developed in Dutch cities. In this respect, Amsterdam probably beats everyone.

setting processes on local housing markets.[132]

One final instrument that provides local governments with the power to intervene directly in the functioning of a local housing market is left. Based on the new legislation on house building subsidies (*Besluit Woninggebonden Subsidies*, 1992) municipalities with more than 30,000 inhabitants have become budgetkeepers with respect to government expenditures on new housing development. Formerly, the national government allocated to municipalities each year new housing contingents (the number of dwellings they are allowed to build), for which the municipalities could obtain subsidies. In the new situation, municipalities are allocated a house-building budget. Within certain limits, the municipalities have relative freedom to spend the money (one restriction: on housing). The most important consequence is that they can save the money until they think the right time has come to build. This results in growing uncertainty with respect to the total number of dwellings that will be completed each year.

The end of this section will discuss the Dutch experience concerning government intervention in the housing sector from an international viewpoint. First, a substantial part of government expenditures on housing in the Netherlands goes to carrying out obligations from the past: subsidies on operating costs to housing associations. This sets limits to starting new policy directions (see Chapter Eight).

Second, in recent years severe cutbacks on housing subsidies have characterised the government's involvement in the housing sector in the Netherlands. However, this is in contrast with the still unlimited tax deduction possibilities for owner-occupiers with regard to mortgage interests (see also Cultureel Planbureau, 1994). Since the owner-occupied sector keeps growing, the national government misses an increasing amount of tax income.

Third, the total amount of housing subsidies per dwelling in the Netherlands probably exceeds housing expenditures in most other Western countries. This may imply that and/or be the consequence of these generalisations:

(1) housing consumption is relatively cheaper in the Netherlands;
(2) the quality of new dwellings in the Netherlands is better;
(3) private developers and/or the building construction industry operate less efficiently, e.g. because their behaviour is too much based on risk reduction: the degree of 'risk acceptance' in the Netherlands is lower than in other West-European countries. As a result they may miss potential development gains (and need subsidies to be compensated);
(4) the development gains for private developers and/or the profits for the building construction industry are on a higher level;
(5) the real costs of (land)development (servicing the land) in the Netherlands are higher;
(6) the locations on which housing development takes place are better situated and therefore more expensive;
(7) Dutch housing associations operate less efficiently than their counterparts in other countries and/or have built up large capital reserves (as they are allowed to do);

---

132 Developers who have been consulted during the preparation of the plan have probably obtained an information lead in comparison to developers who haven't taken part in the consultation rounds. The first group of developers (sometimes it is only one developer) may therefore be better prepared to fullfil the municipality's wishes with respect to the implementation of the plan.

(8) relatively, in the Netherlands more dwellings per capita are developed than in other countries.

Chapters Seven and Eight will extensively refer to these issues.

6.5. Strategies of the actors

Tables 6.5 and 6.6 show, respectively, the gross investments in buildings, by type of financing and by principal in 1993, and the gross investments in housebuilding, by type of financing and by principal in 1993.

TABLE 6.5
Gross investments in buildings, by type of financing and by principal, 1993

	maintenance/ renovations	newly built dwellings	agricultural buildings	business buildings	special buildings (schools)	government buildings	TOTAL
	(x mln gld)						
state government	71	0	1	7	70	442	591
municipalities	224	154	0	141	330	213	1 063
housing associations	564	2 415	-	23	88	-	3 090
financial institutions	54	307	-	219	-	-	580
speculative developers	116	5 907	0	881	18	14	6 937
private persons remaining institutions and firms	1 330	3 742	853	4 373	1 961	29	12 288
TOTAL	2 359	12 522	854	5 644	2 467	689	24 549

Note: Land acquisition costs are not included in building investments
Source: CBS Statistics

TABLE 6.6
Gross investments in housebuilding, by type of financing and by principal, 1993

	social rental housing	premium rental dwellings	premium assisted owner-occupied dwellings	owner-occupied dwellings with one-time allocation	non-subsidised owner-occupied dwellings	TOTAL
	(x mln gld)					
state government/ municipalities	202	8	5	1	13	229
housing associations	1 701	92	72	37	96	1 998
financial institutions	3	93	18	34	269	444
speculative developers	34	135	752	505	4 009	5 465
private persons, remaining institutions and firms	33	14	31	16	2 334	2 428
TOTAL	1 973	342	878	593	6 748	10 534

Source: CBS Statistics, reworked EvdK

In 1993 gross investments in buildings amounted to Dfl. 24.5 billion. Half of all building investments concerned new housing development, Dfl. 5.6 billion was invested in business buildings and Dfl. 2.5 billion was invested in special buildings (schools, hospitals, etc.). Compared with these categories, investments in agricultural buildings and government buildings were small. About 10% of all building investments concerned investments in maintenance and renovation.

Table 6.5 distinguishes six different categories of principals. The category 'private persons, remaining institutions and firms' commissions half of all new building development by value. Note that this is a heterogeneous group of agents. Private persons build mainly new dwellings for their own use, remaining institutions are particularly involved in the development of special buildings, while firms commission mainly the development of new business buildings for their own use. Private developers invested in 1993 almost Dfl. 7 billion in new buildings; the larger part of this figure concerned new dwellings. Housing associations invested Dfl. 3 billion in new buildings -- naturally mainly new dwellings. The shares of the national government, municipalities and financial institutions in total gross investments in buildings were small.

Table 6.6 focuses exclusively on the housing sector.[133] This table indicates that housing associations commission almost all new social rented housing (no surprise) and that speculative developers and private persons are jointly responsible for almost all investments in non-subsidised owner-occupied dwellings, owner-occupied dwellings with one-time allocation and premium-assisted owner-occupied dwellings. Otherwise, investments in premium rental dwellings, premium-assisted owner-occupied dwellings and owner-occupied dwellings with one-time allocation are small, compared to the size of the investments in social rental housing and non-subsidised owner-occupied dwellings. Finally, table 6.6 shows that as much as Dfl. 8.2 billion -- on the total of Dfl. 10.5 billion gross investments in housebuilding -- goes to new housing development in the owner-occupied sector.

I will now pay attention in turn to the strategies of the different categories of principals on the housing market.

Private developers build mainly in the non-subsidised owner-occupied sector. As was argued above, their profits in the housing sector depend on their specific position as 'risk takers' in the development process. Moreover, private developers in the Netherlands derive their gains almost exclusively from speculative building development; they are not -- but this is currently changing -- occupied with speculative land development. Property developers usually buy building plots in land-use plan areas that already have been serviced. In general, they do not hold land banks. In fact this strategy can be labelled as risk-avoiding behaviour: for a developer it means no risk of capital losses and no expenditures on managing the land bank. However, this risk-avoiding behaviour might have changed somewhat recently, as a result of the early reservation of new locations for house building (for further discussion, see Chapter Eight). Moreover, developers do not keep new dwellings in stock -- again because risks are too high. New dwellings are expensive and holding costs are substantial; moreover, both the demand for and the price of new dwellings fluctuate considerably.

The possibilities for private developers to profit from speculative housebuilding development, and thus also their willingness to build, are determined by the development of land and building costs, by the returns on housing development (selling prices), and by the size of the demand for new dwellings. However, this point must be viewed in the light of a number of aspects that are typical to the housing market. These aspects have to do with profit making in housebuilding development processes.

First, professional suppliers of new dwellings must 'compete' with non-professional one-off suppliers of second-hand dwellings (the owner occupiers). Each of them responds differently to changing (economic) circumstances. Second, regional variations in selling prices of dwellings are substantial. This means that regional variations in returns on speculative housebuilding development may be substantial as well (although differences are partly annulled, because of variations in building plot prices). Third, as soon as the demand for owner-occupied dwellings increases, prices will rise as well, because extension of the supply of dwellings usually takes up a relatively long time. Furthermore, it is not to be expected that present owner occupiers will respond quickly to price changes. This will

---

133 The difference in total housebuilding investments between table 6.5 and 6.6 has to do with the fact that the figures in table 6.5 are derived from CBS statistics of 'building permits issued,' while the figures in table 6.6 relate to CBS statistics of 'dwelllings completed.'

aggravate the slow market response to changes in demand. The position of home owners on the housing market is usually not based on the possibility of making profits on the sale of their property. They are primarily concerned with maintaining their position on the owner-occupied dwelling market.

Fourth, and related to the other aspects, both price fluctuations and regional variations in prices are typical to the owner-occupied housing market. It seems at least doubtful whether property developers sufficiently take account of these aspects of the housing market. Within the group of private developers, we must pay some extra attention to the *building entrepreneurs*; as building construction firms they can also be rated among the private developers. However, their development strategies are in principle different: they act as developers not in the first place to derive development gains out of the development process, but to guarantee their own future building production.

Private persons are responsible for a considerable part of new housing development in the owner-occupied sector. In this respect they can be considered as 'principals/future users.' They are typically one-time principals. We may expect them, as developers, to operate less efficiently than speculative developers do, probably resulting in higher development costs. Other implications of their specific role on the housing market are that the use-value of a new dwelling is for them the decisive factor in the development process instead of development gains. Next to the use-value, of course development costs are relevant to their decision to build, as well as the alternative possibility of buying the wished-for dwelling on the second-hand housing market, the development of loan capacity, and the developments of rents. We may assume that possible development gains play no role at all in their decisions to build and that they respond both to fluctuations in house prices, and to fluctuations in loan capacity. Summarised, a private person decides to build a new dwelling for reasons other than those a speculative developer would use to decide. Finally, private persons prefer, most likely, to build in non-urban areas, generally in the more expensive sector of the housing market.[134]

Housing associations develop new dwellings with the intention to let them to (low-income) households; the dwellings remain their property. Thus, their decision to build depends not on changes in house prices, but rather on the development of costs and, related to this, the availability of building subsidies. Table 6.7 shows the number of dwellings owned by housing associations and municipal housing departments. Jointly, they own more than one-third of the total housing stock in the Netherlands. (See also Appendix A1 and A2, concerning respectively 'the number of housing associations and municipal housing departments, by size of their dwelling stock, 1991' and 'the investments of housing associations and municipal housing departments, 1989-1991'.)

---

134 As an indication of this, compare average building costs of new dwellings built by, respectively, speculative developers, private persons and housing association. In 1993 these building costs amounted to Dfl. 134,530 for a dwelling built by a speculative developer, Dfl. 154,679 for a dwelling built by a private person, and Dfl. 91,145 for a dwelling built by a housing association.

TABLE 6.7
Number of dwellings owned by housing associations and municipal housing departments, 1989-1991

	1989	1990	1991
	(x 1000)		
housing associations			
TOTAL	1860	1856	1909
of which:			
cities > 100.000 inhabitants	624	638	680
four large cities	313	323	335
municip. housing departments			
TOTAL	320	301	289
of which:			
cities > 100.000 inhabitants	134	124	125
four large cities	110	100	102

Source: CBS Statistics

As a result of the process of privatisation, three different types of housing associations have come into being (see also NIROV, 1994):
(1) housing associations owning dwellings in 'centres of urban growth.' Their financial position is, generally, fairly good;
(2) housing associations owning dwellings in small towns, in rural areas. Their financial position is good;
(3) housing associations owning dwellings in Amsterdam, Rotterdam and The Hague. Their financial position is poor.

The 'poverty-stricken' housing associations face problems with respect to the maintenance of their property and they have only few opportunities to build new dwellings. On the other hand, the housing associations in the centres of urban growth and in the rural towns do have the financial opportunities to build new dwellings, but the government's housing programme does not always provide for a substantial extension of the housing stock in these towns. As has been mentioned above, new dwellings are to be built mainly in the Randstad; more precisely, for a large part in the conglomerations of Amsterdam, The Hague, Rotterdam and Utrecht. It is expected that, as a result of this situation, mergers between 'rich' and 'poor' housing associations are inevitable.[135] Moreover, when housing associations are really going to act more 'market-orientated,' it may also be expected, for instance, that they decide to sell a part of their property -- especially when house prices are rising.

---

[135] An alternative strategy might be that housing associations located in one town are going to build new dwellings in another town. Jointly, the 'rich' housing associations have at their disposal a capital reserve of Dfl. 15 billion. They can decide for themselves when they are going to use it (see *de Volkskrant*, 24 June 1994).

The remaining groups of agents distinguished in table 6.6 play no significant role as principals on the housing market. *Financial institutions* build mainly in the profit-rental sector. However, they do not own much property. They want to finance the development of new property instead of owning/managing it. *Municipal housing departments* used to build a considerable part of the new dwellings. However, as a consequence of the privatisation processes on the housing market, most of them are now privatised.

Implications
Chapter Eight will demonstrate that, during the research period, the costs of housebuilding construction show a continuous tendency to rise. This is an important fact with respect to the analysis of housing-development processes. It will be argued that the continuous increase of building costs forms a significant factor with respect to the profitability of housing development. As such the consequences of this tendency must be involved, for instance, in the interpretation of the housing-production shortages. It would be interesting to know whether the strategies of the agencies involved in housebuilding, together with the typical 'technical' characteristics of dwellings, have contributed to this tendency. Not aiming to provide a complete answer to this question for the moment, I am still able to indicate some directions for an explanation. First, the specific characteristics of the building product have always impeded the introduction of cost-reducing mass-production methods. On the other hand, section 6.3 reported that the building construction industry, for the most part consists, of small firms with low production outputs. It is to be expected that such a composition of a branch of industry does not lead to a high degree of innovation. As a result, it is likely that building costs are not reduced.

The second point is connected with the fact that the housing market is a typical stock market. The selling price of new dwellings is determined on the second-hand housing market. The next chapters will show that house prices continually fluctuate. It will be argued that these fluctuations of house prices determine private developers' development gains. The increase of building costs does not substantially alter the profits of the private developers, since the level of profits is mainly determined by the fluctuations in dwelling prices.[136]

Third, keep in mind the path dependency of the strategies of the agents involved in house building. For one thing, the important position of housing associations on the development market is typical for the Dutch housing sector. Furthermore, the share of owner-occupied dwellings in the total housing stock is still relatively small. The issue here is why, in a West-European context, this share of owner-occupied dwellings is low. Is it related to the fact that the willingness of households to own a dwelling is smaller in the Netherlands (e.g. because the quality of social-sector dwellings is relatively high), or is the development industry responsible for the low degree of owner occupancy -- the development industry failed to turn the opportunities for building owner-occupied dwellings to account? Why is it that private developers didn't start to build owner-occupied dwellings earlier and to a larger extent? Why has land development always been the specific task of the local governments? What is the impact of the strategies of the 'one-off producers' -- the households building for their own -- for the functioning of the housing development market? Although clear answers are yet unavailable, I assume that these aspects certainly play a role in the present problems

---

[136] In other markets, i.e. non-stock markets, usually the development of selling prices and the development of building costs go simultaneously.

with respect to house building. Alternative strategies of the different groups of agents -- and, with this, alternative market outcomes -- are certainly not inconceivable.

6.6. Institutional Economic Relations between the Agents

Thus far I have discussed the strategies of the producers of new dwellings. I will now pay some attention to the financiers of housing development (see also EIB, 1992). Investments in buildings can be financed either by someone's own funds or by loans on the capital market. In general, financial institutions (mainly pension funds, insurance companies) are able to finance their investments in house development themselves. However, the larger part of their funds is invested in long-term loans (among other things, to finance new housing developments by housing associations. Housing associations, on the other hand, finance housing development either with their own capital reserves or by long-term loans on the capital market.[137] This appeal on the capital market has been facilitated by the foundation of the Special Fund for Housing.

No information is available about the way in which private developers finance their investments in house building. Either they make use of their own funds, or they appeal to the capital market. Sometimes they are linked to financial institutions; in these cases, financing is no problem.

Private persons who build a new dwelling for their own use finance, on average, 75% of their investments by negotiating a mortgage and 25% by their own funds (estimations by EIB, 1992). Table 6.8 shows the newly registered mortgages on real estate from 1990 to 1993. The number of new registrations sharply increased in this period, from 247,187 in 1990 to 379,000 in 1993. In 1993 the average mortgage amounted to about Dfl. 225,000. Most mortgages are provided by banks (49.5%, in 1993), mortgage companies and building funds (20.8%), insurance companies and pension funds (13.0%) and remaining institutions and companies (12.3%). Note that table 6.8 does not focus exclusively on either mortgages for *new* dwellings, or on dwellings only. Mortgages on existing dwellings (which make up the larger part of the new registrations) are also included, as well as mortgages on other buildings. However, what can be concluded from this table is that the *number of transactions* on the housing market has substantially increased.

---

[137] From 1988 on, housing associations are entirely committed to the capital market, since government loans have been abolished.

TABLE 6.8
Newly registered mortgagees on real estate, by total number of registrations and total amounts and by market share of mortgagees, 1990-1993

	1990		1991		1992		1993	
	new registration	amount (mln gld)	new registration	amount (mln gld)	new registration	amount (mln gld)	new registration	amount (mln gld)
	247 187	67 004	251 874	59 681	278 960	62 997	379 163	85 191
market shares mortgagees (in %)								
-mortgage companies and building funds	18.2		19.5		20.8		24.6	
-insurance companies, pension funds	9.2		11.9		13.0		12.2	
-saving funds	5.1		3.6		2.5		2.8	
-general and cooperative organised banks	46.0		47.4		49.5		44.8	
-remaining institutions and companies	9.7		15.4		12.3		11.3	
-private persons and firms without corporate personality	1.8		2.3		2.0		2.4	
average rate of interest on newly registered mortgages on real estate	8.72		9.23		8.84			

Source: CBS Statistics

Finally, an estimation can be made of the total call on the capital market, as a result of investments in new housing development (see EIB, 1992). It is assumed (1) that financial institutions do not call to the capital market, and (2) that owner-occupied dwellings are, on average, financed for 25% by own means. This implies that in 1991, when total investments in new dwellings amounted to Dfl. 14.1 billion, the call to the capital market was approximately Dfl. 10.8 billion.

6.7. Summary

Badcock (1994: p. 427) cites Neutze when he suggests a framework for judging the efficacy of property systems. He favours a property system that:
(1) enables urban development to be managed in an efficient and orderly way;
(2) avoids high speculative costs of land for housing and public purposes;
(3) siphons off the increases in land values that accompany urban growth into the public purse (i.e. via a levy on the betterment or development gain)

Needham *et al.* add to these the desiderata that property prices should not move too erratically, and that private property should not be too unevenly distributed within society (Needham *et al.*, 1993: pp. 210-212).

Badcock continues by arguing that 'generally, public policy has to be able to influence not only the amount and location of land and buildings coming onto the market (the sufficiency of supply criterion), but also its nature and use if these conditions are to be met. Also, if the property market is to operate in an orderly manner, there needs to be a predictable and stable administrative framework guiding the decisions of investors' (Badcock, 1994: p. 427). Probably the Dutch property system would pass this test fairly well. On the other hand, I have tried to make the point in this chapter that a uniform (positive) judgement of the Dutch property system -- the structure of land and building provision -- is hard to make. Although on the face of it numerous characteristics of the Dutch property market seem to indicate that the judgements should be positive, several typical features of the Dutch property market, i.e. the housing market, nonetheless point out that this conclusion is at least premature. The propositions that have been drawn up in this chapter concern these aspects of the Dutch property market and their possible effects for the outcome of market processes. The case study of the Dutch housing market will be helpful in examining these propositions critically. Chapter Nine will discuss this issue more profoundly. The evaluation of the property system will then take place, based on two concepts: the allocative efficacy and the productive efficiency of the Dutch property system.

This chapter analysed the institutional organisation of the Dutch housing development market. With respect to this *structure of building provision* -- related to the productive efficiency of the housing market -- we can already draw a number of conclusions. First, the national government has withdrawn itself in financial terms from the housing market. Severe cutbacks on government expenditures to the housing sector have taken place. The implications are as yet unknown with respect to building production levels. If in the future the total number of dwellings built by private agencies will not decrease, despite the reduction of public money for housing development, this should make questionable the necessity of the large amount of government money that was allocated to the housing sector in the past. Wouldn't it have been possible to build the same number of dwellings with less government money?

Second, housing associations have become a 'new' group of agents on the housing market; they can be classified now as social entrepreneurs, which can be divided into rich and poor housing associations.

Third, private developers occupy a significant position on the housing market. Surprisingly, they have never (until recently) shown any interest in land development and/or land banking. Chapters Seven and Eight will argue that their lack of initiative on the land market is an important aspect of the Dutch property system.

Fourth, a considerable part of new completed dwellings are commissioned by private persons that can be considered as one-off producers. In contrast to private developers, these private persons take account only of the costs of building; development gains are of no interest to them.

Fifth, the building construction industry is characterised by a majority of small-scale firms, a low content of innovation, and risk-avoiding behaviour. Chapter Eight will relate these issues to, among other things, the development of building costs and show that, as a consequence, building costs show permanent real growth.

Sixth, financiers play only a minor role in housing development processes. In general, they are probably willing to invest in new development projects, since risks are relatively low.

Chapter Six has provided the context for a more detailed study of housing development in the Netherlands. The results of this study will now be presented in Chapters Seven and Eight.

7 TRENDS IN HOUSING PRODUCTION AND STRATEGIES OF MARKET PARTIES

7.1. Introduction

Trends in housing production will be used in this chapter as indicators of structural changes, both on the housing market and within the housing-development industry. Changes with respect to the number and type of dwellings that have been built and with respect to the level of building investments that have taken place within the research period, in about 25 years of time, tell us something about the *producers* as well. For instance, the analysis of these trends makes it possible to study how various groups of agents respond to changes in house prices and building costs, to changes in demand and to changes in other, exogenous variables (like economic growth rates and rate of inflation and interest). The outcome of this analysis makes clear how the composition of the group of actors involved in housing development as well as the institutional relations between the agents change over time. Subsequently, both housing investment levels and the number of completed dwellings in the Netherlands will be placed in an international context.

The above is subject of sections 7.2 and 7.3. Next to an analysis of housing production, this chapter contains an analysis of the housing stock (section 7.4). Post-war house building has been responsible for substantial changes with respect to the housing stock. Not only has the size of the housing stock increased immensely, but this has been accompanied by shifts in, among other things, the age, tenure status and quality of the housing stock. Moreover, the composition of the group of house owners has changed. As a result, the spatial structure of most cities has undergone a complete change.

In line with the argument in Chapter Six (that speculative housing development is sensitive to price fluctuations on the second-hand housing market), the next step in the analysis in the present chapter is made by the reproduction of the fluctuations that took place with respect to dwelling prices and land prices (section 7.5). The intention is to make clear the links between speculative housing development and the functioning of the second-hand housing market. Finally, the consumption of housing and the level of demand for new dwellings are analysed (section 7.6). Housing consumption patterns depend largely on the way new dwellings are produced as well as on the ownership relations on the housing market. The development of housing expenditures of tenants and owner-occupiers are analysed, regional variations in housing rents and house prices are compared with each other, and the development of the loan capacity of households is related to the trend in selling prices.

This chapter aims to show the trends in housing production and market prices that are relevant to the functioning of the Dutch housing market. Starting from this point, hypothetical explanations can be provided for the way the organisational structure of the housing development industry has its effect on, for instance, changes in the level of production, the location of new developments, housing consumption patterns and ownership relations. In addition, I will try to make clear how the functioning of the second-hand housing market determines new housing-production levels. In this respect, the most attention will go to the influence of fluctuations in selling prices on the owner-occupied housing market on the profitability of new-housing development.

Chapter Seven focusses on the *changes* that have taken place with respect to housing development and the *consequences* of these changes in production output for the housing stock. The changes in production output are related to the institutional organisation of the housing development market, which has been described in Chapter Six. Chapter Eight discusses potential *sources* of institutional change -- that is, changes in the structure of housing provision. Furthermore, institutional changes with respect to the organisational structure of the development industry and the strategies of the agents are discussed. In the end, I will draw conclusions with respect to the consequences of these changes for the functioning of the housing market and for the output of this market -- the housing stock.

7.2. The Production of New Buildings and Renovations: Investment Trends

Investment in housebuilding rose from Dfl. 8 billion in 1975 to Dfl. 12.1 billion in 1981, then collapsed to Dfl. 9.5 billion in 1984, and were back on the 1981 level (current prices) in 1993 (fig. 7.1).[138] House-building investments appear to be subject to large fluctuations.[139] The growth of investment in the second half of the 1970s -- mainly due to the increased activity of private principals on the owner-occupied housing market -- went together with the growth in both demand and housing prices in this market. Investments still increased until 1981; the larger part of house-building production was then, however, already taken over by the housing associations.

The private developers soon lost their faith in the owner-occupied housing market. This happened when the demand for dwellings broke down at the end of the 1970s as suddenly as it had risen in the years before. Especially rising mortgage rates and disappointing economic expectations were responsible for the sudden collapse of the housing market in the early 1980s.[140] The anti-cyclical -- but costly -- building policy of the national government was to be thanked for the initial continuation of building investments in the early 1980s.

After 1984 (1982 and 1983 were together the 'years of disaster' of the Dutch housing market), the housing market slowly recovered. Private principals (from 1987 on in CBS statistics divided in three categories) started to invest again in house building. Both the category of private developers and the category of private persons substantially increased their investments on the housing market. The share of housing associations in house-building investments, on the other hand, fell to register the lowest figures of the last two decades. It is remarkable that the category of private persons -- consisting mainly of households building a house for their own use -- appears to be responsible for an increasing part of the stock of new dwellings. Taking into consideration that the costs for owner-users to build a house themselves are probably higher than if they would buy a completed dwelling, and

---

138 Investments in land development are not included in these figures.

139 Figure 7.1 would give a different impression of the development market if investments were in real prices. Particularly the peak in investments in the second half of the 1970s is relatively higher than the present level of investments, when inflation figures are taken into consideration.

140 See Janssen (1992) for a detailed study of these developments.

assuming that this category builds new dwellings mainly in the more expensive sectors of the housing market, a possible explanation for this phenomenon relates to the (mal)functioning of the housing market. Perhaps, private developers have been unable to satisfy -- in time -- the demand of these households for new dwellings, and the overheated second-hand housing market leaves them insufficient choice. Are private developers unable to fulfill household's demands? Are profit margins on speculative building development too small? Do municipalities -- in their role as land developers -- delay development processes?[141]

FIGURE 7.1
Gross investments in housebuilding, by principal, 1975-1993 (current prices)

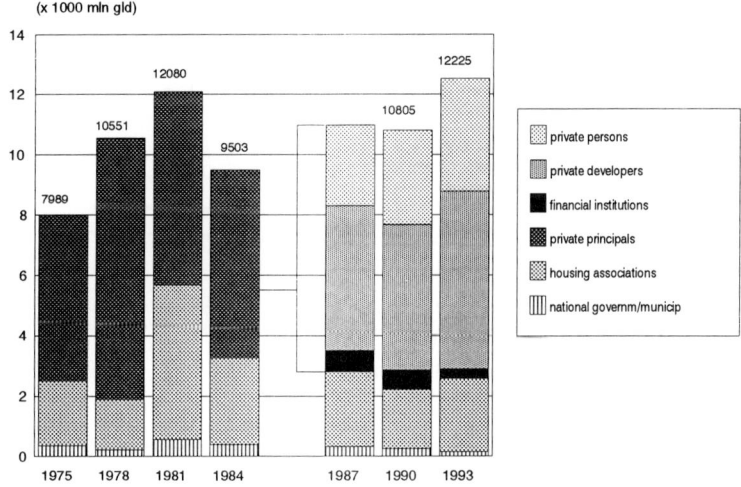

note: from 1987 on the category of private principals is divided in 'financial institutions', 'speculative developers', and 'private persons'.
source: CBS Statistics

Figures 7.2 and 7.3 concern, respectively, indices for gross investments in housing, business buildings and total building activity and the annual percentage of change in the absolute figures for the same categories of building investments.

---

141 I realise that such suggestions are highly speculative. Comparable data on house-building investments by private persons is unavailable for a longer period in time. Thus, it is unknown whether the present increase of their investments is unique or recurring in time.

FIGURE 7.2
Indices for gross investments in housing, business buildings and total building investments, 1974-1993 (1980 = 100; current prices)

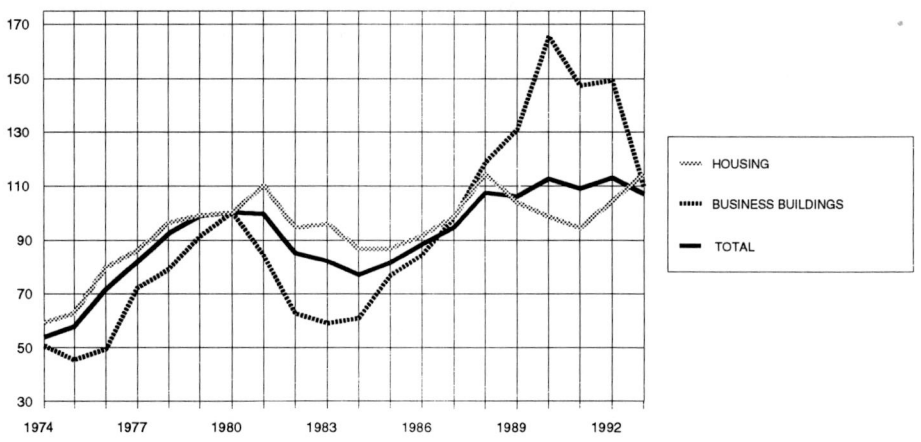

source: CBS Statistics, reworked EvdK

FIGURE 7.3
Gross investments in housing, business buildings and total building investments, annual % of change, 1974-1993

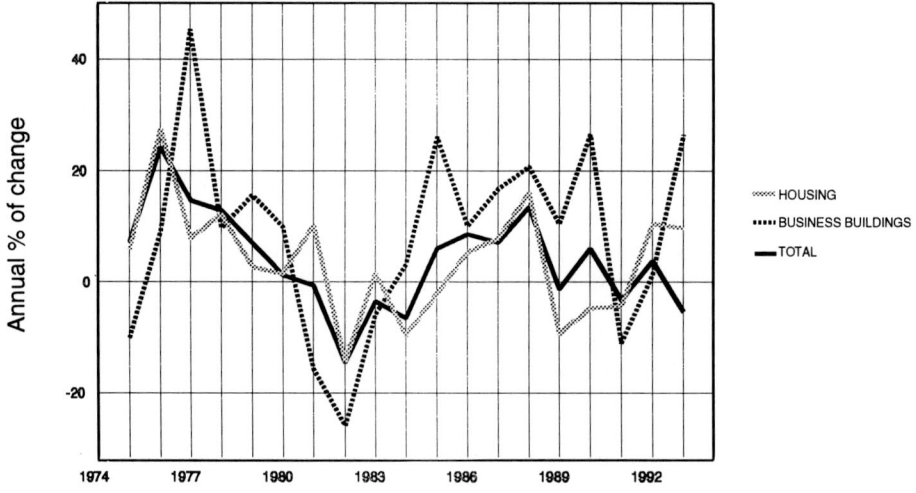

source: CBS Statistics, reworked EvdK

The comparison of investments in housing, business buildings and total building shows a more or less similar trend for the investments in each of the categories. Nonetheless, the fluctuations in investments in business buildings seem to be 'sharper' than the fluctuations in housing investments. Probably this has to do, on the one hand, with the national government's anti-cyclical building policy on the housing market and, on the other hand, with the fact that firms, building for their own use, more directly respond to fluctuations in economic growth than speculative house builders are supposed to do.[142] The demand for housing is of course determined by other factors than the demand for business buildings (see also section 7.6). This is supported by figure 7.3; again, the fluctuations in the annual percentage of change of investments in business buildings are sharper than the annual changes in housebuilding investments.

In an international -- West-European -- context, the level of building investments in the Netherlands takes up a position in the middle (fig. 7.4). The same goes for the share of investments in residential buildings in total investments in building construction. With respect to this point the Netherlands takes up an average position as well (fig. 7.5).

FIGURE 7.4
International comparison of gross fixed capital formation in building construction, as a percentage of gross domestic product, 1980-1992

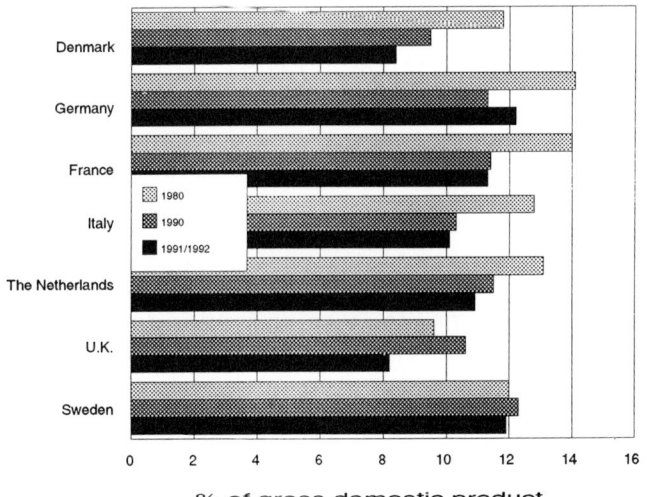

source: CBS Statistics

---

142   The larger part of new investments in business buildings is commissioned by future users; private developers are responsible for a substantially smaller part of the investments in this sector.

FIGURE 7.5
International comparison of gross fixed capital formation in residential buildings as a percentage of gross fixed capital formation in building construction, 1980-1991/1992

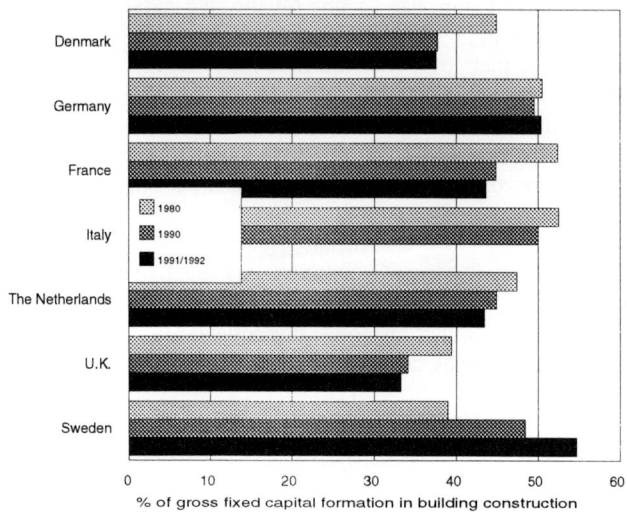

source: CBS Statistics

The investments in residential buildings in most countries take up between 40 and 50 per cent of all building investments. However, in Sweden this share is considerably larger, while in Great Britain the share of housing investments in total investments is significantly lower. Total investments in building construction were also low in Great Britain, indicating that this country clearly stays behind with respect to housing production.

7.3.   The Number of New Dwellings, by Year and by Way of Financing

In the beginning of the 1960s, around 80,000 dwellings per annum were completed. This number increased rapidly from 100,000 dwellings in 1964 to 120,000 dwellings in 1971. From 1971 to 1974 housing production rose to record numbers: respectively, 137,000, 152,000, 155,000 and 146,000 dwellings were completed. This increase in housing production was due mainly to the large number of dwellings that were built in the premium-assisted sector (fig. 7.6). After 1975, the production level fell again to 120,000 completed dwellings. From 1975 until 1989 the number of completions fluctuated between 110,000 and 120,000 per year. Only in 1979 and in 1985/6 did the number of completions dropped to a lower level, respectively 87,500 dwellings, 98,000 dwellings and 103,000 dwellings. In 1979, substantially less dwellings were completed in the premium-assisted sector, while in 1985/6 a relative small number of social sector dwellings were completed. From 1990 on the number of completed dwellings definitely drops to a lower level, around 80,000 dwellings per annum.

FIGURE 7.6
Dwellings completed, by tenure status and by way of financing, 1960-1993

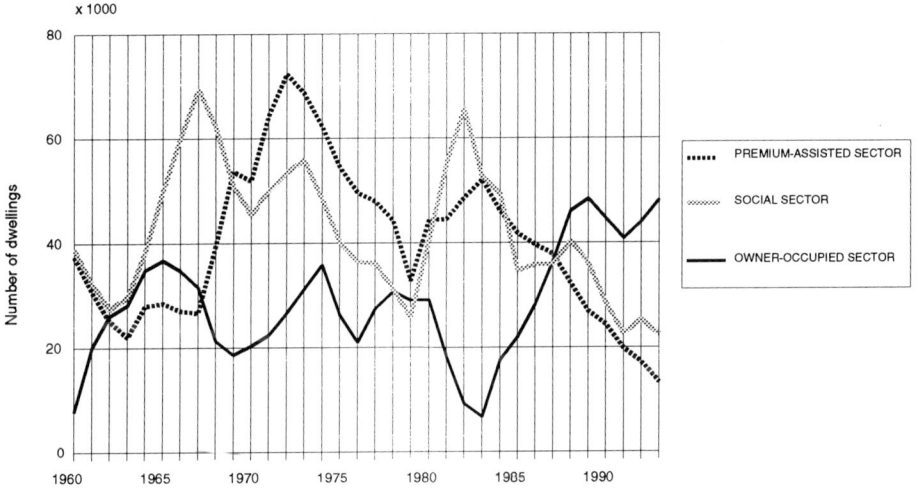

source: CBS Statistics

All sectors of the house-building market show significant fluctuations. At the beginning of the 1980s we clearly see the result of the national government's anti-cyclical house-building policy. The decline in housing production in the owner-occupied sector was compensated by the development of a larger number of social-sector dwellings. In overall house building construction, the social sector has always held an important position, being the logical consequence of the national government's housing policy. The housing associations' declining role in house building construction in recent years also fits in with the goals of national housing policy in the 1990s (see Chapter Six). The share of the premium-assisted sector in new house building varies from less than twenty percent in the second half of the 1960s and in recent years to more than forty percent in the 1970s. Relatively seen, the owner-occupied sector has long been of minor significance compared to new house building -- despite the continual attempt by the national government to realise the reverse. Until 1987, its share never exceeded a quarter of the annual number of completed dwellings -- between 20,000 and 30,000 dwellings per year. In 1982 and 1983 completions in the owner-occupied sector even dropped to almost negligible figures - 6,500 dwellings in 1983.

FIGURE 7.7
Dwellings completed, by tenure status and by way of financing, as a percentage of the total, 1960-1993

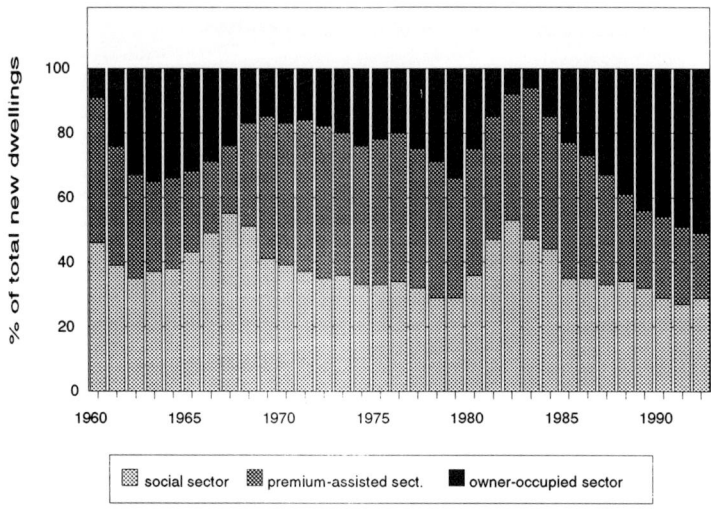

source: CBS Statistics

Although empirical evidence is lacking, it seems that in the Netherlands, until the shift in the second half of the 1980s, a substantial potential of demand for new owner-occupied dwellings has been ignored. Why did the owner-occupied sector not expand in the 1960s and 1970s in the Netherlands, in contrast with the trend in most other West-European countries? Have the larger part of Dutch households never been interested in owner-occupation, either because their loan capacity was relatively small or because they had good alternatives in the social sector? Or is it just because households are unfamiliar with the owner-occupied housing market? Have private developers not thrown themselves on this market, because profits were out of proportion with development risks, or because they have underestimated the potential demand for owner-occupied houses?[143]

Unfortunately, the statistical information necessary to answer these questions properly is unavailable. However, several issues are relevant to the discussion. First, Dutch housing policy (in comparison with that of other West-European countries) has not, until recently, been directed toward promoting the spread of owner-occupation among the Dutch population. This point is related to the fact that the quality of social-sector dwellings is

---

143   In a perfect market, a situation in which demand exceeds supply would automatically lead to an increase in prices. As a result, the supply will grow. However, in a market that is not perfect, several constraints may hinder the smooth functioning of the price mechanism. In the housing market it is possible that demanders lack information about the opportunities to buy a house. It is even more likely that a kind of habitual behaviour -- households are *used* or *satisfied* to live in social-sector housing -- holds households back from buying a house. In the latter cases, developers could try to arouse a demand for owner-occupied dwellings by using a marketing approach directed at providing information to households and changing the habitual behaviour.

generally considered to be relatively good: households do not need to buy a house. Second, private developers have apparently not been particularly interested in building cheap owner-occupied dwellings.[144] If development profits are indeed small in the Dutch owner-occupied housing sector, due to the specific structure of this market in the Netherlands, it is most likely that they are smallest in the cheaper parts of the owner-occupied sector. Third, the specific composition of the Dutch housing development industry might play a role. As has been mentioned before, we know little about (changes in) the composition of the group of private builders involved in housing development (see also fig. 7.8). One possibility is that originally this group of agents consisted mainly of building entrepreneurs that did not want to be confronted with substantial risks in housing development, and that speculative developers, in the true sense of the word, became active in this market only more recently. Perhaps, this also has to do with the fact that market parties in the Netherlands have never been actively involved in land development, as I discussed earlier, leading to smaller development gains for private developers. Finally, figure 7.6 demonstrates that the resulting number of completed dwellings fluctuates largely from year to year. This implies that the size of the production output changes likewise (see also section 7.2): the housing market is unstable by nature. For the building-construction industry, this means that the production of new dwellings is surrounded with many uncertainties. They cannot hold stocks of new dwellings, but it is also difficult for them to speed up the production process in order to respond sooner to changes in demand, mainly because it takes time to purchase and develop new building land. Chapter Eight will discuss this further.

A number of conclusions can be drawn from this figure. In none of the other countries was the decline in the number of dwellings completed per 1000 inhabitants between 1980 and 1991 as substantial as in the Netherlands. In 1989 the number of dwellings completed per 1000 inhabitants in the Netherlands still exceeds the number of dwellings completed in other countries. Between 1989 and 1991, this number in the Netherlands suddenly dropped quite substantially from almost eight new dwellings per 1000 inhabitants to slightly more than five dwellings per 1000 inhabitants, while, for instance, completions in Great Britain remained almost the same between 1980 and 1991 at four. The need for housing apparently remained for a longer period on a high level in the Netherlands than it did in other West-European countries. However, figure 7.9 also makes clear that the production of new dwellings in most other countries is more stable than in the Netherlands.

---

144 Logically, the relatively low share of the owner-occupied sector in the Dutch housing market is a consequence of the fact that the majority of middle-class income groups, who *do* own a house in other West-European countries, do not own houses in the Netherlands. High-income groups in the Netherlands mostly *do* own houses.

FIGURE 7.8
Dwellings completed, by principal as a percentage of the total, 1960-1993

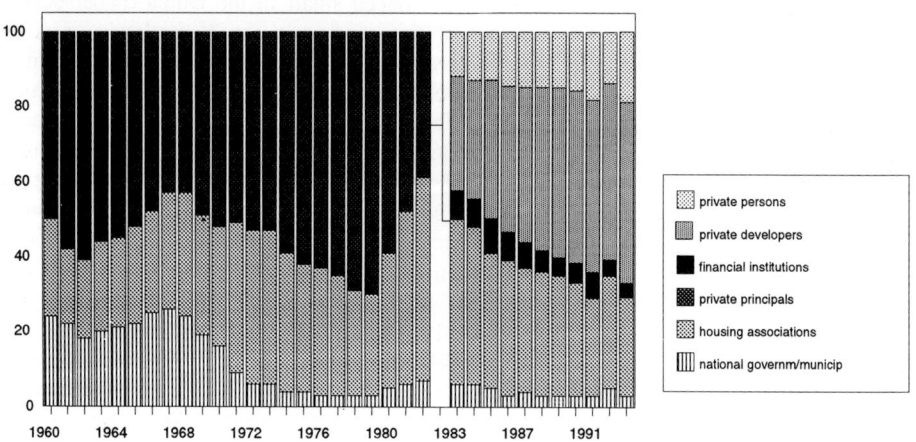

note: from 1983 on the category of private builders is divided in 'financial institutions,' 'private developers,' and 'private persons.'
source: CBS Statistics

Figure 7.9 shows the trend of housing development in the Netherlands in an international framework.

FIGURE 7.9
International comparison: dwellings completed and rate of change of population, 1980-1992

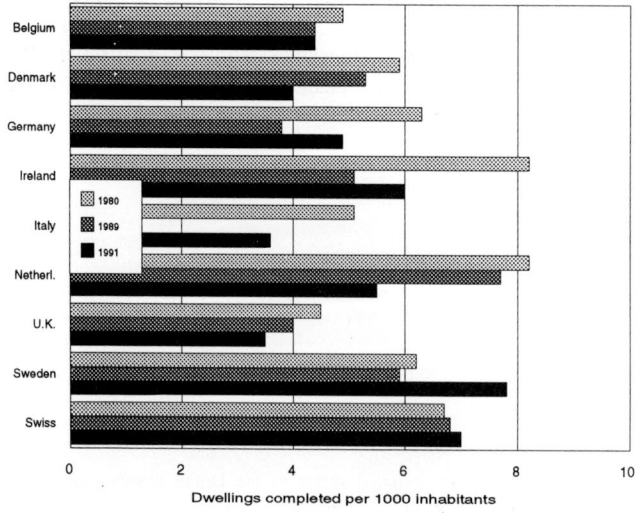

source: CBS Statistics

7.4. Changes in the Housing Stock: Age, Tenure and Quality

What happened during the research period with respect to the housing stock? This section will discuss changes that took place with respect to the stock of existing dwellings. In 1993 the housing stock consisted of more than 6 million dwellings. Between 1970 and 1993, around 2.6 million dwellings were added to the housing stock.[145] Annual addition to the housing stock was maximal in the early 1970s -- around three percent per year; in the 1980s the annual addition of new dwellings to the housing stock was reduced to around one per cent per year. The pace of replacement of obsolete dwellings has remained more or less unchanged during the research period: between 10,000 and 15,000 dwellings per year. This low level indicates that the housing stock is rather well maintained, due to good management by the owners and to government subsidies on renovation. Especially housing associations, which jointly own a considerable part of the housing stock, and owner-occupiers may be expected to be good managers. Private landlords, notorious for neglecting their property, own only a small part of the housing stock in the Netherlands. Moreover, the national government has successively stimulated housing associations to purchase property formerly owned by private landlords that is in a bad condition.

Figures 7.10 and 7.11 concern respectively 'the dwelling stock by date of building' and 'the average estimated value per dwelling, by date of building.' In accordance with the above, these figures demonstrate that the larger part of the housing stock is of a relatively recent date. The estimated value of pre-World War II owner-occupied dwellings is high compared to the estimated value of dwellings that have been built after 1945, especially when the difference in age is taken into consideration. Evidently, the majority of the ante-war owner-occupied dwelling stock consists of large, high-quality dwellings, while in recent years apparently cheaper owner-occupied dwellings have been developed.

Except for 1965-69 and 1975-79, the expansion of the housing stock has been constantly larger than the growth of the number of households (fig. 7.12). Between 1960 and 1985, the growth of the number of households fluctuated between two and three percent per year. However, after 1985 the growth clearly slowed down. The increase of the housing stock has been subject to larger fluctuations (compared to the growth of the number of households). The consequence of this would usually be -- that is, in most market types -- that the degree to which the housing market is characterszed by scarcity will vary as well.

Figure 7.13 shows the development of the share of owner-occupied dwellings in the total housing stock. The share of owner-occupied dwellings has increased from 35% in 1970, via 42% in 1980, to 48% in 1994. In the 1970s most new owner-occupied dwellings concerned premium-assisted dwellings; in recent years, however, the larger part of the new owner-occupied dwellings are non-subsidised, more expensive dwellings.

---

145   In 1970 the housing stock consisted of 3.7 million dwellings.

FIGURE 7.10
Dwelling stock, by date of building, 1 January 1992

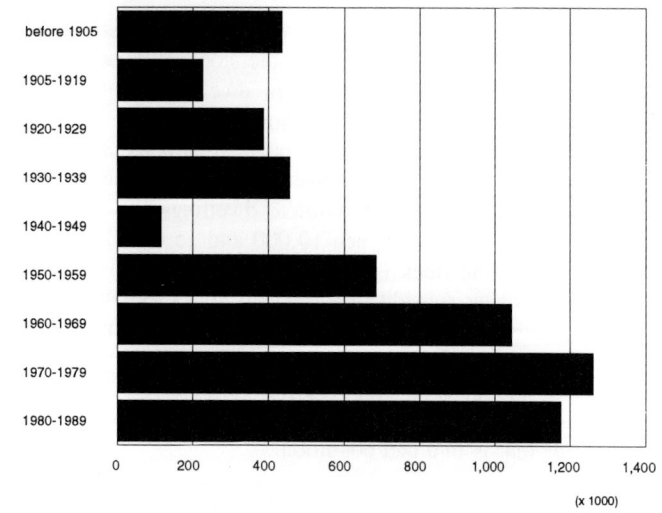

source: CBS Statistics

FIGURE 7.11
Average estimated value per dwelling, by date of building, 1 January 1992 (prices 1992)

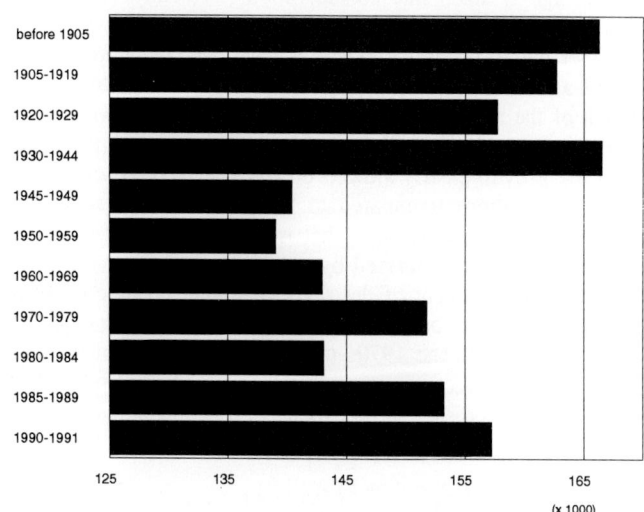

source: CBS Statistics

Trends in Housing Production 153

FIGURE 7.12
Annual % of change of the total stock of dwellings and the number of households, 1960-1994

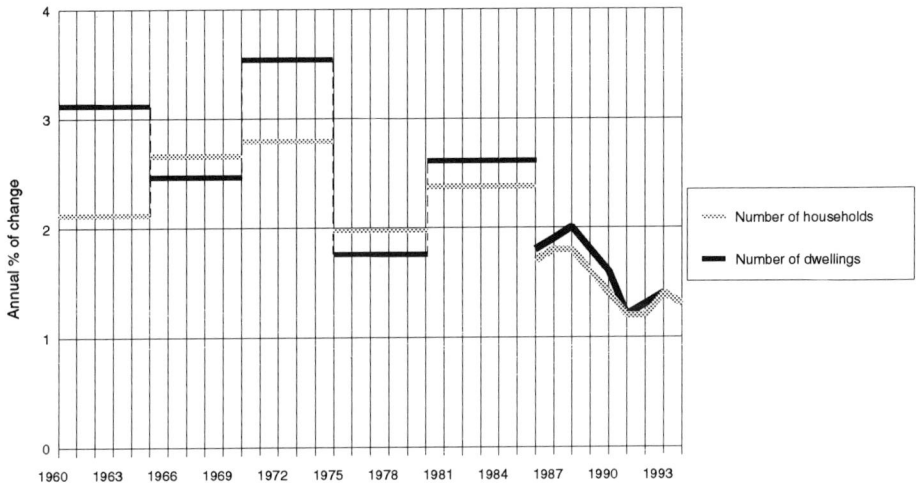

source: CBS Statistics

FIGURE 7.13
Owner-occupied dwellings, as a percentage of the total building stock, 1970-1994

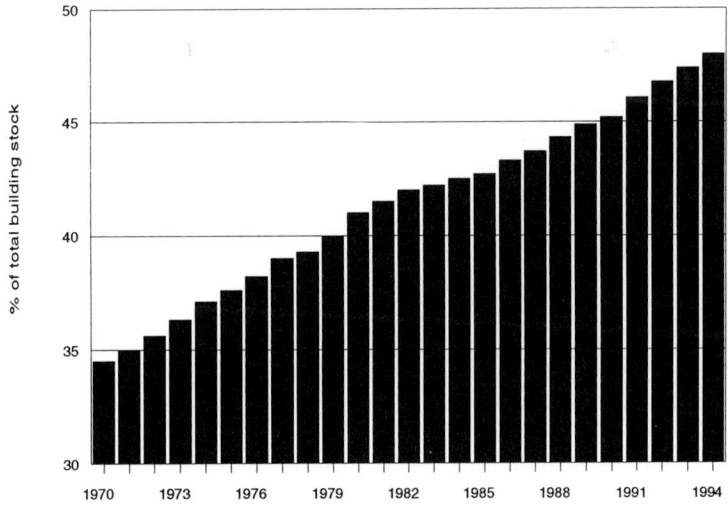

source: CBS Statistics

The above-mentioned figures draw attention to a number of issues. What are the consequences for the functioning of the housing market of the relatively low share of owner-occupied dwellings, on the one hand, and the substantial growth of it in recent years, on the other hand? One guess is that in the Netherlands the national government spent more money on housing than in other countries, because the housing associations -- 'representing' the public sector -- took the responsibility for building and managing the larger part of the housing stock themselves. Second, local governments may miss income from land development, because land prices for social sector and premium-assisted dwellings are set on norm prices. Land prices for owner-occupied dwellings are usually higher (see section 7.5). Third, in most West-European countries owner occupation is commonly better spread among different income groups. Evidently, lower income groups in these countries can afford to buy a house. There is no reason to assume that households in similar income groups in the Netherlands shouldn't be able to buy a house -- especially since in recent years this is actually happening. Does this imply -- as already stated in section 7.3 -- that private developers have ignored a potential demand (for relatively cheap owner-occupied dwellings) or does it mean that development gains in the Netherlands are lower? I will discuss this further in Chapter Eight. Nonetheless, this point is in line with my argument that the present state of the housing market is shaped by the path it has taken in the past.

Fourth, the larger share of owner occupation in other West-European countries indicates that in those countries probably a larger part of lower income groups participates in owner occupation. The financial risks for these income groups -- for instance, when mortgage interests suddenly rise -- are of course larger than for high-income groups, sometimes leading to compulsory sales. Otherwise, in countries with widespread owner occupation among lower income groups, the possibility of making money gains on property comes within their reach (if house prices rise) -- while in the Netherlands they are excluded from this.

Fifth, at this moment in the Netherlands middle income groups increasingly decide to buy a house, leading to an overheated housing market and money gains for existing house owners (see section 7.5). New housing development, on the other hand, takes place especially in more expensive sectors of the housing market (see par. 8.3). The result of both trends is the formation of a move-up market: existing owner-occupiers increasingly move to new, more expensive houses, as a result of the money gains they are able to make on their former property.

Sixth, the Dutch housing market is characterised by a substantial and unwanted skewness (see for instance Dieleman, 1994): middle-income households live in (too) cheap social-sector dwellings. As a result, scarcity in the cheaper part of the housing stock appears. One reason for this could be that the households concerned lack the possibility to buy a house that is within their reach because of a shortage of relatively cheap dwellings in the owner-occupied sector, or because the custom of owning a house is missing within this group. Another reason might be that the quality of social-sector dwellings is relatively good, so that they do not feel the need to move.

Finally, an analysis of the quality of the housing stock should include a discussion of the location of that housing stock as well. It seems that in the Netherlands two different and sometimes conflicting mechanisms have been at work, shaping the locational structure of the housing stock. Local governments, as land developers and being responsible for the implementation of land use plans, have always been able to determine new locations for housing development. In their decisions with respect to the location of building, it has customarily been only the costs of land development that played a role; the real value of the land was left aside.[146] One of the consequences is that social-sector dwellings are now sometimes situated on potentially attractive locations for other users. Without public sector regulation with respect to land development, the land would have been allocated to its most profitable use. In fact, this is another type of skewness on the Dutch housing market: attractive locations are occupied by uses that yield only relatively low returns. Note that such a land policy brings forward a financial cost for municipalities; they miss the possibility of higher returns on land development and run the risk at the same time that norm prices for social-sector and premium-assisted dwellings do not cover the costs of land development. Furthermore, the characteristics of the location have never been expressed in rent levels of social-sector dwellings (see also section 7.6).[147] Recently, more specifically since the revival of the owner-occupied housing market in the late 1980s, local governments have become more aware both of the necessity to attract private developers and of the possibility to make profits out of land development.[148] If this is true, then local governments should now increasingly allocate the most attractive locations for the development of new, expensive owner-occupied dwellings.

7.5. House Price Fluctuations and Changing Land Prices

Average selling prices of owner-occupied dwellings vary considerably, both through time and among places (see respectively fig. 7.14 and Rouwendal, 1994). After the 'boom' in housing prices between 1976 and 1979 (house prices increased by almost 40 percent per year), the housing market collapsed as suddenly as it had 'boomed'. Housing prices remained on a low level until 1985. From 1986 on, prices again started to recover, initially quite gradually but in the last two or three years again sharply -- around 12 to 13 percent per year. The historical low level of mortgage interest is one of the reasons for the increase of dwelling prices. The current upturn of the housing market is, not surprisingly, accompanied by the growth of the number of transactions in this market.[149] It is difficult to explain the characteristic instability of housing prices, due to the complexity of the price-setting

---

146 Land costs are usually not the decisive factor in this respect. An optimal spatial structure is of more importance to the public sector.

147 The rent for a social-sector dwelling in the centre of Amsterdam is the same as the rent for an identical social sector dwelling somewhere in a peripheral region. Only recently has this changed somewhat (see, for regional variations in rents, also Rouwendal, 1994).

148 Note that this is a personal opinion of the author; at this moment no statistical or other data are on hand to support this opinion. Chapter Nine will discuss this issue from a perspective based on institutional-economic theory.

149 In 1988 58,950 transactions on the owner-occupied housing market took place; in 1993 this number had already increased to 75,000 (source: NVB, 1994).

process (however, see Janssen, 1992). Several factors play a role, among them the fact that the stock of housing cannot be expanded rapidly and the fluctuations in demand for owner-occupied dwellings. Households' decisions to buy a house are influenced, *inter alia*, by the means they use to finance transactions -- that is, how mortgage interest develops affects the households' loan capacity (fig. 7.15) -- in combination with the role of moving owners' money gains in their moves (see also Ball, 1983). It is likely that the enlargement of loan capacity makes it possible, in the first place, for more households to buy a house and in the second place incites a larger share of the existing owners to buy a new house -- all the more because the price of their own house has increased. Thus, demand for housing can suddenly expand, while supply cannot respond in time.

From figures 7.16 and 7.17 it can be concluded that the trend of dwelling prices rarely stays in line with the general cost of living index (inflation). Nevertheless, on a longer term both trends *do* evolve more or less similarly. However, such a conclusion must be drawn carefully as it is not yet clear how long the present increase in prices will hold.

FIGURE 7.14
Trend of average selling prices of owner-occupied dwellings, 1975-1993 (current prices)

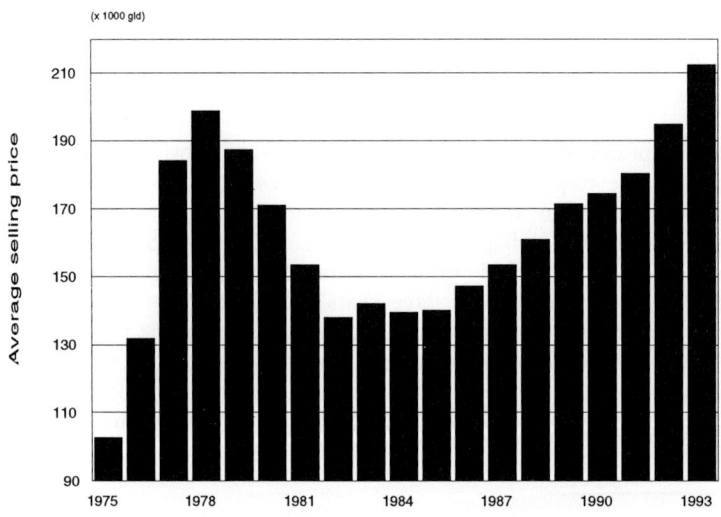

source: NVM

For private developers house price fluctuations are a constant factor.[150] It makes speculative housing development risky, but it gives rise to extra development gains as well. Developers run risks with respect to when the housing market would again suddenly

---

[150] Badcock (1994: p. 431) provides evidence that, compared to other countries (notably the UK and Australia), house prices in the Netherlands are relatively stable. However, when we consider real price developments Dutch housing prices appear to be as unstable as in the UK. Inflation rates in the Netherlands have been much lower than in the UK.

collapse, resulting in a declining demand and falling house prices. Particularly when developers build speculatively -- that is, the future buyers/owners are not yet known -- and the production of new dwellings is already underway, they face financial problems in such a market situation. This is what happened during the collapse of the market in the early 1980s. Developers held a large quantity of new dwellings in stock which they were not able to sell, bringing them into serious financial trouble (Elsevier, 1994). For that reason they try to avoid risks now as much as possible (see Chapter Eight). Sharp increases of house prices, however, can also lead to substantial development gains for speculative developers. The development of building costs is autonomous and does not follow the fluctuations in house prices. Developers can probably best take advantage of a sudden rise of house prices when they hold land banks. By land banking, speculative developers are able to respond in time to sudden market fluctuations. Large-size developers should be able to do so, but in the Netherlands they have never tried.[151]

FIGURE 7.15
Development of average house prices and average loan capacity, 1975-1993

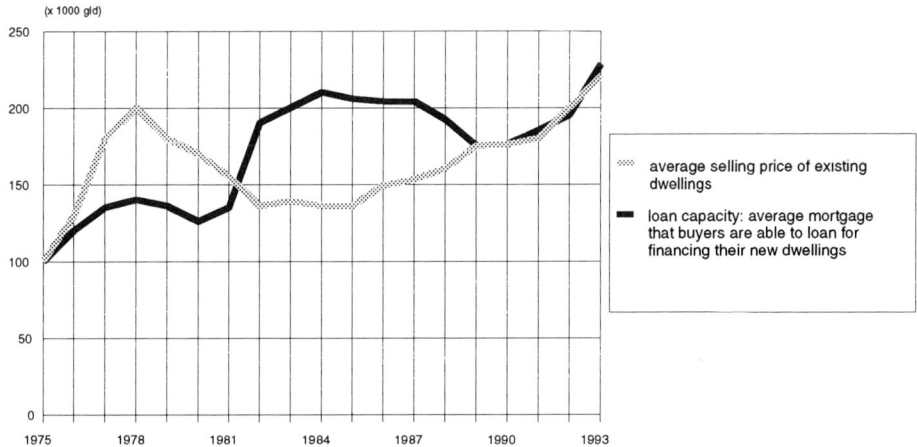

source: VEH (Organisation for house owners)

---

[151] Reliable information on this subject is lacking. There is some reason to believe that this has changed recently: developers appear to have bought land on the VINEX locations. We know from Ball's study (Ball, 1983) that in Great Britain developers *do* hold land banks.

FIGURE 7.16
Price indices of the average selling price of owner-occupied dwellings, 1975-1993 (1975 = 100; current prices)

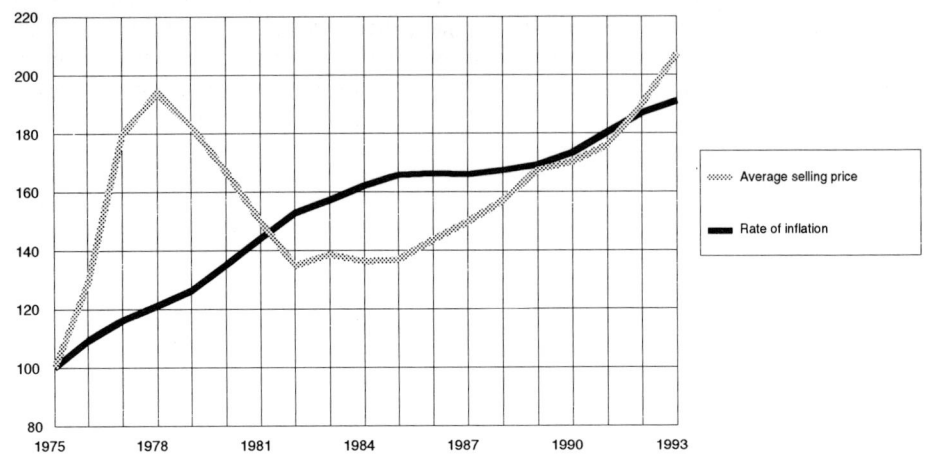

source: NVM / CBS Statistics

FIGURE 7.17
Average selling prices of owner-occupied dwellings and rate of inflation: annual % of change, 1975-1993 (current prices)

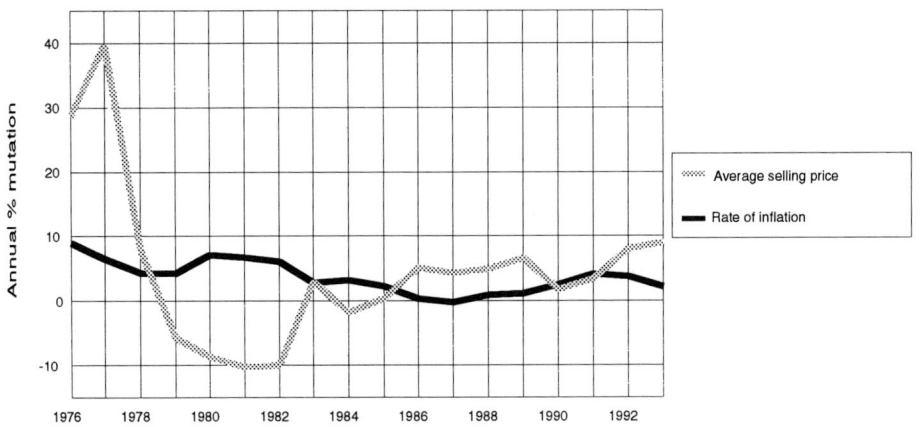

source: NVM / CBS Statistics

This brings us to the functioning of the land market. The analysis of the functioning of urban land markets is frustrated by the incompleteness of statistical information about this market. Nevertheless, some information from empirical studies is available. Land prices in the Netherlands are, in contrast with housing prices, characteristically stable (fig. 7.18; fig. 7.19). Yet, average building plot prices for owner-occupied dwellings decreased substantially at the beginning of the 1980s. Probably this was due to the sharp fall in housing production in this period; local governments held a large amount of building land in stock that burdened them sometimes with considerable financial losses (see Kortenoever, 1989). Therefore these municipalities presumably sold building plots at bulk-purchase prices. It is likely that this concerned an extreme situation. Local governments may have sold building plots at prices that did not cover their costs. Usually they charge prices that at least recover the costs of the total land-use plan.[152]

FIGURE 7.18
Average building plot prices for owner-occupied single-family dwellings in new expansion areas, by way of financing, 1982-1991 (prices 1990)

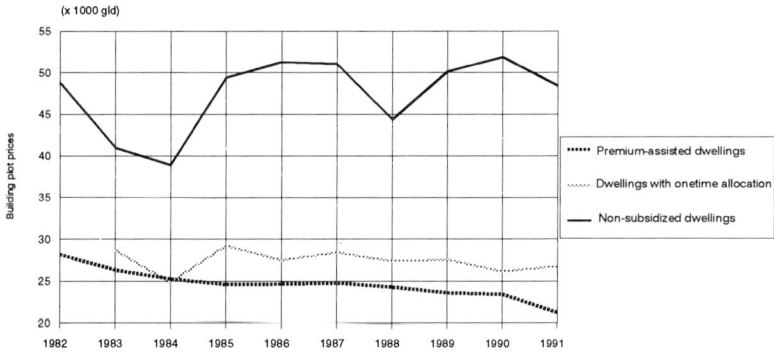

source: TAUW Infra Consult, 1993

FIGURE 7.19
Average building plot prices for social sector dwellings, 1965-1993 (prices 1993)

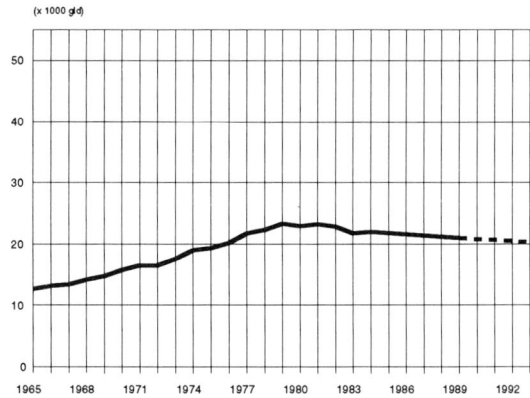

note: figures relate both to the social rented sector and to the social owner-occupied sector (premium-assisted dwellings)
source: EIB, 1988 / TAUW Infra Consult, 1993; reworked EvdK

---

152   Again, reliable statistical information on this point is not available.

Building plot prices for social-sector dwellings and premium-assisted dwellings were based on norm prices that are defined by the Ministry of Housing. If these norm prices do not cover the local governments' costs of land development, subsidies are available. The general state of affairs is that local governments calculate the costs on the development of the land-use plan as a whole. The starting point is that the development of the land-use plan needs to be cost-covering. Cross-subsidising within the plan may take place between the development of social sector dwellings and owner-occupied dwellings.[153] Market mechanisms are thus partially eliminated. In a 'perfect' market, land prices would be expected to follow more or less the fluctuations in housing prices. Positive effects of the Dutch property system are that affordable housing can be developed, that local governments are able to realise new housing on optimal locations, and that negative effects of land speculation can be avoided. However, negative effects are that local governments run the risk of financial losses on land development and that the 'incentive' for speculative housing development is partially taken away. The active participation of local governments on urban land markets leads to low market prices and only minor fluctuations. This behaviour makes it almost impossible for developers to participate in this market (see also Chapter Eight).

As far as building plot prices per squaremeter for owner-occupied dwellings are concerned, prices appear to fluctuate to a larger extent (fig. 7.20). Recently, especially squaremeter land prices for 'dwellings with one-time allocation' and 'non-subsidised dwellings' have increased. Interpretation of fig. 7.18 and fig. 7.20 teaches us that building plots in these categories have become smaller. This implies that either local governments have started to act more 'cost-conscious' (market-orientated) or that relatively more building plots have been sold in urban areas (and less in expansion areas).

FIGURE 7.20
Average building plot prices per m2 for owner-occupied single-family dwellings in new expansion areas, by way of financing, 1982-1991 (prices 1990)

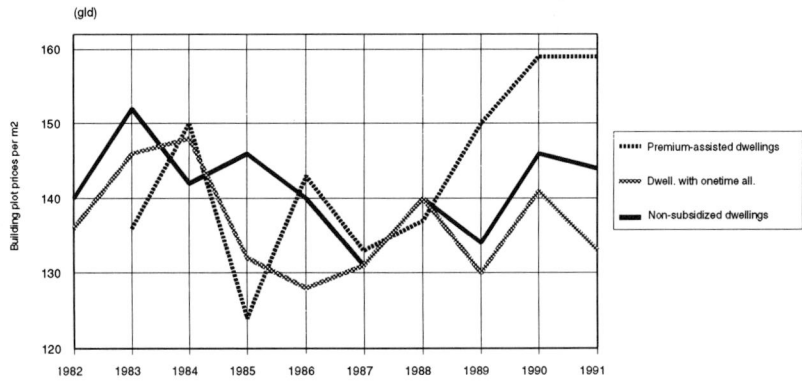

source: TAUW Infra Consult, 1993

---

153 See Needham (1993) for a theoretical explanation of the functioning of the Dutch land market.

Table 7.1 indeed shows that building plot prices substantially vary among regions and that there is a clear variation in building plot prices between existing urban areas and new expansion areas.[154]

TABLE 7.1
Average building plot prices and building plot sizes for owner-occupied single-family houses, by type of area, by region and by way of financing, 1990/1991

	premium-assisted		onetime allocation		non-subsidized	
	price	m2	price	m2	price	m2
Expansion areas						
four large cities*	28 400	125	27 900	136	72 300	275
WEST	22 500	147	26 700	154	51 100	256
NORTH	21 200	226	27 500	260	45 400	441
EAST	23 300	182	27 500	211	51 800	355
SOUTH	22 800	169	26 100	193	52 500	378
TOTAL	22 800	163	26 800	166	51 100	346
Existing urban areas						
four large cities	23 400	125	31 800	118	58 700	240
WEST	21 300	131	21 900	113	91 200	374
NORTH	23 600	452	-	-	59 600	490
EAST	23 200	181	24 800	197	72 400	468
SOUTH	26 100	171	34 900	231	59 600	382
TOTAL	23 100	152	23 900	130	75 300	414

* Four large cities: Amsterdam, The Hague, Rotterdam and Utrecht

Source: TAUW Infra Consult, 1993

---

154 For instance, building plot prices in new expansion areas run from Dfl. 45,400 in the Northern region to Dfl. 72,300 in the Randstad-cities; building plot prices in existing urban areas run from Dfl. 59,600 in the North and in the South to Dfl. 91,200 in the West. Prices per squaremeter vary from Dfl. 103 per m2 in the North to Dfl. 263 per m2 in the Randstad cities.

7.6. The Consumption of Housing

Compared to international standards, housing consumption costs were low in the Netherlands until the end of the 1970s. In 1975 Dutch households paid a moderate 14 percent of their income on housing, while households in countries like Sweden and Denmark paid above 20 percent (Priemus, 1992; quoted in Dieleman, 1994: p. 457). However, this situation changed in the 1980s drastically. Housing costs in the Netherlands increased substantially compared to France, Germany, the UK, Denmark and Sweden. Housing costs are now comparable to those in France, Germany and the UK.[155] The fact that differences between average housing costs for Dutch households and other West-European countries have levelled out is not surprising; it is in line with the Dutch national government's efforts to bring housing rents closer to market levels. Nonetheless, the increase of housing consumption costs took place exclusively in the rented sector; housing costs for owner-occupiers were actually reduced (fig. 7.21).

FIGURE 7.21
Indices for the development of housing expenses for tenants and owner-occupiers and rate of inflation, 1981-1992 (1981 = 100; current prices)

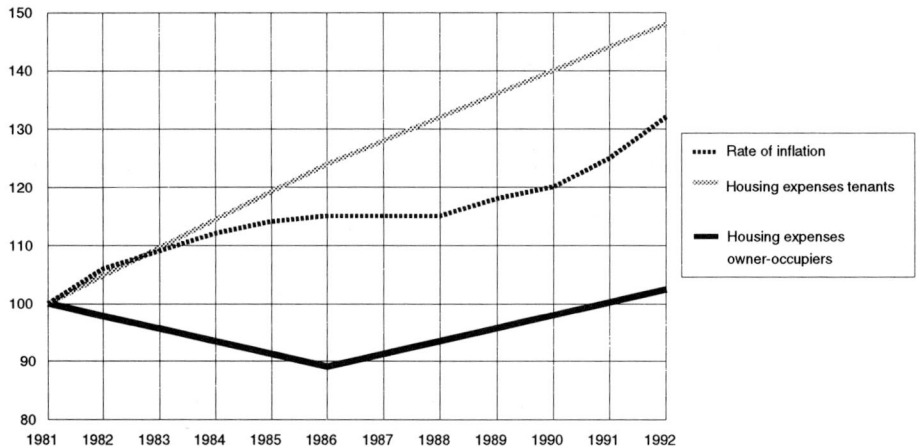

source: CBS Statistics / Ministry of Housing; reworked EvdK

Between 1981 and 1990 the net housing quotum for owner-occupiers declined from 16.6 to 12.9%, while the net housing quotum for tenants increased from 15.8 to 19.7%. This is certainly remarkable, but is related to the fact that at the beginning of the 1980s house prices dropped and that at present the mortgage rent is low. Moreover, account must be taken of the fact that homeowners are often able to capture money gains when they sell their house;

---

155 See Boelhouwer *et al.* (1991), Ministry of Housing (1992); quoted in Dieleman, 1994: p. 457.

this diminishes their 'real' housing expenses even more.

Figure 7.21 does not address variations in rents between social-sector dwellings and profit-sector dwellings. However, since we know that in the social sector regional differences are only slightly expressed in the level of rent, we can assume that rents in the profit sector usually exceed rents in the social sector.[156] Fig. 7.22 gives some evidence of this. The profit-rented sector concerns mainly dwellings with rents in the categories of Dfl. 700 per month and more -- in total around 12 percent of all rented dwellings. In 1992 the average rent was Dfl. 510 per month; for a considerable part of dwellings in the social sector, however, rents are lower.

FIGURE 7.22
Relative frequency distribution of housing rents, per 1 July 1992

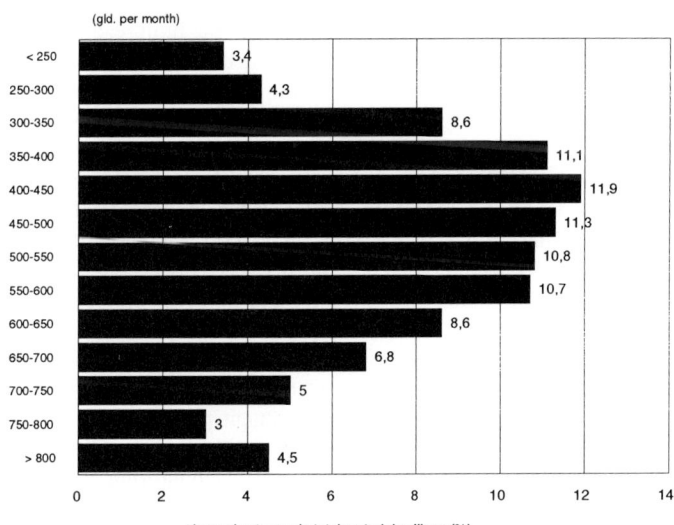

source: CBS Statistics

7.7. Conclusions

This chapter has analysed the trend in housing production, the investment strategies of the principals in the house building process, the number of new dwellings that have been completed every year, the changes with respect to the housing stock concerning age, tenure and quality, the fluctuations of house prices and land prices, and aspects of housing

---

156   See also Rouwendal, 1994.

consumption. The intention was to show the trends of housing production and market prices, as well as the resulting consequences for the housing stock and the consumption of housing. Interpretation of these diverse developments has taken place by linking the results of the analysis to the specific structure of housing provision in the Netherlands; more specifically, to the typical organisational structure of the Dutch property-development industry and other characteristics of the property system. The analysis in this chapter has provided data that can also be used as indicators of institutional changes that may have taken place with respect to the organisational structure of the property-development industry and/or the property system.

One of the statements in this chapter was that annual housing production output and number of completions have in fact always been strongly influenced by the development of housing need and that the influence of trends in development costs and selling prices have been of less significance (compared to their influence on other products, such as computers and video recorders). The number of new dwellings to be built each year has, in turn, always been fixed by the Ministry of Housing. Note that this is a conscious choice made by the national government. The consequence is that both the development of building costs as well as fluctuations in returns and profit margins have never really influenced overall production levels. It is true that the non-subsidised owner-occupier market has shown periods of decline, alternated with periods of growth, yet this was always 'compensated' by the subsidised housing program, including social-sector housing and premium-assisted owner-occupied housing. Thus, the way the housing market has evolved contrasts with the way many alternative markets have evolved. For instance, market mechanisms related to cost reductions have never had much influence on the housing market.[157] Of course, that does not alter the fact that the diverse groups of agents involved in house building constantly adjust their strategies to changing market circumstances. If average building costs increase and/or returns of speculative housing development drop, these agents will certainly attempt to reduce the total development costs of their development projects -- i.e. they will demand more government assistance. An alternative strategy, with respect to the development of non-subsidised owner-occupied dwellings, would be to try enlarging development gains in the development process. This is, they would confine their building activities to the more expensive sector of the owner-occupied housing market, preferably at the most attractive locations.

It has also been argued that price fluctuations on the second-hand housing market influence the profitability of speculative housing development. The tendency of existing owner-occupiers to sell their property -- related to the evolvement of a move-up market -- affects house price fluctuations and the level of demand for new owner-occupied dwellings. Other specific characteristics of the Dutch property system that affect the profitability of speculative housing development concern the active participation of municipal land departments on urban land markets and the risk-avoiding strategies of property developers.

Moreover, we have seen that the quality of the housing stock is relatively good, due to good management by the housing associations, that the share of owner-occupation in the housing market is still low (but increasing), and that housing consumption in the Netherlands is relatively cheap -- especially for owner occupiers.

---

157   In many markets, i.e. the video or computer market, cost reductions have enabled producers to lower market prices. The reduction of market prices has expanded sales possibilities for these producers enormously.

Finally, here is a summary of the most significant issues covered by this chapter that are relevant to the discussion in Chapter Eight:

(1) The returns of speculative housing development are determined by the development of housing prices on the second-hand owner-occupied housing market. Prices in this market are continually fluctuating;

(2) The way costs of housing production develop (a more-or-less constant relative growth), probably influenced by the organisation of the building-construction industry. This branch of industry is dominated mainly by small-scale firms. The nature of the building product certainly plays a role in this respect;

(3) Municipalities have traditionally taken responsibility for the development of house building locations. As a result, the land market has always been stable. Possibly, the profitability of speculative housing development -- in a negative sense, and the overall costs of social sector house building -- in a positive sense, have been influenced as well;

(4) Both housing associations and private developers have, for a long time, been assured (within limits) of (financial) government assistance. This means that development risks for market parties were low;

(5) The instability of the owner-occupied housing market favours, in principle, large developers and large building entrepreneurs above small firms. Large developers are able to act counter-cyclically, while small firms generally lack this possibility. However, it must be questioned whether large speculative developers in the Netherlands benefit from this in the most optimal way.

8 A CRISIS IN HOUSING PRODUCTION: INSTITUTIONAL CHANGES, PATH DEPENDENCY AND FUTURE TRENDS

8.1. Introduction

The previous chapter explained that between 1960 and 1993 the annual production of new dwellings has fluctuated quite substantially. Consequently, the way in which these continuous changes in production output are interconnected with the functioning of the housing market was studied. This chapter relates these changes in production levels to *institutional change*. What have been the sources of the institutional changes that have taken place with respect to the *structure of housing provision* (section 8.2)? In section 8.3 the institutional changes that took place will be discussed. More explicitly, I will try to explain which factors have influenced the strategies of the actors that are involved in the property-development industry. Section 8.4 focuses on the profitability of speculative land and housing development. A better insight into the development gains of speculative house building and the way in which these gains are made up is vital to a proper understanding of housing development. Fluctuations in the profitability of speculative house building, together with other structural features of the Dutch housing market, will subsequently lie at the bottom of my interpretations with respect to the production of new dwellings. In particular, section 8.5 will relate the present shortage in housing production to both general characteristics of housing markets and the typical organisational structure of the property development industry in the Netherlands. Finally, section 8.6 will combine the results of the Chapters Six, Seven and Eight and use them to discuss the supposed relation between the typical structure of building provision in the Netherlands, the production of new dwellings, and the 'output' of the market. Institutional-economic theory will be used to interpret various aspects of this relation.

As has already been stated in the introductory paragraph to Chapter Six, Chapter Eight aims, first, to investigate the sources of institutional changes and the institutional changes that took place with respect to the institutional organisation of the housing-development market. Ultimately, this chapter aims to contribute to a better understanding of the structure of housing provision in the Netherlands, to make clear the way this typical organisational structure of the housing development industry, in combination with more general characteristics of housing development, determines housing production, housing market functioning and urban spatial structures.

8.2. Sources of Institutional Change

Chapter Five identified different types of potential 'sources of institutional change': fundamental changes in relative prices, notably changes in the ratio of factor prices, technological innovations and changes in information costs, and changes in ideas, norms, and values. This section will analyse these sources of institutional change and the way they have influenced housing development in the Netherlands. The objective is to analyse why and by which processes institutional changes with respect to housing development have taken place.

I will start with a discussion of the way changing ideas and norms have affected housing development (section 8.2.1). In sections 8.2.2 and 8.2.3 I will discuss changes in the ratio of factor prices. Section 8.2.4 analyses the meaning of technological innovations in housing development processes. Section 8.2.5 will pay attention to changes in information costs.

8.2.1. Changing ideas and norms

Changing ideas and norms irrefutably play a significant role on the housing market.[158] Three important shifts in thinking can be distinguished that have structured the performance of national, regional and urban economies in the last fifteen years:

(1) the development of an environmental consciousness;
(2) the withdrawal of the government from the market, combined with the introduction of a new, entrepreneurial style of policy making;
(3) an internationalisation tendency;

Particularly with respect to housing-market functioning in the Netherlands, shifts in ideas and norms concerning the demand for housing are also relevant, such as the spread of homeownership among a growing group of households, changes in location preferences of some groups of households (i.e. the willingness of high-income groups to live in inner-city areas), and the continuing decrease of the average size of households.

First, the development of an environmental consciousness has indirectly led to, among other things, rising land-development costs, because of soil pollution, to a restriction of potential expansion areas, because areas of high environmental value protected, and to rising building costs, because extra demands have been placed on the way of building and the use of building materials. Restriction of new housing development to locations in the proximity of existing urban areas has been one of the reasons that average building costs have increased. Fig. 8.1 shows that average building costs per cubicmeter (m3) vary by degree of urbanity. Building costs for non-subsidised dwellings in urban areas (category 5) far exceed the costs of building in other 'categories.' The development of a dwelling in category one will be less expensive than building an identical dwelling in category 5.[159] From fig. 8.2 it can be deduced that building costs in the Netherlands tend to rise faster than those in other West-European countries. It might be that this relates to the influence of the national government's spatial policy in the Netherlands, directed to a concentration of new developments in existing urban areas.

---

158   A division of the research area is necessary at this point. I analyse the changes that have occurred in general ideas and norms, as far as the functioning of the housing market is concerned, and the resulting institutional changes with respect to the structure of housing provision. However, I leave aside the reasons why these ideas and norms change -- this is not part of my research.

159   Note that probably not only the building costs per m3 vary by degree of urbanity, but the 'quality' of the new dwellings, as well. It may be expected that in non-urban areas higher quality dwellings are built than in urban areas. This explains why building costs in category 1 and 2 exceed building costs in category 3 and 4.

FIGURE 8.1
Variations in building costs per m3 of new dwellings, by degree of 'urbanity' and by tenurestatus

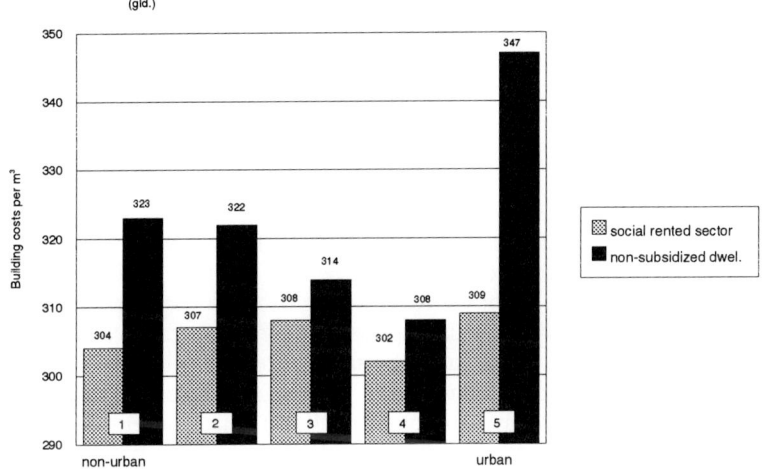

note: the degree of urbanity is related to the 'addresses density' per square kilometer: a larger density implies a higher degree of urbanity
source: CBS Statistics

FIGURE 8.2
International comparison: Price indices for average building costs of new dwellings, 1980-1992

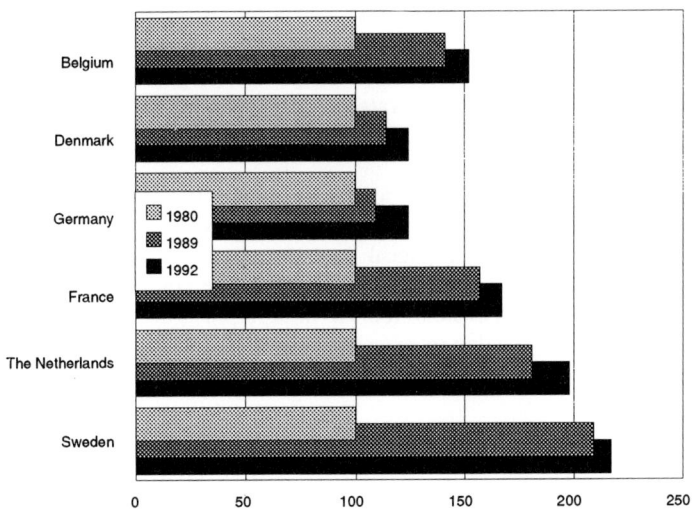

source: CBS Statistics

However, it is not inconceivable that the relative rise of building costs in the Netherlands is also determined by a tendency that more dwellings are now developed in expensive sectors of the housing market.

Second, the reorganisation of the housing sector, including the financial privatisation of the housing associations, is clearly connected to the national government's wish to withdraw from the housing market. The government has traded in its financial involvement with house building and exploitation for a new regulatory role. The current transformation of government policy has been inspired by the need of substantial savings on government expenditures on housing. On the other hand, the new entrepreneurial role of the public sector may have brought local governments to an increased financial consciousness. For instance, potential building locations are increasingly allocated to the use that yields the highest price. Third, many studies of urban development mention the internationalisation of the economy as one of the sources of the restructuring of urban spatial patterns. Its influence on real estate markets, particularly with respect to commercial real estate, is also recognised. However, in contrast to commercial real estate markets, housing markets remain highly localised markets. The increased competition for 'space' possibly affects the *relative* profitability of housing development to commercial real estate development. As a result, development processes in each sector are different. For example, on the housing market mainly local private developers participate in the development process, while in commercial real estate projects large (inter-)national developers participate. This may put extra pressure on the availability of housebuilding location.

Moreover, a number of changes that directly affect the demand for dwellings have taken place. The group of owner-occupiers has substantially expanded. The number of private individuals that decide to build their own new dwelling has extended significantly. It may be expected that the costs of new dwellings that are commissioned by private persons usually exceed the costs of new housing projects commissioned by speculative developers or housing associations. The differences in building costs depend on the fact that private persons are likely to build less efficiently and yet on the fact that they build higher-quality dwellings. Fig. 8.3 examines this: the building costs of single-dwelling projects, of which we can assume that they are usually built by private persons, amount to about Dfl. 335 per m3, while the costs of multi-dwelling projects, on average, never exceed Dfl. 310 per m3.

The willingness of high-income groups to live in inner-city areas has brought forward a larger demand for apartments and dwellings in more expensive sectors of the housing market in inner cities. As a consequence, many local governments have initiated the development of new expensive apartments in inner-city locations. Finally, the continually diminishing size of Dutch households has been responsible for an unexpected extra need for new housing. Especially in recent years this has led to severe problems in housing production.

FIGURE 8.3
Variations in building costs per m3 of new dwellings, by project size (by share in total of new dwellings) and by tenure status, 1992

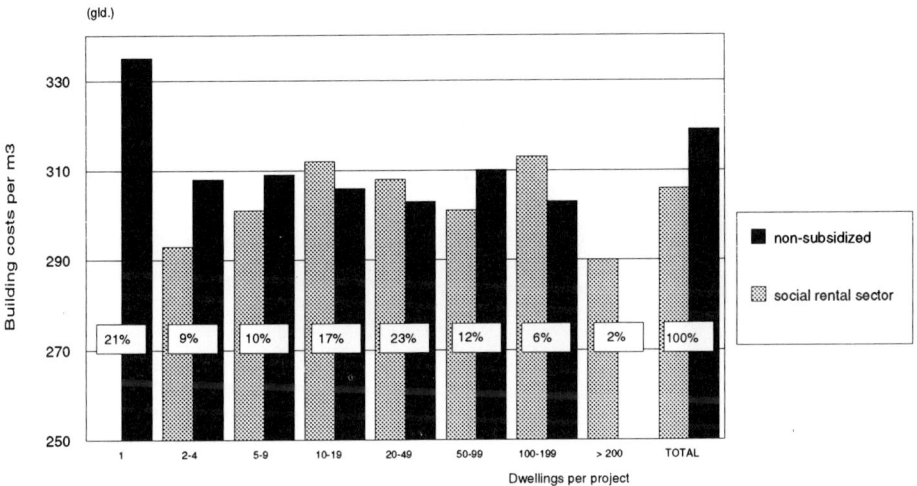

source: CBS Statistics

8.2.2. Changes in relative prices: building costs

Figures 8.4, 8.5, 8.6 and 8.7, concerning average building costs of new dwellings, mutations of average building costs, average building costs per m3 and mutations of average building costs per m3, jointly show the development of average building costs of new dwellings between 1975 and 1993.

Fig. 8.4 indicates that especially building costs of non-subsidised dwellings fluctuate considerably. A comparison of fig. 8.6 with fig. 8.4 (in fig. 8.6 variations in size of new dwellings are eliminated) reveals that from 1984 on, building costs per m3 of the three distinguished sectors tend to come closer to each other. From this, it can be concluded that the size of new dwellings varies by sector, yet the quality of social-sector dwellings approaches the quality of non-subsidised owner-occupied dwellings (while the quality of premium-assisted dwellings lags behind).

FIGURE 8.4
Average building costs of new dwellings, by sector, 1975-1993 (current prices)

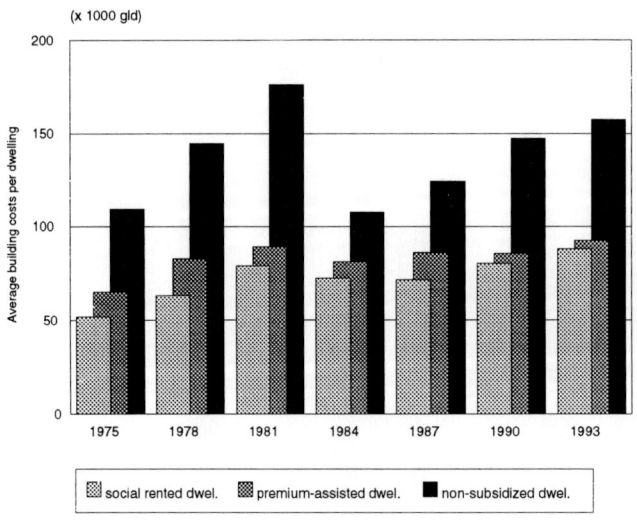

source: CBS Statistics

FIGURE 8.5
Mutations of average building costs per dwelling, by sector, 1975-1993 (corrected for inflation)

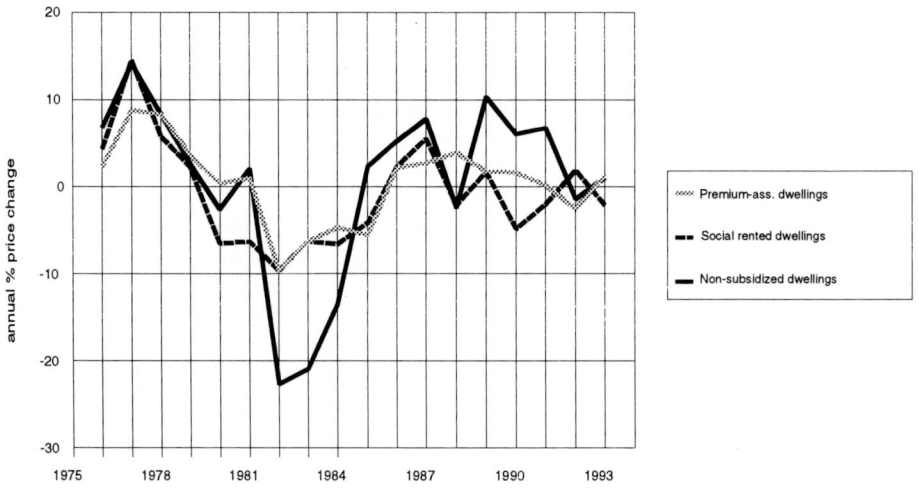

source: CBS Statistics; reworked EvdK

FIGURE 8.6
Average building costs of new dwellings per m3, by sector, 1975-1993 (current prices)

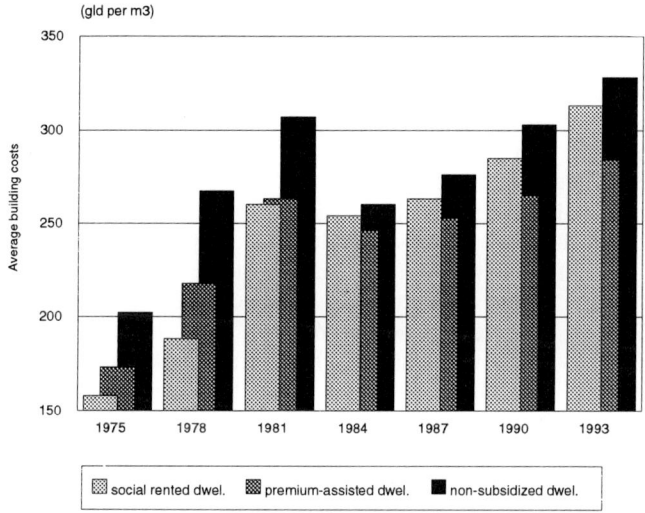

source: CBS Statistics

FIGURE 8.7
Mutations of average building costs per m3, by sector, 1975-1993 (corrected for inflation)

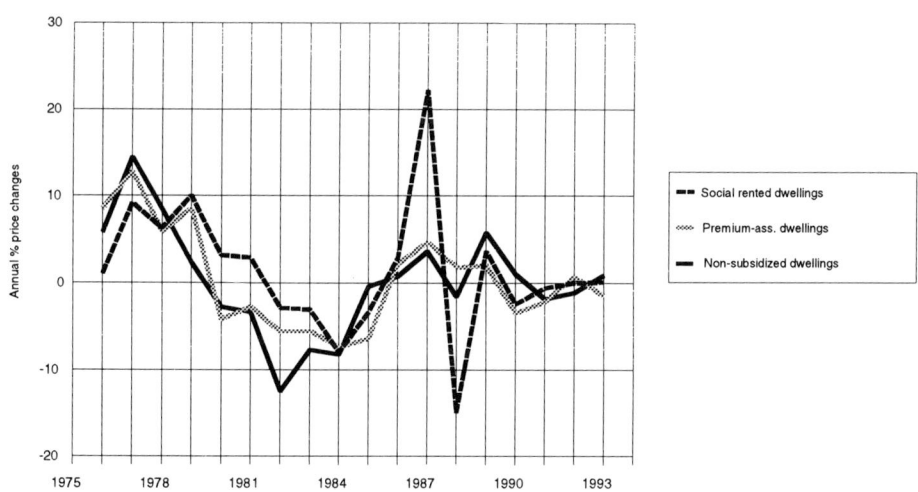

source: CBS Statistics

Figures 8.5 and 8.7 show the annual mutations in building costs, corrected for inflation. Annual mutations appear to deviate almost unremittingly from the trend of inflation. Particularly in the 1970s a permanent relative increase of building costs determined building developments. In the early 1980s this trend became a decline of building costs in relative terms. This shift most likely relates to the collapse of the housing market at that time; average building costs dropped because of a lower quality of new dwellings and as a result of the fact that building construction firms, out of necessity, had to be satisfied with lower profit margins.[160] The second half of the 1980s showed a renewed increase of relative building costs, while in the 1990s average building costs tend to follow inflation trends.

The building-costs developments that are reproduced in these figures lead to an important conclusion: when we assume that the share of new dwellings in cheaper categories of the housing market in the total amount of new dwellings has increased (the quality of new dwellings has generally declined),[161] then it appears that building costs show a tendency to rise faster than inflation. That is, the real building costs of two identical dwellings characteristically vary through time, on the understanding that average building costs in one year exceed the average building costs in the previous year. Moreover, building cost developments are autonomous; they are independent of the development of housing prices. This suggests, in turn, that the ratio of total costs to housing prices is subject to continuous changes (see figures 8.8 and 8.9).

Note that the ratio of total development costs to housing prices is not absolute, since the data in figures 8.8 and 8.9 concern average figures. Therefore, fig. 8.8 shows only that the relation of costs to prices varies through time, indicating that profit margins for developers vary as well (see section 8.5). The *causes* of the relative rise of building costs are supposed to originate from the specific structure of the building-construction industry. Ball (1983), however, provides an additional explanation with respect to the relative increase of building costs in the 1960s and 1970s in Great Britain. He claims that the profitability of speculative housing development is mainly determined by the development gains that speculative developers are able to make by their speculative strategies, i.e. land banking; the development of building costs is of only minor influence on their profit margins. With help of land banks, developers can anticipate fluctuations in housing prices in their building activities. As a result they did not really try to reduce building costs.

---

160 A similar line of argument can be found in RIGO (1987).

161 I assume that the quality of new dwellings in expensive categories exceeds the quality of dwellings in less-expensive categories.

Institutional Changes, Path Dependency and Future Trends 175

FIGURE 8.8
The total costs of new dwellings in the owner-occupied sector (with onetime allocation and premium-assisted), versus average selling prices of all owner-occupied dwellings, 1984-1992 (current prices)

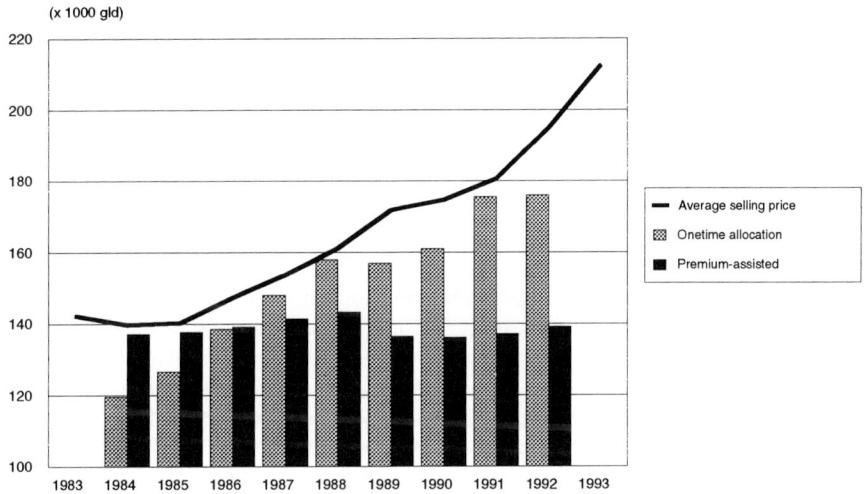

notes:
* the costs of new dwellings in this figure include both building construction costs and land development costs;
* the costs of new non-subsidised owner-occupied dwellings are excluded from this figure
source: Ministry of Housing / NVM

FIGURE 8.9
Price indices for the total costs of new social-sector dwellings and new subsidised owner-occupied dwellings, 1975-1993 (1984 = 100, current prices)

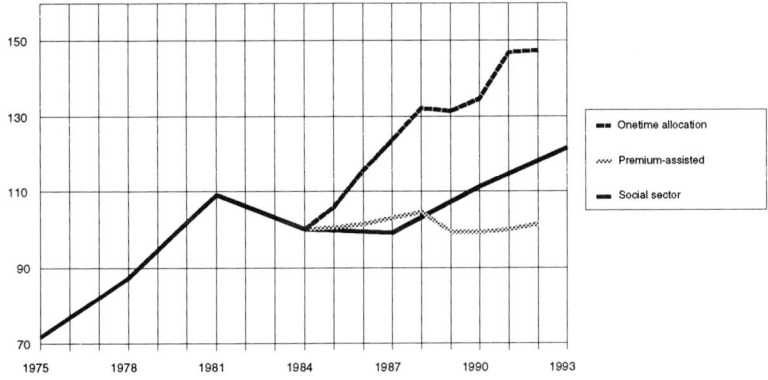

note: figures for new subsidised owner-occupied dwellings are only known for 1984-1992
source: CBS Statistics

Apart from the question whether this point is also valid in the Dutch situation (I will discuss this in section 8.3) the *consequences* of the relative growth of building costs are similar in both countries. Because production costs are continually rising and the market price of new dwellings is determined by price fluctuations on the second-hand market, the profit margins of the development of owner-occupied dwellings will decrease, as soon as housing prices drop (unless developers find other ways to reduce their operating costs). If this is true, then it is to be expected that private developers will look for alternative ways to guarantee sufficient profit margins: they can, for instance, restrict their development activities to the expensive sectors of the housing market on attractive locations (for more discussion see section 8.3).

8.2.3.   Changes in relative prices: land and property values

According to general land-price theory, the value of land is determined by the returns of the building (or alternative use) that is on it.[162] This would mean that when market prices -- the 'returns' for the developer -- are rising and development costs remain more or less the same, the value of land should rise as well. Then, the share of the land in total value increases, as well as the average market value of land. As a result it may be expected that:
(1) the property of existing land owners will increase in value;
(2) speculation on land -- land banking -- is in principle profitable;[163]
(3) the ratio of land prices for housing to land prices for alternative uses is not constant;
(4) from a pure financial point of view, the moment in time when land should be reallocated -- and the existing building on the land demolished -- constantly changes.

However, the above line of argument is a theoretical one. In the Netherlands the share of land costs in total development costs takes up only about 20 percent. The starting point for defining land prices in the Netherlands is usually the development costs (see figures 7.17 and 7.19 in Chapter Seven); as a result, changes in the value of land are not reflected in the actual prices that are paid for building plots. More recently, private developers seem to have changed their strategies with respect to land development. They have started to buy undeveloped land in future house-building locations, especially in the VINEX locations, most likely because they want to guarantee their future production. Finally, Chapter Seven concluded that property values on the housing market characteristically fluctuate. The substantial increase of house prices in recent years may have caused institutional changes with respect to the strategies of existing owner-occupiers. They may have started to cash in money gains. As a result, a move-up market may have come into existence (see section 8.3).

---

162   See, for an introduction, Kruijt *et.al.* (1990).

163   Note that land banking in the first place is usually not aimed at deriving profits from land sales. The aim is to anticipate on market developments on the housing market - to be able to start new developments as soon as market circumstances improve.

8.2.4. Technological innovations with respect to housing construction

In many branches of industry technological innovations play an important role regarding the economic growth of the sector concerned. Often, technological innovations are the impetus to institutional change. Yet, compared to other branches of industry, the innovative content of the building-construction industry is relatively low.[164] Fig. 8.10 provides evidence for this statement. Investments per Dfl. 1,000 added value are much lower in the building construction industry than they are in other sectors. Low investments indicate that innovations must be rare.

FIGURE 8.10
Investments per Dfl. 1,000 added value, average for 1983-1989

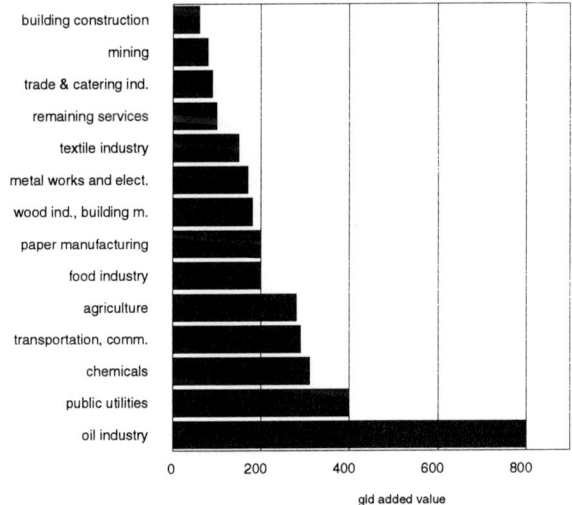

source: EIB, 1992

The MERIT-study indicates that some technological innovations in building construction have indeed been introduced, particularly with respect to the use of new building materials and a shift of activities to preliminary stages (so-called prefab production methods). However, these innovations take place mainly in supply companies. Building-construction firms, themselves, hardly innovate.[165] The low level of innovations in building construction is related to the nature of the product and of the production process:
(1) building construction as a branch of industry is fragmented: design, construction and delivering are spread between different firms. This blocks the introduction of

---

164 Studies by EIB (1992) and MERIT (1990) confirm this image of the building construction industry.

165 According to CBS-statistics, in Dutch firms on average 0.71% of the employees are involved in research and development. In manufacturing this percentage amounts to 2.7%. In the building-construction industry, merely 0.064% of the employees is involved in research and development.

rationalisation processes;
(2) the building market hardly expands and is unstable by nature;
(3) profit margins are relatively small;
(4) many firms that are involved in building construction still operate in a traditional way (because they are small in size), leading, for instance, to risk-avoiding strategies;
(5) 'buildings' as a product offer few opportunities for innovation (compared to, for instance, cars, computers, etc.).

The building-construction industry is an outstanding example of a small-scale branch of industry. We can safely assume that this specific character of the industry frustrates even further the introduction of innovations. Up to 99 percent of this sector consists of small and medium-sized firms; 75 percent of all building construction firms have less than 10 employees (see also tab. 6.3 in Chapter Six). The share of small firms' production output in total production output has even increased since the beginning of the 1970s, perhaps as a consequence of the tendency towards small-scale building projects. The specific features of the building-construction industry have been responsible for the fact that, in contrast to other branches of industry, the growth of demand for new building developments has not been determined by technological innovation.[166] Actually, the opposite is true: the lack of technological innovations has blocked institutional change and even impeded new building development (see section 8.3).

8.2.5. Changes in information costs

Changes in information costs relate to changes of risk and uncertainty and changes in efficiency. The degree of uncertainty affects the institutional organisation of the market, i.e. the role of speculative developers and financiers in speculative housing development, the necessity of a guarantee fund for social-sector housing, government intervention, etc. The strategies of the agents involved in the production process are shaped by the degree of uncertainty. For instance, do they build speculatively or not? Uncertainty, together with the complexity and the nontransparency of the market, also constitutes a significant condition for the presence of development gains on urban land markets.

The degree of uncertainty is of course uncertain, and fluctuates. Fig. 8.11 shows the fluctuations in interest rates and inflation. Interest rates have a strong influence on the loan capacity of households and on the costs of financing new development projects by housing associations and developers. The rate of inflation fluctuates likewise. Shifts in the rate of inflation affect, for instance, the benefits of the ownership of land and/or dwellings to respectively land owners and owner-occupiers.

---

166   For instance, computerisation processes in banking have enabled a strong growth of payments (ME-RIT, 1990).

FIGURE 8.11
Developments in interest and inflation

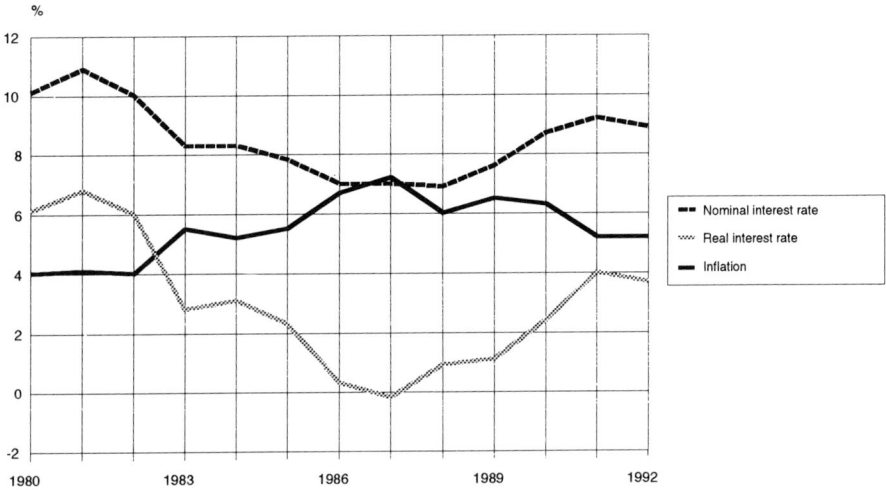

source: CBS Statistics

Government intervention of course also affects the degree of uncertainty in local housing markets. I will argue in subsequent sections that the specific way the government intervenes in the Netherlands -- notably, the local governments active behaviour on urban land markets -- has led, on the one hand, to a reduction of uncertainty with respect to the direction of spatial development in Dutch cities and is responsible for the relative stability of land and property markets, but, on the other hand, has led to a reduction of the possibilities to derive development gains from speculative land and building development as well.

8.3. Institutional Changes with respect to Housing Development

Having distinguished several sources of institutional change on the Dutch housing market, I will now turn to the institutional changes themselves. In what ways and for what reasons has the institutional organisation of the housing market changed? The assumption underlying my argument at this point is that the 'sources of institutional change' give rise to institutional changes with respect to the institutional organisation of the housing development market, because the preconditions for development have been changed. For instance, the profitability of housing development may have been altered, due to changes in building costs and/or returns, or the level of risk may have been changed. The actual *demand* for new housing, as distinguished from the *need* for new housing, is clearly subject to continual fluctuations, etc. It is likewise important to recognise constraints to institutional change -- in this case, we can speak of institutional inertia. For instance, as a result of improving economic circumstances, the demand for new housing may suddenly rise. However, speculative developers cannot respond in time to this increased demand, because local governments fail to provide sufficient building locations, or because developers have neglected to anticipate this development. This brings into play the significance of path dependency on the housing market.

First, I will discuss government intervention (section 8.3.1). Then, changes with respect to the commissioning and financing new developments are analysed (section 8.3.2). Finally, structural changes in the housing construction industry will be investigated (section 8.3.3).

8.3.1.   Government intervention

After World War II, similar to developments in many other West-European countries, a substantial housing shortage occurred in the Netherlands (Boelhouwer and Van der Heijden, 1992).[167] Because of the combined effect of increasing costs of living, escalating building costs, and a high interest rate in the post-war decades, the government had to intervene, in order to solve the housing shortage. Van der Schaar (1987) estimates that around 95 percent of the post-war dwelling stock was developed with some sort of government support. The primacy in house building construction was, in the first stage of reconstruction, with the social sector -- both because of ideological reasons and because of pragmatic reasons. In the 1960s and 1970s government involvement with the housing sector grew in importance -- certainly in financial terms. The prominent role of the housing associations in the social-housing sector started in 1969, when priority was given to housing associations instead of the municipal housing departments as commissioners for new social housing. In the 1970s the national government chose for a mixed housing-subsidy system: building subsidies and subsidies on operating costs to housing associations and individual housing subsidies to households. One of the consequences of this policy was that between 1975 and 1985 government expenditures on both building and individual housing subsidies grew explosively, as a result of high interest rates and the complete collapse of the owner-occupied housing sector. High interest rates brought forward an increase of building subsidies, because housing associations were confronted with a strong growth of development costs -- borrowing money had become more expensive.

Between 1985 and 1995 a turn in public-sector policy took place. According to Boelhouwer and Van der Heijden (1992: p. 66), the introduction of 'new' goals in housing policy was impeded, because present government expenditures in the housing sector were to a large extent (in 1988 around 60% of the government expenditures on housing) determined by obligations from the past. These obligations especially concern the annual long-term contributions to housing associations.

The cutbacks in government expenditures have been accompanied by a shift towards a market-orientated approach, characterised by the improvement of market mechanisms, attempts to stabilise the owner-occupied market, and the guarantee of sufficient house-building production and a satisfactory quality of the housing stock. The *Cultureel*

---

167   The discussion in this section of government intervention on the housing market in a historical context is mainly based on Boelhouwer and Van der Heijden, 1992.

Planbureau writes in its annual Sociaal Cultureel Rapport (Cultureel Planbureau, 1994) that the following changes in housing policy took place: public-sector policy will be focused on target groups (low-income households); a shift from 'steering' to 'regulation' -- a decentralisation process (more powers for municipalities) and a financial liberation process directed at the housing associations; annual rent increases of 5.5% in the social-housing sector, resulting in rising living expenses for households and a substantial growth of the capital reserve of the housing associations; and the *Bruteringsoperatie* (see Chapter Six). The shift in the national government's financial involvement with house building is clearly visible in figures 8.12 and 8.13. After 1984, the gross expenditures of the Ministry of Housing with respect to housing dropped both in absolute terms and in relative terms (as a percentage of net national income).

FIGURE 8.12
Gross expenditures Ministry of Housing with respect to housing, 1970-1994 (current prices)

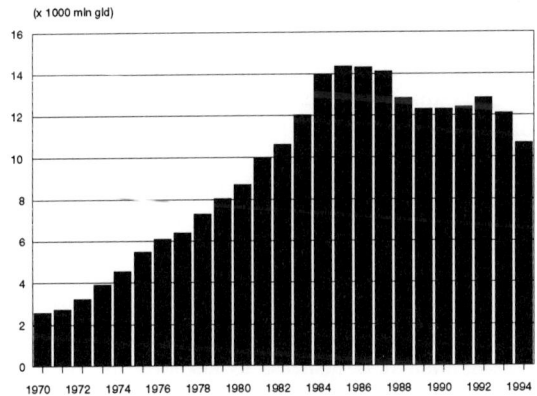

FIGURE 8.13
Gross expenditures Ministry of Housing with respect to housing, as a percentage of net national income, 1970-1991

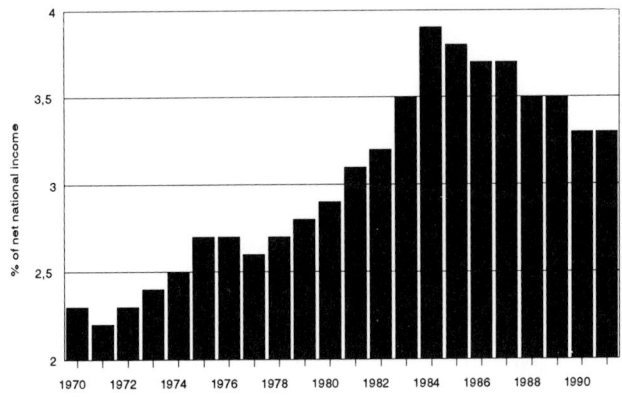

source: Ministry of Housing

Figures 8.14, 8.15, 8.16 and 8.17 provide more information with respect to the trend in the government's financial interference with the housing sector. According to fig. 8.14, the average government expenditure per dwelling, taking the total housing stock into consideration, has increased until 1984. After 1984 the average expenditure per dwelling dropped substantially.

Fig. 8.15 indicates that, as I just mentioned, obligations from the past put severe pressure on current government expenditures. It can be concluded from the data that the average government expenditure per newly built dwelling in recent years is still increasing, while total annual government expenditures have substantially been cut down.[168]

Figures 8.16 and 8.17 concern subsidies in the owner-occupied sector and social sector subsidies. In the owner-occupied sector, the average subsidy per newly built dwelling has diminished since 1985.[169] Note, however, that from 1985 on the share of non-subsidised dwellings in the total number of completed dwellings in the owner-occupied sector has increased. Thus, if we should add the annual number of completed non-subsidised dwellings to the total number of subsidised owner-occupied dwellings in fig. 8.16, then the average subsidy per newly built dwelling in this sector would drop still further.

Fig. 8.17 shows that in the social sector especially the total amount of government money that is spent on building and exploitation subsidies has increased -- between 1975 and 1993 it has been tripled (in real prices).

The information provided in these figures calls into question the productive efficiency of housing development before and after 1984. In the owner-occupied sector, private developers increased building activities in the second half of the 1980s, while the public sector's financial assistance substantially dropped. It is unknown whether private developers were able to do this by improving the efficiency of the production process (reduction of costs); probably after 1984 their returns also increased. If they were indeed able to reduce the total development costs, then it is justified to question the productive efficiency of the housing sector *and* the necessity of the total amount of public-sector money spent on housing before 1984.[170]

---

168 Government expenditures, in this case, include subsidies on newly built dwellings, individual household subsidies as well as contributions to housing associations, meant for exploitation of existing social sector dwellings.

169 However, the tax relief for homeowners remains unchanged. Because the number of households that owns a house has substantially increased, it may be assumed that public money spent on this veiled subsidy to owner-occupiers has risen as well.

170 In other words, I wonder whether the public sector's strong financial involvement with housing development, before 1984, has reduced the private sector's efforts to reduce costs and/or increase returns.

FIGURE 8.14
Development of gross government expenditures with respect to housing, per dwelling (total housing stock), 1975-1993 (prices 1990)

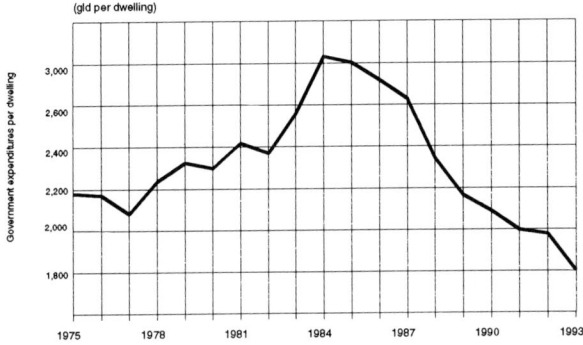

note: government expenitures with respect to housing include building subsidies to housing associations, private developers and owner-occupiers, subsidies on operating costs to housing associations, urban-renewal subsidies, household subsidies to individuals, renovation subsidies and remaining subsidies
source: Ministry of Housing / CBS Statistics; reworked EvdK

FIGURE 8.15
Development of gross government expenditures with respect to housing, per newly built dwelling, 1975-1993 (prices 1990)

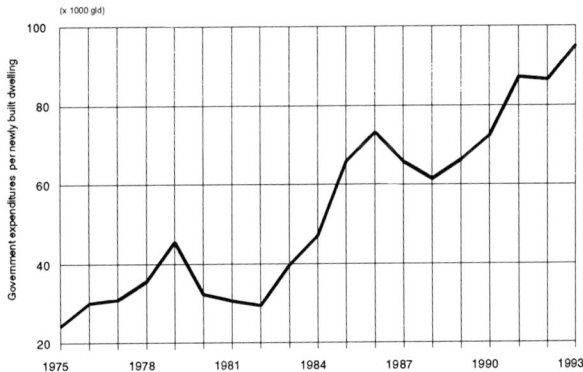

note:
* government expenditures include urban-renewal subsidies, land-development subsidies, building-costs subsidies social rental sector and owner-occupied sector, and subsidies on operating costs in the social rental sector;
* government expenditures with respect to housing in one year are not necessarily spent on the dwellings that are completed in that year. They may be spent on dwellings that are completed in the next year. However, the figure gives an indication of the trend;
source: Ministry of Housing / CBS Statistics; reworked EvdK

FIGURE 8.16
Development of gross government subsidies with respect to the owner-occupied sector per newly built dwelling, 1975-1993 (prices 1990)

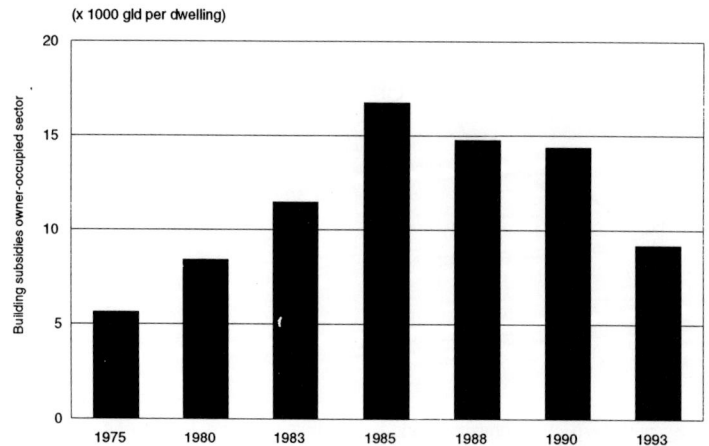

note: figures include subsidies regarding premium-assisted rented dwellings
source: CBS Statistics

FIGURE 8.17
Development of gross government subsidies with respect to the social rented sector per dwelling (total social housing stock), 1975-1993 (prices 1990)

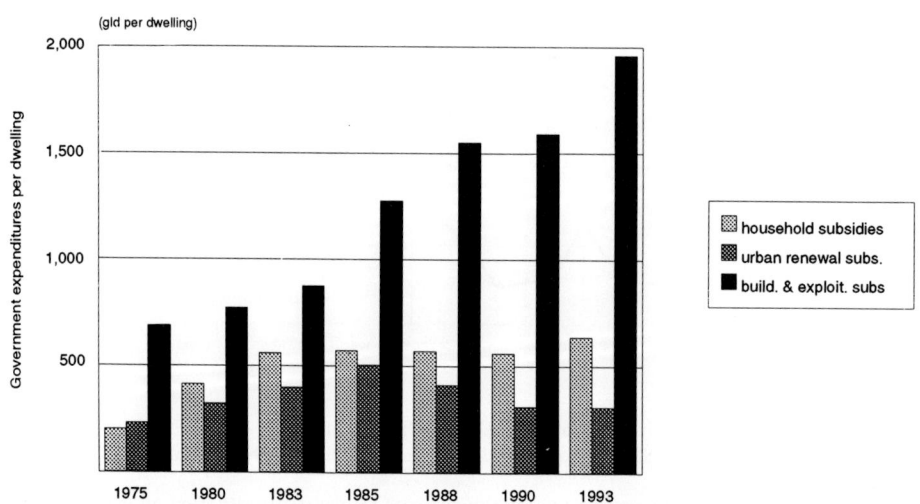

note: it is assumed that urban renewal subsidies go mainly to the social-rented sector
source: CBS Statistics; reworked EvdK

Who benefits from government subsidies on housing and what are, in this respect, the effects of the national government's policy to cut down on grants? In the owner-occupied sector, government subsidies enlarge private developers' opportunities to develop new dwellings. Future owners, who are able to acquire a subsidised owner-occupied dwelling, benefit in financial terms as soon as they decide to sell the dwelling, assuming that house prices follow at least inflation rates. In the social-rented sector, households can now live in dwellings that they otherwise could not have afforded.

The national government's financial withdrawal from the housing sector can be considered to be an institutional change itself. However, as a side-effect, other institutional changes may occur -- i.e. changes with respect to the profit margins of housing development, the division of profits among the agents in the development process, the development costs, the consumption of housing, etc. These changes concern, in fact, changes in market circumstances and may affect the strategies of the 'builders.' The feasibility of social-housing development and the profitability of speculative owner-occupied housing development are to a large extent determined by these changes in market circumstances. The national government's current policy in the housing sector is apparently based on the expectation that the 'market' should be able now to produce more owner-occupied dwellings with less government assistance. This is at least a dubious assumption that is, moreover, inconsistent with actual facts. Such a policy can, after all, only be successful if the profitability of the development of owner-occupied dwellings should have improved recently. Perhaps, profit margins in the owner-occupied housing sector have recently indeed increased because market prices of owner-occupied dwellings have sharply risen. However, we know that the housing market is unstable by nature: a shift in current trends is always possible. Moreover, we have seen that building costs characteristically tend to rise in relative terms. If dwelling prices in the future drop, and building costs indeed keep rising, it will probably become difficult for private developers to build new owner-occupied dwellings on the same level as they do now.

One of the factors that determine developers' gains in housing development processes concerns the location of the new dwellings. The location of new-housing development depends both on the national government's spatial policy and on the local governments' land policy. In this respect, the effects of the national government's spatial policy and the local governments' land policy on both the costs and returns of housing development are obvious. For instance, I already mentioned the consequences of the national government's policy to concentrate the majority of future housing development in the proximity of existing urban areas in the Randstad. It is to be expected that land development costs in these urban areas exceed the costs of land development in expansion areas in peripheral regions.[171]

Another example concerns the urban renewal plans that have been carried out in most cities in the 1970s and 1980s. One of the goals of the urban renewal policy was to provide affordable social sector housing to low-income households in inner-city areas. Note that this is primarily a political decision -- and, in that respect, a justifiable point of view. However, the financial consequences of the political decision to designate potential 'top locations' as low-cost housing zones seem to have been underestimated. The Ministry of Housing was burdened with substantial financial obligations (which still put pressures on the Ministry's

---

171 On the other hand, market prices on housing markets in Randstad cities -- and thus, for private developers, also returns on the development of new dwellings -- exceed dwelling prices in peripheral regions.

budget) and municipalities were relieved of the possibility to obtain gains from land development. The ratio of development costs to returns from sales would probably have been better balanced if part of the inner-city areas were allocated to alternative uses.

In conclusion, both changes in direct government intervention in the housing sector and shifts in the national government's and the municipalities' spatial policy continually affect the performance of the housing market. The impact of this influence is particularly relevant to the feasibility of new social-sector housing and the profitability of speculative owner-occupied housing development.

8.3.2. Commissioning and financing new housing development

The analysis in Chapter Seven showed the way housebuilding investments have evolved during the research period. The analysis also provides information with respect to the participation of different groups of agents in housing development. On the face of it, the intensity of the activities of each of these groups on the housing-development market varies according to fluctuations in demand for both social-rented and owner-occupied dwellings, and, regarding owner-occupied dwellings exclusively, according to changes in the profitability of housing development. Section 8.3.1 demonstrated how the pace at which these institutional changes take place is shaped by the combined effect of the government's housing and spatial policy. It has also been argued that this intervention is sometimes the result of a conscious choice, but may also be an unforeseen side-effect of the implementation of alternative government goals.

The analysis of building investment, however, still makes for a rather superficial investigation of institutional change. Are we able to carry out a more detailed analysis of the changes that took place with respect to the organisational structure of the property-development industry? That is, in what sense have the strategies of the agents and their position in the development process changed and what happened to the institutional relations between the agents, including the financing of new developments?

Figures 8.18, 8.19, 8.20 and 8.21 give some insight into recent shifts in the strategies of housebuilders. Housebuilders represented in these figures include all the distinguished groups of agents, notably speculative developers, housing associations, private persons, financial institutions, and government bodies.[172] First, average building investments per project by type of building are compared (fig. 8.18 and 8.19). Although figures are only known for a short period of time, still some conclusions can be drawn. Both the average investment per project and the average investment per m3 in the housing sector appear to be considerably smaller than in the other sectors that are distinguished. The differences between the housing sector and the other sectors in fig. 8.19 appear to be more significant than in fig. 8.18, indicating that in the housing sector (on average) more buildings per project are developed. We see that average investments per project in the housing sector between 1988 and 1993 are relatively stable. This is in contrast with the trends in the other sectors. The

---

[172] Detailed information on each of the groups of agents seperately is not available with respect to these points.

size of development projects in business sectors and the size of projects concerning the development of special buildings (i.e. schools, hospitals, etc.) tend to become larger, while the project size of developments concerning government buildings is fluctuating. Although we can hardly speak of a trend (because the research period only takes up five years), this illustrates that in the housing sector increases in scale of the building projects do not take place at all, while in the business sector and the sector of 'special buildings' such a tendency perhaps may have taken place. We may assume that in the latter sectors projects usually consist of one building. Thus, fig. 8.18 indicates that in these sectors the average size of *buildings* is increasing. However, *building quality* does not alter; average building investments per m3 are unchanged.

The conclusion that increases in scale do not occur in house building is further supported by the information that is given in figures 8.20 and 8.21. The average number of dwellings per project is currently decreasing. Especially when single dwellings built by private persons are excluded, a rather remarkable development appears to have taken place (fig. 8.21). While in 1988, on average, still around 18 dwellings per project were developed, in 1993 this number was reduced to merely around 9 (dwellings per project).[173] Housing associations and private developers -- jointly responsible for the completion of the majority of the development projects -- thus (were forced to) cut down the size of their projects by half. It is not likely that this shift in their strategies took place at the initiative of the developers and housing associations themselves. The balance of costs and benefits of small-scale projects, after all, is most likely less favourable than the balance of costs and benefits of large-scale projects. This shift to small-scale development has probably been caused in part by a shortage of large-scale building locations and by an increase of the share of development projects located in (the proximity of) existing urban areas (including urban renewal).

Special attention must be paid to the strategies of housing associations. It has already been argued that in fact two different groups of housing associations can be distinguished: the 'rich' ones and the 'poor' ones. The poverty-stricken housing associations have little financial scope. It is expected that in the near future a flood of involuntary mergers between housing associations will take place (see NIROV, 1994). The rich housing associations, however, have access to substantial capital reserves. They have the right to decide themselves whether they use these reserves immediately to build new dwellings or wait for better times. In the latter case they are obliged to invest the capital reserves to safeguard the real value of the money. The current reorganisation of the social-housing sector has been accompanied by annual rent increases that must guarantee the future income of the housing associations. Housing associations' strategies are not based on profit maximalisation. Therefore they neither suffer nor benefit from fluctuations in returns. In fact, development risks in the social-housing sector are minimal, because occupancy of the new dwellings is generally guaranteed.

---

173 Other CBS Statistics show that the investments in the majority of housing projects do not exceed the Dfl. one million boundary. Just 0.4% of all projects in the housing sector require an investment of more than Dfl. 10 million.

FIGURE 8.18
Average building investments per project (including renovations), by type of building, 1988-1993 (current prices)

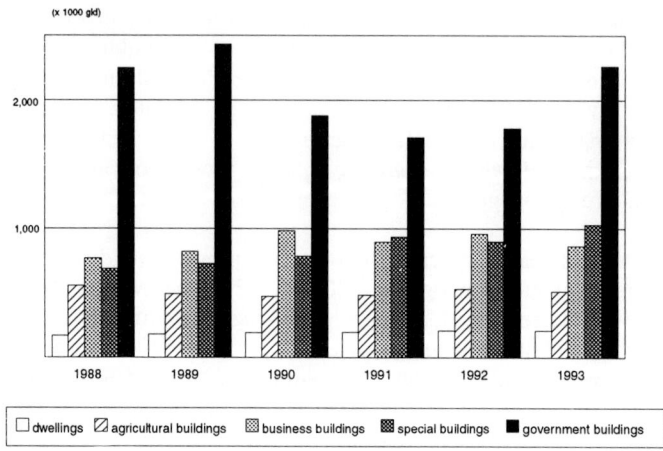

note: figures for 1993 have been estimated
source: CBS Statistics

FIGURE 8.19
Average building investments per m3 (including renovations), by type of building, 1988-1993 (current prices) per project

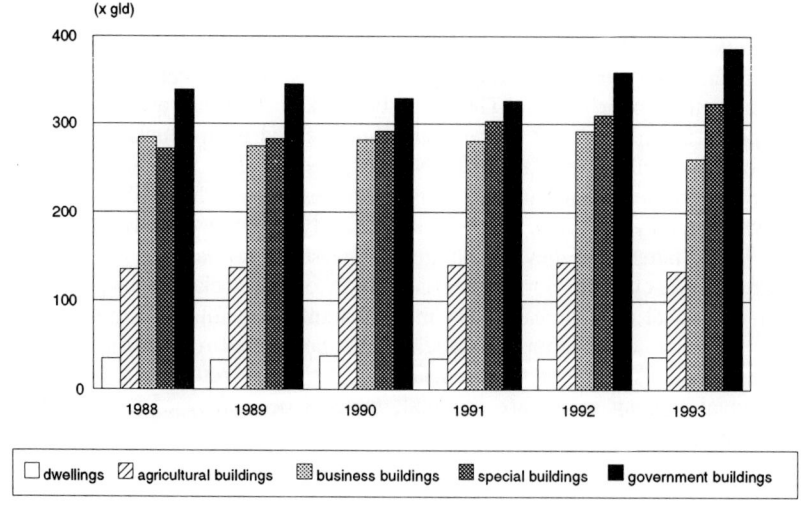

notes:
* figures for 1993 have been estimated
* figures are based on information about investments in building projects
source: CBS Statistics

FIGURE 8.20
Average number of dwellings per project, 1988-1993

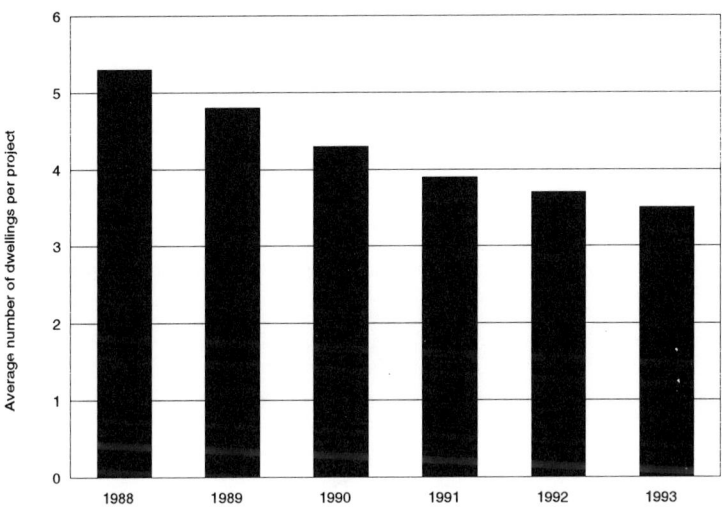

source: CBS Statistics; reworked EvdK

FIGURE 8.21
Average number of dwellings per project (single dwellings built by private persons excluded), 1988-1993

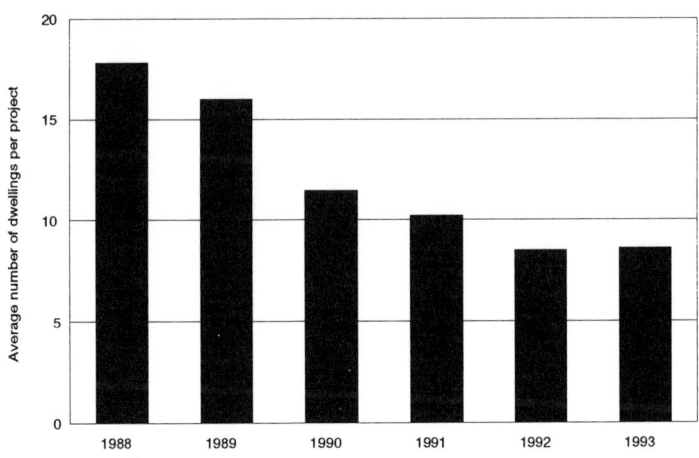

source: CBS Statistics; reworked EvdK

I have just indirectly referred to the financing of new housing development. The reason for this neglect is simple: it does not seem to be much of a problem. No evidence exists that private developers face any problems with respect to financing their development projects. Perhaps this is related to the impact of their strategies -- generally based on risk-avoiding behaviour. If this is true, then we may expect that they restrict their investments to relatively 'safe' projects that do not raise financing difficulties. Housing associations face few problems with respect to the financing of their projects. Investment risks are substantially reduced by the creation of a guarantee fund (the *Waarborgfonds*).

With respect to mortgage financing on the owner-occupied housing market, substantial fluctuations can be observed with respect to the trend of newly registered mortgages. These fluctuations depend on market circumstances and shifts in mortgage rates (fig. 8.22). In 1993 the low rate of interest caused a spectacular rise of newly registered mortgages.

FIGURE 8.22
Trend of newly registered mortgages on real estate and average rate of interest on newly registered mortgages on real estate, 1970-1993

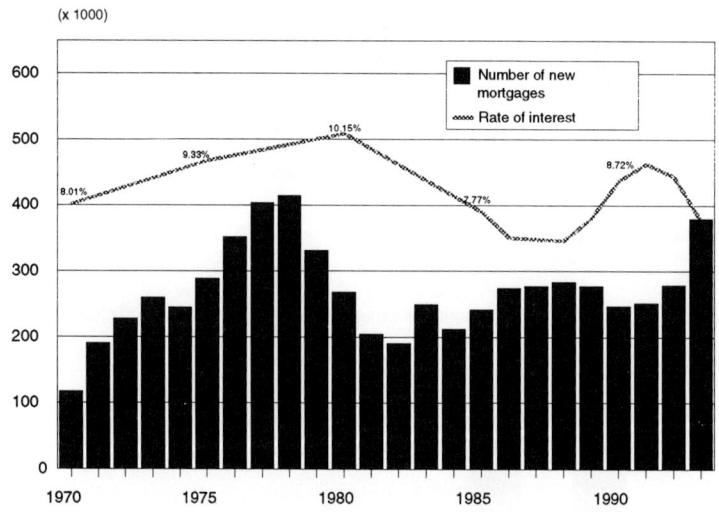

source: CBS Statistics

8.3.3.   Structural changes in the housing construction industry

Section 8.2.4 already referred to the low content of innovations in the building-construction industry, which is related to the typical structure of this branch of industry. Fig. 8.23 shows that between 1960 and 1988 the domination of small-scale firms in this sector remains unchanged. Nevertheless, a number of large-scale enterprises -- the building entrepreneurs -- *do* participate in this sector. Jointly, in 1987 they accounted for 32 percent of the total gross turnover in building construction (fig. 8.24). Remarkably, their share in total gross turnover has declined during the 1980s -- from 39 percent in 1983 to 32 percent in 1987. In the same period, small-scale enterprises have considerably expanded their share in the total volume of trade in this sector.

Institutional Changes, Path Dependency and Future Trends 191

FIGURE 8.23
Number of firms in the construction industry, by size of firm, 1973-1988

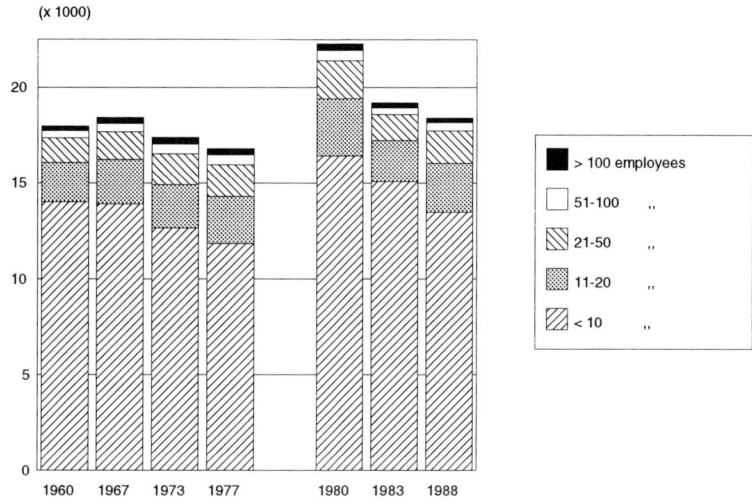

note: interruption of trend in 1978-79; figures for 1960-77 and for 1980-88 are based on different sources
source: EIB, 1980 / CBS Statistics

FIGURE 8.24

Gross turnover by firms in construction industry, by size of firm, 1981-1987 (current prices)

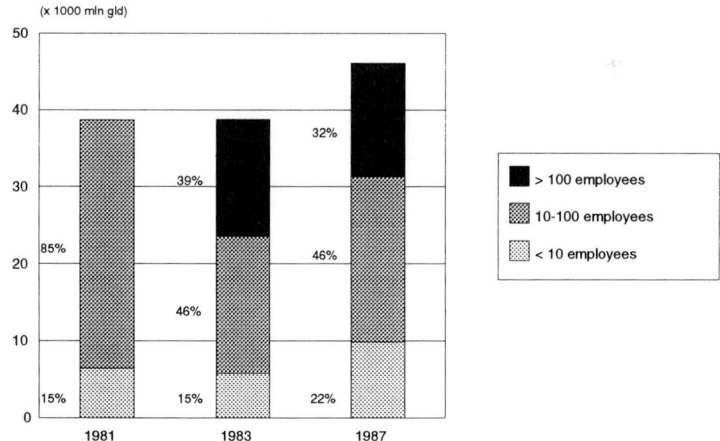

note: for 1981 the category of firms with 10-100 employees also includes firms with more than 100 employees
source: CBS Statistics

Apparently, in building construction small enterprises are equal in competition to large enterprises. This relates to the fact that it is almost impossible to realise any 'advantages of scale' in building construction -- i.e. development costs of large-scale house building projects are equal to the development costs of small projects.[174] Fig. 8.25 subscribes to this viewpoint. Between 1980 and 1988, average labour productivity increased for all firms in the building-construction industry.[175] Although labour productivity in large enterprises still surpasses labour productivity in small firms, the difference between them has substantially decreased, mainly because labour productivity in small firms has increased relatively faster than in large firms. The strong, and apparently even improved, position of small enterprises in building construction is also connected with the fact that average building projects are rather small in size and the trend is that they will further decline in size. Table 8.1 demonstrates that the size of projects that are carried out by large construction firms has declined; the annual number of projects in progress has, on the other hand, increased (see also fig. 8.21).

FIGURE 8.25
Trend in labour productivity, by size of firm (average turnover per employee), in 1980, 1983, and 1988 (current prices)

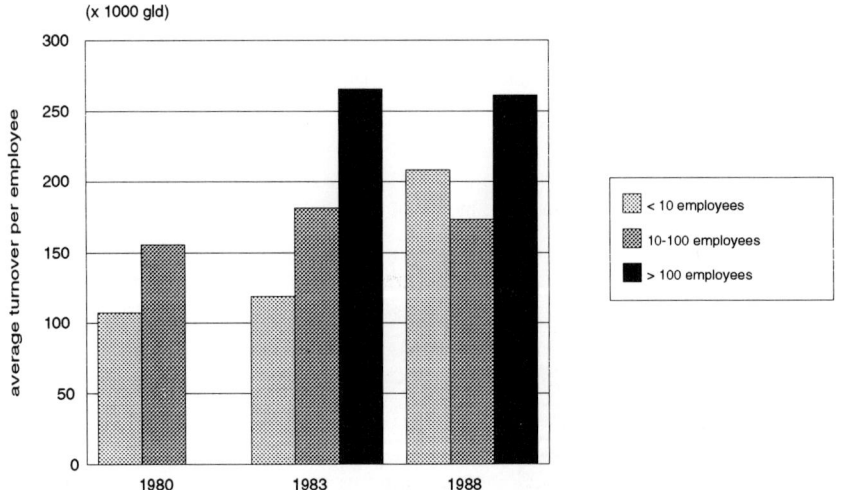

note: for 1980 the category of firms with 10-100 employees also includes firms with more than 100 employees
source: EIB, 1992 / CBS Statistics; reworked EvdK

---

174 See also MERIT, 1990. The conclusion with respect to advantages of scale in the Dutch building construction industry contrasts with Ball's conclusion concerning the English building construction sector. Ball (1983) suggests that large enterprises in building construction *are* able to achieve advantages of scale, mainly because they hold land banks and can act counter-cyclical.

175 Variations in labour productivity are supposed to express variations in organisational structure among firms. As such, they can be interpreted as potential advantages of scale.

TABLE 8.1
Average project size (A) and annual number of projects in progress, by building construction firms (B), by size of firms in 1980, 1983, and 1988 (prices 1987)

size of firms in 'number of employees'	1980		1983		1988	
	A	B	A	B	A	B
	(gld)		(gld)		(gld)	
1-10	18 000	33	11 000	39	18 000	81
11-50	52 000	78	42 000	99	44 000	139
> 50	687 000	94	1 000 000	89	594 000	118

source: EIB

The conclusion must be that the building construction industry is still more or less dominated by traditionally operating small-scale firms. Although the specific characteristics of the building product obstruct large-scale innovations, the traditional character of the industry itself has certainly contributed to the low content of institutional change, as well. One of the main consequences of this situation is that cost reductions related to the introduction of new technologies almost never occur on the house-building market (see also section 8.2.2). This is certainly no exclusively Dutch phenomenon; in other West-European countries more or less similar developments take place. However, although little is known on this point, we know from Ball (1983) that developments with respect to building construction in Great Britain have been somewhat different. The position of large building firms in England has improved, among other things because of their counter-cyclical strategies. They buy land when the housing market is in recession and land prices are depressed; as soon as the housing market recovers they are able to respond immediately and start new development projects. Thus, in Great Britain large building firms take advantage of market fluctuations in two ways: they are able to acquire building land for relatively low prices and they are able to respond immediately to a revival of the housing market.

The line of argument in this paragraph subscribes one of the main points that I have tried to elaborate on in this case study, namely the profitability issue with respect to housing development processes and the factors that influence the degree of profitability. The next section is entirely dedicated to this issue.

8.4. Development Gains in Housebuilding Development Processes

This section focuses on the profitability of housing development and on the significance of development gains in development processes. Development gains influence the profitability of development projects on the housing market. The results of previous sections concerning costs, returns and subsidies with respect to land and building development, will be used in order to estimate the profitability of housing development. Precise calculations of development gains and profit margins are not possible to glean from the available data. Nevertheless, a number of interesting indications of gains and profits can be presented.

8.4.1. Profit margins in the land development process

In the Netherlands municipalities traditionally participate in the land-development process. They acquire agricultural land, 'develop' it (servicing and infrastructure) and sell it to market parties. Municipalities have always considered it their task to arrange the supply of sufficient building land. Their active participation in urban land markets is commonly held responsible for the stability of this market. With respect to selling prices of building plots, municipalities have been satisfied with prices that enable them to recover the total costs of housebuilding schemes. (Fluctuations in) profits have therefore never played an important role in the land development process. Nevertheless, this seems to have changed recently. Municipal land departments increasingly take notice of the difference between costs of land development and the market price of land.

Due to gaps in statistical data, our knowledge about trends in land development costs and building plot prices is, unfortunately, rather incomplete. Fig. 8.26 contains information regarding trends in land-acquisition costs, land-servicing costs and building plot prices for dwellings. The trends have been partially estimated.[176] The affect of subsidies on costs and prices have been left aside.[177] The exact determination of the development of profit margins in the land-development process -- the difference between costs and returns -- is not possible from these data. The data concern averages for the Netherlands as a whole. The determination of profit margins from average figures would not make sense, because both development costs and market prices of building land typically vary among locations. These variations cannot be deduced from fig. 8.25. Nevertheless, fig. 8.26 gives some indications of profit margins in land-development processes.

We can gather from this figure the relative costs of development and the relative returns of development in proportion to each other. Comparison of both trends with each other gives a rough indication of the 'costs/returns relation' through time, and thus of the development of profit margins as well. Theoretically, it can be assumed that the relation between costs and returns is at least equal to zero: if costs should exceed returns, land is not developed (note that this does not follow from fig. 8.26, because this figure concerns index numbers). It becomes clear from fig. 8.26 that the trend of land development costs and the trend of building plot prices for, respectively, non-subsidised owner-occupied dwellings, premium-assisted owner-occupied dwellings and social-rented dwellings go quite gradually. The trend of land-acquisition costs deviates from the others. However, land acquisition costs are usually only a small part of total land development costs (in relation to the costs of servicing the land). The conclusion must be that the relative relation of costs and returns in the land-

---

176   Because the land market shows a more or less constant development, these estimations are assumed to be fairly reliable.

177   Because I make use of index numbers, this doesn't matter; the trends remain equal.

development process has remained constant.[178]

FIGURE 8.26
Index numbers of the trends of land acquisition costs, land servicing costs and building plot prices for dwellings, 1965-1991 (1972 = 100; current prices)

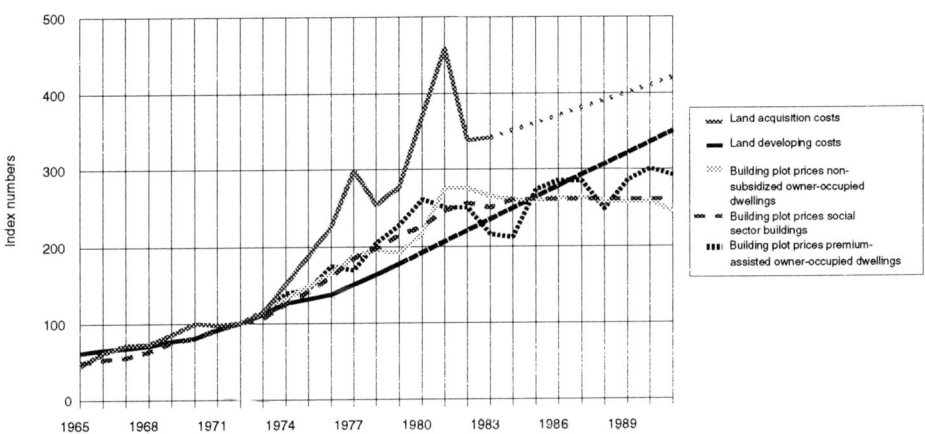

notes:
* land-acquisition costs concern the prices that municipalities pay for agricultural and remaining land (with the intention to develop it). Prices are known for 1965-83; figures for 1984-91 have been estimated. In 1983 the average price for undeveloped land was Dfl. 31,- per m2;
* land-development costs concern the costs of servicing the land (commissioned mainly by municipalities). Index figures are based on CBS Statistics on the development of costs of land servicing and (aqua-)infrastructural works. Prices are known for 1965-78; figures for 1979-91 have been estimated;
* building plot prices for social-sector dwellings and premium-assisted and non-subsidised owner-occupied dwellings are based on figures 7.18, 7.19, and 7.20. In 1983 the average prices for building plots were Dfl. 100,- per m2 (social-sector dwellings, estimated), Dfl. 133,- per m2 (premium-assisted dwellings), and Dfl. 138,- per m2 (non-subsidised owner-occupied dwellings).
source: CBS Statistics / SEO, 1987 / EIB, 1988; reworked EvdK

8.4.2.   The profitability of speculative housing development

The profitability of the development of owner-occupied dwellings obviously depends on the evolution of costs and returns in this sector. Development costs consist of building costs, land costs, and additional costs. Possibly, these costs are reduced by subsidies. Figures for returns in the development process are based on selling prices of the completed dwellings.

---

178 This conclusion leaves unimpeded that on specific locations profits on land development may be substantial, just as on other locations land development may create losses.

Figures 8.27 and 8.28, concerning the non-subsidised owner-occupied housing sector and the premium-assisted owner-occupied housing sector, give an indication of the fluctuations through time of the profitability of owner-occupied housing development. Note that the figures do not consider precise profit margins in absolute figures, but rather the annual fluctuations of relative profits through time. The figures are based on index numbers (see notes to fig. 8.26); the use of absolute numbers would cause insurmountable problems. The use of index numbers makes it possible to reproduce the relative development of profit margins in house building. For instance, fig. 8.27 indicates that profits on the development of non-subsidised owner-occupied dwellings in 1993 clearly surpass profits from this sector in 1983. However, fig. 8.27 gives no clues with respect to the absolute degree of profitability in 1983 or in 1993.[179]

FIGURE 8.27
Index numbers of the profitability of speculative house building, owner-occupied dwellings, non-subsidised sector: development of returns versus development of costs, 1975-1993 (1983 = 100; current prices)

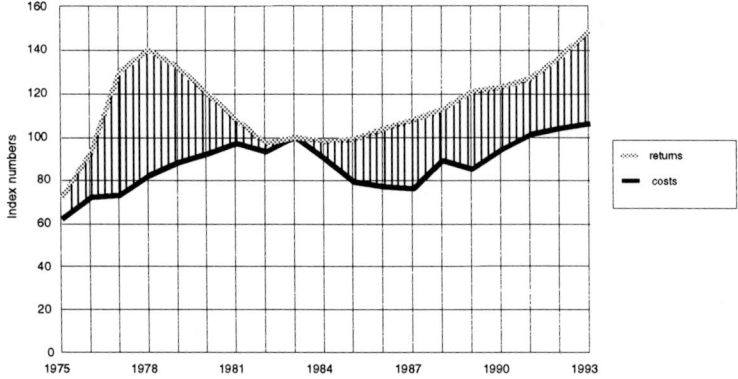

notes:
* 1983 is taken as the starting point for both returns and costs. Note that this figure tells nothing about the abosule margin between returns and costs in 1983 (or in any other year). The figure shows how both returns and costs develop each year in relation to 1983 and in relation to each other year;
* 'returns' are based on average house prices per year;
* 'costs' include building costs and land-development costs, but exclude extra costs. It has been assumed that the share of extra costs in the total costs is stable;
* land-development costs and total costs have been partially estimated
source: various figures in Chapters Seven and Eight; estimations EvdK

---

179 The year 1983 is deliberately taken as the 'starting point' for costs and returns -- that is, index numbers for 1983 are set at 100 -- because in this year housing prices reached rock bottom. It may be expected that profit margins in this year were at a low point as well. Note, however, that it is not suggested that the absolute profit margin in 1983 is equal to zero.

FIGURE 8.28
Index numbers of the profitability of speculative house building, owner-occupied dwellings, premium-assisted sector: development of returns versus development of costs, 1975-1993 (1983 = 100; current prices)

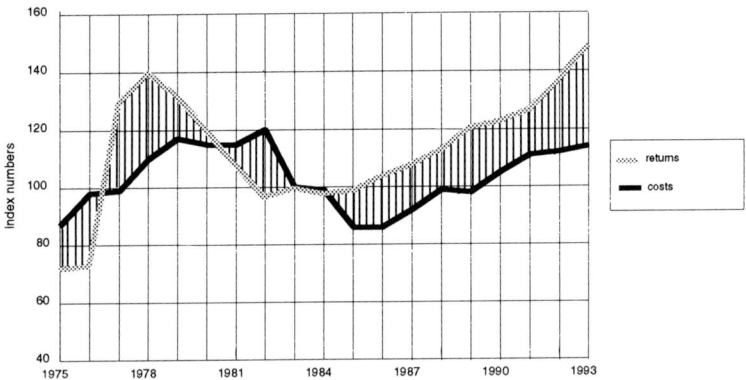

note: similar to notes in fig. 8.27; moreover, subsidies have been deducted from the total costs
source: various figures in Chapters Seven and Eight; estimations EvdK

The reproduction of the annual fluctuations of profit margins is only indicative. A number of assumptions underlie both figures. First, the annual level of returns is based on average selling prices in the owner-occupied housing market. It is assumed that price fluctuations, in relative terms, are identical in all submarkets. Moreover, selling prices of new dwellings are expected to be determined by price developments in the second-hand housing market.

Second, the index numbers for 'building costs' -- being part of the total costs -- are based on 'building costs per m3'. Thus, shifts in the average size of new dwellings (i.e. in the 1980s the average size of new dwellings dropped) cannot obscure the actual development of building costs. We have no access to data with respect to the trend of additional costs. However, it can safely be assumed that extra costs do not affect the overall development of costs through time. The calculation of the overall development costs is based on the supposition that, on average, around 75 percent of the total costs is made up by building costs and 25 percent by the costs of land acquisition.

Third, 'costs' also include the developers' costs that are involved with the acquisition of building land. These land-acquisition costs are deduced from the statistical information that is available on building plot prices. Data are available only for 1982-91, but no reason exists to believe that price development in the land market has undergone large fluctuations. Besides, land costs take up only about 25 percent of the total costs, so that price changes can hardly affect total cost development. It is assumed that developers do not develop the land themselves; they buy it from municipalities.

Fourth, in both figures I have left aside possible time differences between the moment that a dwelling is built and the moment that it is sold in the market.[180] A new dwelling may be developed in one year -- building costs are defined at the start of the building process --

---

180 A similar time difference may exist between the moment that building land is purchased (determining the land costs) and the time that the completed dwelling is sold.

and sold the next year. The profitability of a single development project may seriously change when market prices on the second-hand market suddenly change during the development process. However, this is not really relevant to figure 8.27 and 8.28, because it does not affect the long-term trend of profitability.

Fifth, with respect to fig. 8.28, the development of average subsidies per newly built owner-occupied dwelling has been taken from fig. 8.16 in section 8.3. In addition, fig. 8.29 indicates to what extent subsidies affect the overall costs of the development of premium-assisted dwellings.

FIGURE 8.29
Index numbers of the total costs per m2 of speculative housebuilding, owner-occupied premium-assisted sector, with and without government subsidies, 1975-1993 (current prices)

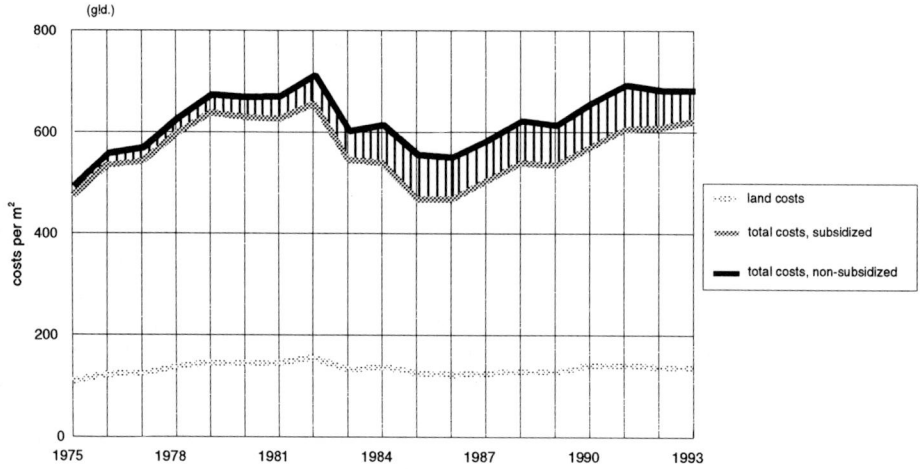

source: various figures in Chapters Seven and Eight; estimations EvdK

Although the above assumptions prevent pronouncements with respect to absolute profit margins in speculative housing development, we can still derive from both figures the fluctuations in the profitability of housing development through time. The profitability of premium-assisted dwellings is subject to even larger fluctuations than the profitability of non-subsidised dwellings. These fluctuations are caused both by shifts in returns and shifts in costs. It may be expected that these fluctuations will continue in the future. We may add to this that regional variations in house prices, and thus in 'returns' on speculative development as well, are substantial. This demonstrates that regional variations in the profitability of housing development occur as well, since development costs hardly vary among regions. The irregular development of the profitability of housebuilding through time and the regional variations in profitability are important preconditions to speculative housing development. In general it can be assumed that in the Netherlands development gains are only of minor significance with respect to the profitability of housing development. Private developers can make development gains by buying agricultural land when it is cheap and develop it only when returns on housing development are high. However, land prices are stable, so there is no need for developers to purchase land early. Nevertheless, one comment must still be made. Figures 8.27 and 8.28 show that the profitability of housing development *does* fluctuate. For this reason it might be profitable for developers to keep land in stock. As soon as the profitability of housing development increases they can immediately start to build.

8.5. Explanations for the Crisis in Housing Production

One of the reasons to undertake this study was the present commotion with respect to shortages in building production on the Dutch housing market and the related imminent housing shortage. The most common explanation for these shortages refers to the state of affairs on urban land markets. A shortage of available building locations impedes the progress of building production. Chapter Six argued that this interpretation of the present shortages in building production is too short-sighted. We should at least ask ourselves why this shortage has developed.

As an alternative approach to this issue, Chapter Six suggested taking into consideration the specific structure of housing provision in the Netherlands. Might it be true that structural features of the housing production system prevent supply adjusting to fluctuations in demand for housing? The analysis of the functioning of the Dutch housing market points out, for one thing, that these fluctuations in demand are characteristic to the housing market, as related to the specific factors that determine the demand for housing. The analysis of the structure of housing provision also provides a better insight into potential supply-side blockages to the smooth functioning of the housing market. This section will gather together the arguments that have been made in previous paragraphs with respect to the way structural market characteristics cause the crisis in housing production.

First, I have shown that the trend of building costs and the trend of housing prices are two autonomous developments. The market price of new dwellings is determined by the price fluctuations on the second-hand owner-occupied housing market. Moreover, building costs show a constant tendency of relative growth. Cost reductions do not take place, because of the characteristics of the building product -- innovations in the production process hardly occur -- and the traditional market strategies of the predominantly small-scale building construction firms. The consequences of this may be that for developers it becomes harder to develop new dwellings. They have hardly any possibilities to reduce development costs. As a result the opportunities that are open to developers to build new dwellings may have been diminished.

The second point is related to the supposed risk-avoiding behaviour of most developers, due to the instability of the demand for owner-occupied dwellings and the uncertainty with respect to the development of market prices.[181] For that reason, they do not risk building

---

181   I have argued that these fluctuations in demand are caused by the combined effect of the factors that influence the loan capacity of households and of the fact that because of sharp increases in housing prices a move-up market has come into existence. With respect to the latter point, owner-occupiers increasingly use the

speculatively (holding costs). That is, many developers reduce their building activities as soon as demand drops and/or market prices fall. Because the development process takes up a rather long time, the market cannot respond immediately to a renewed increase of demand. Again, as a result, shortages of building production are likely to occur repeatedly.

Third, private developers in the Netherlands did not hold land banks, in contrast to their colleagues in Great Britain (Ball, 1983). This behaviour quite possibly cuts down their profits and deprives them of the ability to anticipate market developments. The reasons for this behaviour are unclear. It may be related to the specific character of the Dutch property system. Municipalities have traditionally taken up a monopoly position on urban land markets. As a result land markets were stable and there used to be no scarcity of building locations at all. Market parties had no reason to take over the municipalities' role on urban land markets. Now this situation has changed, market parties may lack the capacity to start acting as land developers.

Fourth and related to the former point, the present shortage of building locations for housing contrasts sharply with the large quantity of business sites most municipalities seem to dispose of more or less permanently. As a result of the substantial economic growth in the second half of the 1980s, which was accompanied by a large demand for business sites, municipalities probably have allocated large quantities of land for business purposes. Local governments compete with each other to attract new firms to their municipalities. Allocating land for business purposes generates more employment and generates more income for them.[182] It is possible that the substantial demand for business sites has reduced the number of potential locations for housebuilding. This calls into question the role of local governments. Municipal land policy, being part of the municipalities' spatial-economic policy, may impede the productive efficiency of the housing-development market (see Chapter Nine).

Finally, the national government's role in the housing market must be questioned. The national government has initiated a reorganisation of the housing sector in recent years. In financial terms, the national government has clearly withdrawn from this sector. However, a contradicting trend has taken place with respect to the national government's spatial planning policy. In the national report on physical planning (the VINEX, Ministry of VROM, 1990), a limited number of locations has been selected in a very early stage of the development process, where the larger part of new housing developments will be situated. As a consequence, alternative potential building locations cannot be developed anymore. Moreover, this policy may be responsible for forcing up land prices and introducing land speculation on the VINEX locations. Both developments would hinder the smooth implementation of the new housing plans even further.

The conclusion forces itself on us that the national government's goal to establish an optimal spatial order has always disregarded differences in the profitability of the development of diverse locations. This might have led, in general, to rather small profit margins in housing development processes and, in consequence, to complications with respect to the implementation of the desired house building program.

---

money gains on the sale of their former property to 'move up' to more expensive dwellings.

182   Selling prices of business sites usually exceed selling prices of building plots for housing.

8.6. Conclusions: A Qualification of the Dutch Property System

Chapter Eight dealt with the sources of institutional change and the institutional changes with respect to the structure of housing provision themselves. It has been demonstrated how changing norms and ideas, changes in relative costs and market prices, (the lack of) technological innovations and changes in information costs have altered through time the significance of government intervention in the housing sector, the strategies of the agents involved in housing development, and the structure of the building construction industry. The analysis has made clear that the organisational structure of the property-development industry and other aspects of the property system are subject to continuous changes. I have shown that changes in the institutional organisation of the housing market sometimes result in a different outcome of housing-development processes. Examples of change concern the changing strategies of private developers on the land market and the new position of housing associations as social entrepreneurs (with the consequence that less social-sector dwellings are being developed). Moreover, the location of new dwellings has constantly been subject to changes in the national government's spatial policy, sometimes with significant consequences for the costs and/or profitability of new development projects. The relation between the second-hand housing market and the development of new dwellings has been analysed, as well as the significance of the long-term trend of building costs to housebuilding production.

The case study has extensively analysed the way dwellings are *produced* in the Netherlands and the influence of typical features of housebuilding production in the Netherlands on the functioning of the housing market (number and type of new dwellings, quality, location, etc.) By concentrating on the supply side, I was able to discuss a number of issues that have, in the Netherlands, received only minor attention. These issues include:

(1) the efficacy -- from a social point of view -- of government expenditures on housing, not only concerning government subsidies to housebuilding production, but also with respect to municipalities' land policy;
(2) the conflicting perspectives of the national government's spatial policy and housing policy;
(3) the impact of the strategies of both private and public agencies on the housing market on the development of housing and the profitability of the development of new dwellings;
(4) several reasons for the present shortages in housing production that are related to the way new dwellings are produced in the Netherlands and to government policy;
(5) the path dependency of the functioning of the housing market -- the impact of decisions that have been made in the past concerning, notably, the position of housing associations, land policy of local governments, the strategies of private developers, the spread of new dwellings over the Netherlands, and the location of dwellings within a city -- and, as I mentioned above, the meaning of institutional change to the functioning of the Dutch housing market.

Finally, what has been the contribution of the institutional economic approach to the field of housing studies and to our understanding of the functioning of housing markets? The case study has examined a number of themes that are usually not addressed. I have tried to demonstrate the relevance of these issues, which are all related to the production of new dwellings and, to the functioning of housing markets. Institutional economic theory has thus set the direction for research. With respect to this *structure of housing provision*, I have particularly emphasised, with help of institutional economic theory, the influence of the institutional organisation of the housebuilding market on housing development processes. The significance of institutional change and path dependency has already been mentioned, but throughout the previous chapters I have also focused on the impact of information problems on the strategies of both public and private agencies and on the different rationalities that underlie the behaviour of different groups of agents. The framework for analysis has thus directed the attention to changes in housing development processes, to the fact that in some situations changes in development processes fail to appear (while, from a purely economic point of view, we expect them to appear), and to the strategies/behaviour of the agents that are involved in housing development. The importance of institutional change, path dependency, information problems, and the different rationalities of strategic behaviour will again be considered in the subsequent chapter.

Chapter Nine will make use of the results of the case study to discuss the propositions that have been drawn up in Chapter Six. With respect to these propositions I will explicitly stress the significance of these institutional factors. The answers will, in turn, be used in Chapter Nine to assess the allocative efficacy and the productive efficiency of the Dutch housing market.

PART IV   TOWARDS A BETTER UNDERSTANDING OF PROPERTY DEVELOPMENT PROCESSES

INTRODUCTION

The final part of this book serves two different purposes. Chapter Nine will evaluate the Dutch property system. This chapter focuses on the allocative efficacy of the Dutch property system, related to the 'output' of real estate development processes, on the one hand, and on the productive efficiency, related to the efficiency of the way real estate is produced, on the other hand. It will be argued that a public-sector strategy directed at improving the allocative efficacy of a national property system sometimes worsens the conditions that determine the productive efficiency of the property system.

However, Chapter Nine goes beyond examining the role of public sector policy. Its concern is with the significance of the institutional organisation of the real estate market -- including public-sector policy, but also referring to the strategies of market parties and the meaning of information problems and path dependency -- to the functioning of this market, the outcome of real estate development processes and the transformation of urban spatial patterns. Can we conclude that the Dutch property system leads to an efficiently operating real estate market? Does it lead to a desirable outcome of development processes and is the way in which Dutch cities 'transform' preferable to transformation processes of cities in other countries?

Chapter Ten will investigate different directions for urban regeneration policies. Chapter Ten analyses the relations between real estate development and the functioning of the urban economy and the way the public sector should take these basic relations into consideration. The nature of real estate development processes and the ways that are open to the public sector to intervene in these processes are linked to urban economic growth. Two issues will be analysed. First, can property-led urban regeneration policies be a useful instrument in the more general effort of the public sector to stimulate urban economic development? On the other hand, the various ways in which local governments may try to stimulate real estate development -- from providing subsidies to supplying building sites -- are examined.

The subjects of both chapters are related to each other. Allocative efficacy implies, among other things, that the optimal spatial structure with respect to urban economic growth has been accomplished, referring to the location of new business sites for instance, or to the availability of business sites. The discussion of the allocative efficacy of the Dutch property system calls into question whether the output of real estate development processes serves the urban economy well. Furthermore, the discussion of the productive efficiency -- or inefficiency -- of the real estate sector directs our attention to the obstructions the real estate sector can raise to the functioning of urban economies: the suppy-side constraints that were mentioned in Chapters One and Two.

Chapters Nine and Ten will use the findings of the previous chapters of this book. The issues discussed in Chapters Nine and Ten will be analysed from an institutional perspective. The assessment of the efficacy and efficiency of the Dutch national property system in Chapter Nine will take place with help of the operational theory that has been developed in Chapter Five. I will base my argument primarily on the discussion of the significance of information problems, the different rationalities of the behaviour of the agencies involved in the development process, both the sources and consequences of institutional change, and the significance of path dependency. Moreover, Chapter Nine will refer to the social problems related to property development that have been summed up in Chapter One, and to the hypotheses concerning the functioning of the Dutch housing market that have been drawn up in Chapter Six. Chapter Ten means to fill the remaining gap in the operational institutional theory of Chapter Five (see section 5.3). It is concerned with the consequences of the special characteristics of the Dutch real estate market for urban economic growth. The objective is, ultimately, to judge the national government's urban and regional economic policy: (1) to evaluate the ways in which the public sector deals with the links between real estate development and urban/regional economic development -- in other words, the impact of the national government's urban and regional economic policy on real estate development and the conditions that the real estate sector imposes on urban/regional economic growth; (2) to evaluate the *social efficiency* of public sector investments in real estate development and in urban/regional economic development.

9 THE INSTITUTIONAL ORGANISATION OF THE DUTCH REAL ESTATE MARKET: EVALUATION

9.1. Evaluating the Dutch Property System

This chapter aims to evaluate the consequences of the way the Dutch real estate market is organised for the outcome of real estate development processes and, ultimately, for the spatial-economic restructuring of Dutch cities. Essentially, the objective is to link the characteristics of the Dutch property system -- the term is identical to 'institutional organisation of the real estate market' -- to the key outcomes of real estate market functioning and to the driving forces behind development processes. These 'key outcomes' and 'driving forces' are, in turn, related to urban economic growth patterns. With respect to this *institutional organisation*, the role of the public sector on urban land and property markets will be examined. The public sector affects the outcome of real estate development in a variety of ways. It is a well-known fact, for example, that local governments, as suppliers of building land, play a key role on the urban land market. However, less is known in the Netherlands about the impact of the local governments' role on urban land and property markets on property prices, the costs and profitability of real estate development, risks, and the location and nature of supply. Moreover, the public sector influences the structure of the development industry, the opportunities for market parties to participate in real estate development, and the availability of necessary 'sources,' like land and capital.

Clearly, when considering the nature of the property system, we must take into consideration the organisational structure of the development industry, the institutional relations between the actors involved in this industry, the set of rules that regulate the market and the status of ownership rights. The significance of each of these aspects of the property system will be addressed at two different levels of enquiry. First, the outcome of the housing market study will be analysed in the context of Chapter Nine's objective. How well is the Dutch housing market organised and what are the positive and/or negative consequences of the way housing provision in the Netherlands takes place? Second, a number of examples of supposed non-optimal outcomes of real estate development in Dutch cities are investigated. In what sense is the functioning of the Dutch real estate market influenced by inefficiencies in the property system? The scope of this analysis is, however, limited by the fact that these examples are only a small selection of real estate development processes that actually take place in Dutch cities. The evaluation of the Dutch property system will take place from two different perspectives. This chapter aims to assess, respectively, the allocative efficacy and the productive efficiency of the Dutch property system. I will argue below that this distinction is especially important in situations in which the *outcome* of real estate development processes may be optimal from a policy point of view (for instance, with respect to the number, type, and location of new dwellings), but in which the building production process is inefficient (for instance, production takes place only heavily subsidised), or vice versa. To make sense, criteria are needed that determine the allocative efficacy and productive efficiency. One of these criteria will refer to the relation between real estate development and urban economic growth. The latter point links Chapter Nine to Chapter Ten.

The set-up of the chapter is as follows. Section 9.2 starts with a discussion of the criteria that should be used in order to appraise the allocative efficacy and productive efficiency of a national property system. In section 9.3 the results of the housing market case study are then interpreted with help of these criteria. Section 9.4 attempts to examine the relevance of inefficiencies in the property system to a number of 'social problems' related to real estate market functioning in Dutch cities. Finally, section 9.5 makes some concluding remarks with respect to the efficacy of the Dutch property system.

9.2. The Institutional Organisation of Urban Real Estate Markets: Criteria of Allocative Efficacy and Productive Efficiency

In the *summary* of Chapter Six I already mentioned the criteria that are suggested by Badcock (1994) for judging the efficacy of property systems. Needham, Koenders and Kruijt (1993: pp. 210-212) propose a comparable set of criteria:

1. There should be a sufficient supply of property. Needham *et al.* (1993: p. 210) argue that 'sufficient relates to need as well as demand, supply should be sufficient for each type of use, including the needs and demands of poorer people and non-commercial activities.' Moreover, they argued that the supply should be at the right location and that the supply should be able to react quickly to changes in need and demand.
2. Public policy must be able to influence not only the amount and location of the property but also its nature and use (for instance, in case of negative external effects).
3. The private ownership of property should not be too unequally distributed.
4. Prices for property should not fluctuate greatly. 'Fluctuating prices cause uncertainties that can destabilize the property market (and possibly other markets as well), and they can cause speculation in property, which interferes with a steady supply' (*ibid.*, p. 211).
5. The processes on the property market, and not only the outcomes, should be visible and socially acceptable. This point relates to, among other things, the status of ownership rights: for instance, private actors should not be subject to unpredictable or unreasonable use of compulsory purchase powers.

Application of these criteria to the functioning of urban land and property markets is not without difficulties, because the definition of the criteria still leaves open various interpretations. For instance, what should be understood by a sufficient supply, to what extent should public policy be able to influence the amount, location, and use of property, and how far are property prices allowed to fluctuate, etc. Nevertheless, a property system that measures up to the standards listed above may be expected to operate fairly well from a point of view that favours the public welfare. The criteria listed above refer to the allocative efficacy of the property system: does the property system -- the structure of building provision -- lead to a desirable output of property development processes and to a desirable distribution of the output? However, the judgement of the Dutch property system should also be based on the evaluation of the productive efficiency of building provision. Productive efficiency refers to the optimal output *in proportion to* the input, regardless of the distribution of the output. It brings into question whether the production of land and buildings is efficiently organised -- the land supply system, the strategies of developers -- and whether the production is profitable. Productive efficiency also relates to the way both public and private agencies respond to changes in demand and to institutional and technological change.

As argued in the introduction to Part IV, it is important to make this distinction, because several situations can be found in which the allocation of land and property is judged as optimal -- for example, public sector policy has been implemented successfully -- but in which the production of land and property may cause inefficiencies in the production process. Or, the development of real estate may take place efficiently, but this need not necessarily result in the most desirable allocation of land and property from a public sector point of view.

In fact, these points relate to the contradictions in interest that exist between the producers of land and buildings and the consumers of land and buildings. Regarding the interst of consumers, I mean the policy of the public sector with respect to the consumption of land and buildings. Producers benefit from an optimal productive efficiency, the public sector strives for an optimal allocation and distribution of land and property to the joint benefit of all consumers. Contradictions in interests appear on at least three levels. First, should the outcome of real estate development processes lead to an urban spatial structure that serves the public benefit, or is maximum urban economic growth the goal? When we strive, for instance, for maximum urban economic growth, the consequence may be that non-commercial activities are driven away from attractive locations. Second, should the property system operate on behalf of the user of the building, the developer, or the investor? In particular, the significance of conflicting interests between developers and investors is often underestimated. With respect to new building developments, the public sector often holds an orientation to property that generally favours the developers (instead of an investment orientation). Municipalities try to improve the conditions for economic growth by taking care of a sufficient supply of building land. However, as Healey remarks in a recent paper, '(t)his illustrates clearly the tension between a financial orientation to property as an investment asset and a production-orientation to property as an input to production. If industrial land is to be supplied according to the first orientation, then the strategy should be to limit supply to force values up. This could deter companies from moving into the region if land and property values are higher than in other regions where they are considering locating' (Healey, 1994: p. 193). Investors, obviously, want high returns, minimal risks, and increasing property values. On the contrary, the prime interest of the users (firms, households, etc.) with respect to property is high quality, low costs, sufficient, and optimal location. Third, considering both the allocative efficacy and the productive efficiency of property systems, conflicts may exist between local and national interests. Local authorities often compete each other in attracting new firms to their region. Unless it concerns an international migration, firms moving from one region to another contribute to the economy of the region they move too, but put the economy of the region they leave at a disadvantage. Thus, public money (subsidies) is 'wasted' in this process of competition, with no benefit for the national economy.

We must thus be careful when assessing the efficiency and/or efficacy of property systems. The criteria mentioned in Needham *et al.* (1993) point to the allocative efficacy of property systems. In addition, criteria related to the productive efficiency must be recognised: the level of development costs, uncertainty, risks and returns, profitability, the distribution of costs and benefits, flexibility of supply, etc. It is clear that the assessment of the efficacy/efficiency of the property system is thus more complicated, since the criteria are often contradictory. Sections 9.3 and 9.4 will take account of the different conditions for optimal allocation and distribution as well as optimal efficiency.

9.3. How Well Does the Dutch Housing Market Work?

The case study of the Dutch housing market analysed the impact of the institutional organisation of the housing market on the functioning of this market. This section will draw a number of conclusions on the allocative efficacy of this institutional organisation and on the efficiency of housing production in the Netherlands. When judging efficacy and efficiency we have to take into consideration the special characteristics of the housing market (see section 6.1). A low efficacy level or an inefficient production system may cohere with some of the typical qualities of this market (so the property system is not to be blamed).

One of the reasons to undertake the case study was the observation that at present the production of dwellings lags behind the need for new dwellings. We could easily take the present shortages in housing production as a temporary situation that poses no serious challenge to the efficacy of the market's functioning. However, I have argued that such a conclusion may be too hasty. The way new dwellings are produced in the Netherlands is in some respects inefficient. Considering the efficacy and efficiency of the Dutch system of housing provision, a number of issues deserve our attention. These include:

* *the long-term development of building costs;*
* *development gains of speculative land development (e.g. determined by the location of a new housing estate);*
* *the consequences of fluctuations and regional differences in the prices of owner-occupied dwellings;*
* *fluctuations in the profitability of housebuilding and the factors that affect the profitability (e.g. the size of new building projects, the local authorities' land policy);*
* *the amount of government money that is involved with housebuilding;*
* *the consequences of changes in the strategies of market parties;*
* *the inconsistencies in the government's spatial and financial-economic policy;*
* *the low degree of innovations in the housebuilding industry;*
* *the consequences of land speculation on future housebuilding locations;*
* *the rigidity in housebuilding production (the supply side often responds delayed on fluctuations in demand, while these fluctuations are just characteristic for the housing market).*

The case study has not provided decisive evidence supporting the suggestion that the present shortage in housing production is structural and caused by the developments above. Nonetheless, I have brought up several arguments suggesting that we should at least investigate the relevance of these issues more profoundly. This section will use insights from institutional theory in order to support the arguments that have been summed up in Chapters Seven and Eight. To what extent are the above mentioned issues -- and the problems they may generate -- related to the property system? Is there reason to believe that, in situations that this market malfunctions, the typical institutional organisation of the Dutch housing market must be held responsible? It goes too far to label the housing sector as an inefficiently functioning market. On the other hand, the case study indicates that a closer examination of the functioning of the Dutch housing market would probably lead to a more balanced assessment of the efficacy/efficiency of this market. I will discuss now the propositions with respect to the organisation and functioning of the housing sector that have been drawn up in Chapter Six (section 6.2), aiming to put the functioning of the housing market in a different perspective.

First, section 8.5 contained a detailed discussion of the reasons for the present low level of housing production in the Netherlands. The complexity of this issue has been explained and the conlusion drawn that the shortage of building locations, which is generally assumed to be the reason of the housing production crisis, is really merely the effect of deep-down characteristics of the functioning of the housing market. These aspects have been summarised in section 8.5. I have questioned the efficiency of both the land supply system and the strategies of the developers. The public supply of building land seems to be a classic example of path dependency. Apparently, the role of municipalities on urban land markets has kept private agencies from taking an active role on these markets. Now it appears that the municipalities have not been able to develop sufficient building land in time. Perhaps, institutional change -- a shift from public supply of land to the development of building land by private land developers -- would lead to better results, but this has been obstructed for some reason.[183] With respect to the latter point, consider also the strategies of the private developers and the rationality behind these strategies. Do they respond "in the right way" to the shifts in demand and supply that currently take place on the land market? Section 8.5 argued that they do not, perhaps because their information of the changes in supply of and demand for land is incomplete.

Second, section 8.4 investigated the profitability of speculative housing development. I have tried to expose the relevance of (fluctuations in) the profitability of speculative house building to total housing production output. The degree of profitability in housing development processes is essential with respect to the strategies of market parties, the necessity of government intervention and the final level of production output. Although the availability of empirical data on this point is limited, it still proved possible to show that the fluctuations in 'profitability' through time (due to rising development costs and fluctuating returns on development) actually represent a form of institutional change. We can only guess whether market parties and local governments sufficiently take account of the fluctuations of the profiability through time and the variations in profitability, due to the attractiveness of locations and the type of dwellings. The same goes for the factors that influence the profitability of housing development. Do local governments realise that the location of building sites, the density of new housing schemes, etc. affect the profitability of

---

183   Note that, to be able to judge the efficiency rightly, alternative research methods must be used, for instance by analysing differences in plan development costs in public and private land development projects.

housebuilding? And what about the consequences of the national government's urbanisation policy for the profitability of speculative housebuilding? I have suggested that the profitability issue is generally neglected in government strategies. Moreover, it has been argued that the government's spatial/urbanisation policy often lowers the profitability of housing development. Note that I do not suggest that public sector policy should therefore be considered as wrong. It is just that different rationales underlie both the public sector's decision to implement a certain urbanisation policy and private developers' strategies to develop new dwellings. It certainly is worth the effort to pay more attention to these issues; until now they have almost never been addressed in housing studies.

Third, I have already mentioned that private developers in the Netherlands, in contrast to their colleagues in Great Britain, do not hold land banks.[184] Section 8.5 made clear that this behaviour may cut down their profits and deprive them of the ability to anticipate market developments. The fact that municipal land departments have always taken care of a sufficient supply of building sites probably must be held responsible for the developers' strategies with respect to land development. Now that market circumstances have changed, developers seem to lack the capacity to shift their strategies. I consider these strategies as part of the organisational structure of the housing market. In other words, the supposed inability of private developers to change their strategies could be a matter of institutional inertia. This may be one of the reasons for the fact that developers at present cannot respond quickly to the increased demand for new dwellings: again an indication of productive inefficiency.

Fourth, it has been claimed that municipal land departments should be careful with bearing the risks that are bound up with land development. It is true that fig. 8.25 shows the stability of the land market, but this figure does not take into consideration the possible instability of the demand for building plots. At this moment, risks for municipal land departments are low. However, if the market should suddenly collapse, they indeed run the risk of substantial interest losses. It is questionable whether municipalities possess sufficient information about these risks.

Fifth, section 8.3 analysed extensively the national government's financial involvement with housebuilding. It has been argued that the current national government's objective to diminish its expenditures on the housing sector raises some questions. Is it possible to keep housebuilding production on the same level as before with less government money? Since there is no reason to assume that the profitability of housing development has structurally improved recently, the 'new' government policy -- to leave housebuilding to the market -- may lead to a collapse of housebuilding production in the future, in the case that prices on

---

184   Recently, they seem to have changed their strategies: they have started to build up land banks, especially on the VINEX locations. In fact, this supports my argument. When they do hold land banks now, why shouldn't they have done it before (assuming that the profitability of holding land banks has not changed)? However, there is still an important difference between Dutch and British developers, concerning their reasons for holding land banks. In Great Britain, private developers hold land banks on *potential* building locations in order to be able to respond quickly to an increasing demand for new dwellings. In the Netherlands, private developers buy land on future building locations to strengthen their negotiation position in relation to the municipalities: they are prepared to sell the undeveloped land to municipalities, but expect in exchange to be involved in the development of new housing schemes.

the owner-occupied market fall.[185] On the other hand (though not yet supported by empirical evidence) it is also possible that the housing market will function quite well with less financial government assistance than before. This line of argument suggests that, in financial terms, the organisation of the housing sector in the past lacked efficiency.

Sixth and related to the former point, the owner-occupied housing market is now 'booming.' The sharp increases of housing prices in recent years have made it easier for private developers to start new non-subsidised building projects, while the average loan capacity of households has increased simultaneously. However, if the owner-occupied housing market should suddenly collapse, private developers will probably be more careful with the implementation of new housing projects. Because government expenditures on housing have been reduced, this cannot be intercepted anymore by expanding social-sector building. The national government seems to overlook the fact that the profitability of speculative housing development characteristically fluctuates.

Efficient or not?
The Dutch property system enables housing development to be managed in an efficient and orderly way, manages to avoid high speculative costs of land for housing and public purposes, has arranged it so that increases in land values that accompany urban growth benefit (at least in part) the public, ensures that property prices are relatively stable, and, finally, takes care that private property now comes within the reach of an increasing group of households. Of course, all that glitters is not gold. In specific cases, house price fluctuations, a collapsing demand, government intervention, etc. cause negative side effects. Apart from these points, I have tried to make clear that there is more the matter: the productive efficiency of the housing development industry seems in some respects suboptimal. Government strategies aiming to accomplish an optimal allocation of new dwellings -- referring to the total number of dwellings, the location of these dwellings, and the distribution of the dwellings among the inhabitants -- impose conditions on the production of new dwellings. The alternative explanation of the housing production shortages in section 8.5, as well as the discussion of my propositions above, points out that the specific institutional organisation of the Dutch real estate market, including these government strategies and the strategies of private developers, the nature of the housing market, and the 'technical' restrictions to the production of new dwellings in some situations jointly impede a smooth functioning of the housing development market. The characteristic instability of the owner-occupied housing market, the low degree of innovation in the housebuilding industry, the continual growth of building costs, the inextricable alliance between housing development and the land market, and the uncertainty with respect to future developments of prices and demand for housing are just a few of the wrongdoers. The section calls into question whether the productive efficiency of the housing provision system can be improved. Directions for public policy will be discussed in Chapter Ten.

---

185 It is no longer possible to compensate for a sudden decrease in the production of owner-occupied dwellings by building more social-sector dwellings (as happened before, in the early 1980s).

9.4. The Dutch Real Estate Market: Examples of Allocative Inefficacy and Productive Inefficiency?

While section 9.3 was concerned with the housing market, this section is focused on the commercial real estate market. The key outcomes and driving forces on local real estate markets depend on, subsequently, the nature of demand, the nature of supply and the institutional organisation of the market. 'Key outcomes' refer not only to the amount, type, nature and location of supply, but also to the profitability of real estate development, fluctuations and regional differences in prices, costs, risks and returns, the pace of replacement of the existing building stock, public benefits and risks, and the distribution of costs and benefits. 'Driving forces' allude particularly to the strategies of developers, investors, the building industry, owner-occupiers, municipalities, housing associations, etc. In fact, driving forces concern the expectations of both market parties and public authorities with respect to, for instance, the profitability of new developments, the returns on investments, or the development gains of land speculation. In the context of the present chapter I am primarily interested in the impact of the institutional organisation of the real estate market on these key outcomes and driving forces. One way of assessing the influence of the property system is to select situations that give reason to believe that the outcome of development processes is not optimal. The efficacy and efficiency of the property system in these situations can then be examined. The aim is to find out whether the property system negatively affects the driving forces behind the strategies of the actors involved in the development process, and, consequently, whether it is responsible for unwanted outcomes of real estate development. Below I will address (a selection of) the examples of social problems related to property development that have been mentioned in Chapter One (section 1.4), intending to analyse whether the institutional organisation of the market must be blamed for these problems.

(1) High vacancy rates exist on the office market -- considered to be socially undesirable because vacant buildings occupy locations that cannot be used for alternative purposes. Of course, a certain degree of vacancy is necessary on every market to guarantee a sufficient circulation. What we are interested in is *structural* vacancy. Vacancies in the office market may be the result of two different 'mechanisms.' Either vacant obsolete buildings are not demolished (because the costs of demolition are too high), or the stock of office buildings is expanded, while no absolute increase of the demand for office space can be noted. In the latter case vacancies may occur in the newly built offices or in the existing building stock. In both cases office space remains unused that in principle meets the needs of the market. In the Netherlands, expansion of the stock of office buildings especially seems to lead to vacancies in existing buildings. This is due to the fact that relatively minor differences exist between the rents of new offices and existing offices. The occurrence of vacancies is typical of *commercial* real estate markets. Companies that rent office space can relatively easily move to a new building, compared to companies that own their property.

Are the present high vacancy rates in Dutch cities connected with an inefficient property system? The answer to this question must be positive. Apparently the market still holds incentives -- in a period in which the market is down -- for developers to develop new property and for investors to invest in the office sector, whereas it is socially unwanted. If the office market would not be dominated by an investment demand, this would not happen. In this respect, the role of financial institutions (as the owner-lessor) is the most important. As long as companies are willing to move to new office buildings, financial institutions may be expected to continue investing in new offices, despite the fact that they run the risk of vacancy (and, as a result, capital losses) in the property they already own. The property developers' part is simple: they keep developing new offices, as long as the financial institutions go on purchasing them. The strategies of these actors are rational -- from their own perspective -- but do not contribute to the public benefit. Institutional change is necessary to 'solve' these problems. The situation will persist, unless the national government intervenes by limiting building activities or the financial institutions jointly agree to reduce new building developments.

(2) The development of the Y-bank project in Amsterdam was dismissed; it is possible of course that the local authorities of Amsterdam and the development industry were jointly just not capable of 'organising' a project of such a large scale: then, we would speak of productive inefficiency. However, it is more likely that the decline of demand, as a result of the economic recession, is the most important reason for the project's demise. With respect to this level of demand, obviously an information problem exists. The involvement in the project of both public authorities and market parties was based on expectations of future demand; these expectations appeared to be false.[186]

(3) The property development industry complains that office development is too decentralised to diverse locations and that international top locations are missing; this state of affairs is connected, among other things, with the entrepreneurial role of the local authorities (see also Chapter Five). They consider it necessary to attract as many companies to their region as possible, mainly by supplying building sites and developing new real estate projects in public-private partnerships. Apart from the fact that in the long run this policy may reduce returns on property investments, the benefits for the municipalities themselves is also questionable. It seems that the costs and benefits of the entrepreneurial role of the local authorities have never been weighed well against each other. There may be a positive employment effect, but this is reduced when new development projects primarily attract firms from within the urban region. Moreover, the projects that are developed in public-private partnerships often require massive financial contributions by the public sector (which could also be used for alternative purposes), the municipalities' revenues from land development turn out to be low (because land prices are low), municipalities risk financial setbacks when development plans are ultimately not carried out, the public benefit of a new business park is modest, real estate owners on existing business sites see their property lower in value, etc. The conclusion must be that the public sector's strategies on this point reduce the productive efficiency of the commercial real estate market and that -- from a financial point of view -- the relation between costs and benefits to the public sector may turn out to be negative.

(4) Rental levels and capital value of property in the Netherlands are rising too slowly, making the investment climate in the Netherlands less attractive than in other countries; this

---

186   The local authorities of Amsterdam are also partly responsible for the dismissal of the Y-bank project, because they go ahead with developing 'Amsterdam-Zuid' and 'Amsterdam Zuid-Oost' -- two alternative locations for office development within the boundaries of Amsterdam. They have deliberately chosen for the dispersal of new commercial real estate development.

point relates to the former point. The way the land and property market functions must be held responsible for this situation. Needham *et al.* (1993: p. 213) produce three reasons. First, suppliers of land (municipalities) try to prevent any shortage of opportunities for building. Property developers grasp those possibilities, so there is no shortage of buildings, so prices do not rise. Second, all suppliers try to provide good locations, so the geographical variations in prices is small. Third, the supply of land is so predictable: it is supplied in accordance with a land-use plan at times and locations decided by public bodies, not by private developers. The consequence is, according to Needham *et al.* (1993), that property developers can make normal profits, but no extra profits (by being able to detect and realise development opportunities that their competitors have not grasped). The reason is that developers are taking up too many of the building opportunities made available to them. Property investors also make normal profits, but no extra profits (because the actual returns reflect the expected returns). The reason is that investors are competing against each other to acquire property, which drives up the prices. This makes it profitable for property developers to supply more property, which drives down the rents. The conclusion must be that the unfavourable conditions on Dutch urban real estate markets (to private developers and investors) are the combined effect of both the typical organisational structure of the development industry that is characteristic for commercial real estate markets, the strategies of the developers and investors, and the role of the public sector on these markets. The effects are, however, negative not only for developers and investors. The relatively low capital value of commercial real estate in the Netherlands must be held responsible for a relatively low building quality, as well. As a result of the low returns on investments, the amount of money that can be spent on the building itself in the Netherlands lags behind the amount of money that is spent on real estate projects on international top locations in other West-European countries (see Van der Krabben, 1993a). Finally, referring to the line of argument above, we must take account of the fact that public money is involved. Since developers/investors can only make normal profits, they demand financial support of the public sector in situations featuring high risks (i.e. because of high redevelopment costs). In these situations the public benefit of the public sector investments should always be examined (see also Chapter Ten).

These examples show, again, that public sector strategies meant to improve the allocative efficacy of the commercial real estate market sometimes reduce the productive efficiency of this market.

9.5. Concluding Remarks

Is it possible now to draw conclusions with respect to the efficacy and efficiency of the Dutch national property system, in comparison to the efficacy/efficiency of national property systems in other (West-European) countries? What are the advantages and disadvantages of diverse property systems? The discussion of the Dutch housing provision system in section 9.3 and of the examples of social problems related to the functioning of the commercial real estate market in section 9.4 suggests that the property system is certainly not optimal in the way it 'organises' the functioning of urban real estate markets. Various problematic situations have been recorded in which the property system plays a crucial role. In a number of cases, the institutional organisation of the market can indeed be blamed for socially undesirable outcomes of the development process. In these cases the different rationales behind the strategies of public and private agencies play a role, as do different kinds of institutional inertia (due to insufficient information). Obviously, we must be careful with an overall assessment of the Dutch property system, solely on the basis of the content of the previous sections. It is, at least, too early to conclude that an alternative institutional organisation of the real estate market would lead to better results. The real estate market is a complicated market, characterised -- inter alia -- by various contradictions in interests (see section 9.2). For instance, Needham *et al.* (1993) argue that 'some kind of concentration policy (on the office market, EvdK) would probably be in the general interest. It would not, however, be in the interest of all municipalities and their inhabitants, nor in the interest of all property developers and investors. Moreover, the benefit to property developers and investors might be a temporary effect caused by introducing the policy, rather than a permanent effect of the continued application of the policy' (p. 215). It can be added to this that such a policy would also increase the expenditures for accommodation of the users of the office buildings.

This dilemma -- with respect to changing the property system or not -- holds in fact for most of the examples mentioned here. Therefore, the conclusion must be that the efficacy of the Dutch property system could be improved at several points, but that in all cases we need to take care of the impact of these changes on a variety of issues -- ranging from profit margins for developers, to the expenditures for consumers and to the public interest -- related to the efficiency of the real estate market.

One final issue has been left unnoticed so far: the impact of the Dutch property system, via driving forces behind property development and the outcome of development processes, on urban economic growth. What is the relevance of variations with respect to the functioning of urban real estate markets to the conditions for urban economic growth? Issues that must be examined in this respect include the absolute availability of land and property, purchase costs of land and property for consumers, regional differences in attraction of cities to trade and industry (push- and pull factors), the impact of city marketing, the competitive position of cities in an international context, and the overall costs and benefits of urban economic growth to the society as a whole. With respect to this relation, again the paper by Badcock (1994) is worth mentioning. He has tried to assess the impact of the Dutch property system on the economies of the Randstad cities (Amsterdam, Rotterdam, The Hague, Utrecht). He maintains that there are three main issues to consider. 'The first relates explicitly to the possible role of the property sector in advancing the 'internationalisation' of the Dutch economy. The second raises the question as to whether property is undervalued in the Netherlands due to the intervening effects of public land supply and the subsidy system; and therefore represents potential revenue lost to the municipalities. The third explores the need for some reorganisation of government as a basis for improving the coordination of development activity within the Randstad' (Badcock, 1994: p. 438).

Regarding the first point, how important is the availability of land 'at cost' insofar as it effects the location costs of foreign firms and the housing costs of their expatriate workforce? According to Badcock, the industry opinion is that the expense of office location is a negligible factor in the operating costs of an international corporation. The second issue brings into question the overall costs and benefits to Dutch society of maintaining the current property system. It seems impossible to answer this question -- among other things because most of the cost and benefits cannot be expressed in exact figures. For instance, how should we assess the benefits to the Dutch population from the high quality of the housing stock and the built environment? With respect to the costs, the same difficulties arise. For instance, the characteristically low land values in Dutch cities 'no doubt helps to hold down the total subsidy bill paid by the central government,' but at the same time 'undervalued land and structures represent revenue foregone by the municipalities' (Badcock, 1994: p. 440). The third issue, regarding the coordination of development activity within the Randstad, is again difficult to answer. 'In principle, regional reorganisation would help to alleviate the internecine conflict between municipalities that arises over space for expansion at the edge of the 'big four cities,' as well as paving the way for a coordinated office policy for the Randstad. However, in practice, the need to coordinate land policy across much larger urban regions will inevitably complicate and draw out the decision-making process' (Badcock, 1994: p. 442).

Badcock's final conclusion is that 'assuming that the move to greater regionalisation of urban government within the Randstad does overcome some of the obvious problems of coordination, and given the demonstrable failure of the system in Britain and Australia in the late 1980s (...), *it would be unwise to begin to dismantle a system that has served the Dutch comparatively well*' (Badcock, 1994: p. 442). Badcock's conclusion may be correct; in my opinion, however, his argument still falls short. The relation between real estate development and urban economic growth is obscure (and at present, as we will see in Chapter Ten, the subject of intense debate). Badcock has restricted his analysis to the way the property system 'conditions' urban economic growth. His main concern is with the possible barriers the property system may put up against the proper functioning of the urban economy. However, equally important is whether 'the property system' enables the public sector to stimulate urban economic growth by way of property-led urban regeneration policies. The latter issue will now be examined in Chapter Ten.

10 DIRECTIONS FOR URBAN REGENERATION POLICIES

10.1. Introduction

Chapter Ten addresses two issues. First, it examines the value of *property-led urban regeneration policies* in the context of urban economic growth promotion. Second, and related to the former, the chapter studies the various ways in which the public sector may try to advance real estate development. The motivation for discussing these issues stems from two different developments.

Particularly in Great Britain, a substantial number of studies have appeared in recent years that question possible directions for urban regeneration policies. Property-led urban regeneration policies take up a significant position in the public sector's attempts to stimulate local economic development.[187] They were introduced during the 1980s and, in Great Britain, indicate a clear break with previous policy directions. Real estate development had originally been left to the private sector; from the 1980s on, the public sector started to intervene more directly in this sector. Property-led urban regeneration policies concern various types of policy measures that are directed to promoting private sector property development, in order to improve the conditions for new local economic development initiatives and to encourage firms to establish themselves in the urban region concerned.

This kind of urban policy -- based upon the belief that a strong link exists between real estate development and the urban economy -- has attracted the attention of many authors, leading to an ever-increasing number of studies on the subject. Contributions can be divided into two camps. Some authors argue in favour of property-led urban regeneration policies and emphasise the positive effects of the public sector's support of real estate development projects, while others see serious limits to the success of such policies.

In the Netherlands, urban regeneration policy is not explicitly 'property-led.' However, local authorities have always had a strong influence in the real estate sector, particularly in their role as land suppliers. The municipalities' role in local land markets could indeed be considered as a form of property-led regeneration policy, but has in fact never possessed this status.[188] Dutch municipalities consider it their task always to provide sufficient building land. Public supply of land is, however, not explicitly meant as a policy instrument to stimulate private-sector property development. Whether the local authorities' land policy leads to urban regeneration or not -- via increased activity on the real estate sector -- is only one of the motivations underlying this policy. As a consequence, the phrase 'property-led' urban regeneration policy has no equivalent in the Netherlands. Nevertheless, it is interesting to see how in Dutch cities public-sector policy either directly or indirectly influences the functioning of the real estate market and the outcome of real estate development processes. Do these public-sector real estate market policies generate a positive effect for urban economies? The discussion of these issues also calls into question the social efficiency of public sector investments in real estate development and in urban/regional economic

---

187   Alternative urban-regeneration policies may be directed, for instance, at improving infrastructure, telecommunications, training and education of the workforce, the administrative organisation, etc.

188   Note that in the Netherlands the municipalities' property-led policies (land policy) are concerned not only with redevelopment projects, but with urban expansion projects as well.

development.

A research project that has been recently carried out, initiated by the Dutch Ministry of Economic Affairs, forms the second motivation for analysing the links between the real estate sector and the urban economy (Ministry of Economic Affairs, 1994a,b,c,d,e,f). The research project is meant to support the new National Report on Regional Economic Policy that will be published in 1995. This project investigates the future claims of various sectors of the economy -- notably the business sector, the housing sector, and the recreational sector -- on the land market, and, consequently, relates them to the amount of land that is still available for the specific use. My study is particularly interested in the results of the study of the spatial claims of the business sector (Ministry of Economic Affairs, 1994b). In the Ministry's study the expected level of demand for business sites has been weighed up against the stock of business sites. This research project is exemplary for the growing interest in the Netherlands in the links between real estate development and urban economic growth. However, the supposed relation is more complicated than seems to be assumed in the Ministry of Economic Affairs' research. This chapter will argue that, to be successful, public-sector policy with respect to urban regeneration should include more than just fulfilling the expected future needs of firms for business sites. Moreover, possible side effects of the public supply of business sites -- for instance, regarding the profitability of new development projects -- should be taken into consideration, as well (see section 10.4). It seems rather strange that two different ministries (the Ministry of Housing, Planning, as well as the Environment and the Ministry of Economic Affairs) generate -- from different perspectives -- policies meant to create an optimal spatial structure. It is likely that these policies in some cases contradict each other. This issue, however, I leave aside; the point I want to emphasise in this chapter is that the policies initiated by both Ministries have in common that (the availability of) land and buildings are considered as autonomous factors that are of no concern to regional and urban spatial restructuring (think of the 'service-hatch' argument in Chapter One). This chapter will argue that the way land and buildings are produced needs more attention.

This brings me to the objective of Chapter Ten. I intend to assess the chances of property-led urban regeneration policies and to examine the ways that are open to the public sector to intervene in the real estate development process (with the explicit aim to promote urban real estate development, in order to improve the opportunities for urban economic growth). For this purpose, I will use the existing literature on this topic, interpreting it with the help of the institutional-economic perspective that has been developed in previous chapters of my study. The set-up of the chapter is as follows. Section 10.2 sketches the conceptual links between the real estate sector and urban economic growth. Section 10.3 contains a discussion of the British experience on property-led urban regeneration policies, while the Dutch experience -- shaping the conditions for economic growth -- is the subject of section 10.4. Finally, section 10.5 aims to come to a synthesis: what can be the role of the public sector in stimulating real estate development and can we expect positive effects for urban economic growth?

10.2. The Real Estate Sector and Urban Economic Growth: Conceptual Links

If we want property-led urban regeneration policies to be successful, we must know what kind of links exist between the real estate sector and the urban economy. The public sector may try to promote local economic development by intervening in the property sector. For instance, an improvement of the opportunities available for real estate development, the public sector can attract the development industry to invest in real estate. The thought behind such a policy is that there will be a positive effect to the urban economy. Policymakers hope that firms from outside the region will move to the region concerned, attracted by the availability of business sites and office premises. In this way, thus, the public sector may indeed generate urban economic growth -- but it is certainly not guaranteed. To be more outspoken, is public money being spent efficiently or is it wasted? Moreover, I expect that public-sector interventions in the real estate market will be accompanied by different kinds of side-effects, affecting for instance the value of real estate and/or the profitability of real estate development, which drain possible positive results of this policy. Finally, we must take account of the fact that there is an opposite relation as well: local economic development may also influence the functioning of the real estate market. These pronouncements, not yet supported by empirical evidence, call for a thorough examination of the links between real estate development and the functioning of the urban economy.

Chapter Two already referred to the results of my research carried out in the city of 's-Hertogenbosch (Van der Krabben and Boekema, 1994). In this study I tried to conceptualise the links between real estate development and local economic development. I will summarise the supposed relations now. First, I investigated the impact of local economic development on real estate market functioning. Changing strategies of firms led to an increase in the absolute number of migrations (firms increasingly become 'foot-loose'). As a result, a growth of transactions on the market for second-hand buildings and an increase of new building developments took place. A number of implications for real estate market functioning were noted:

(1) *This implies a more prominent role for the intermediary agents on the real estate market: real estate agents and property developers. In general, the level of and fluctuations in demand for business buildings influence the strategies of the development industry and the profit margins of real estate development. We can speak of institutional change, if the strategies of private developers really change; for instance, they may start to build speculatively and develop more risky projects.*

(2) *Undesirable side effects may appear: vacated, obsolete buildings and high costs of revitalisation in run-down areas and an over-heated land market in the attractive regions.*

(3) *Positive side effects may arise, as well -- particularly in the form of urban renewal.*

(4) *Urban economic growth may directly lead to a scarcity of business sites, resulting in, among other things, rising land prices, rising office rents and rising commercial*

property values, more expensive business accommodation, capital and development gains for the present owners and for property developers, and a considerable growth in the municipalities' revenues from land sales.

(5) *Both the increasing amount of capital that financial institutions pour into the built environment and the changing demands placed on locations and type of buildings by companies have led to the destruction of capital, since buildings are becoming obsolete sooner in functional terms. This is another form of institutional change: the economic life span of business buildings has been reduced, leading to a relatively larger share of new buildings in proportion to existing buildings.*

On the other hand, the special characteristics of urban real estate markets can influence urban economic growth in a number of ways. The impact of the real estate sector on urban economic growth can roughly be divided in *constraints*, on the one hand, and *boosts*, on the other hand. Development constraints have probably received the most attention in the literature.[189] Adams *et al.* (1993) mention different categories of development constraints, including planning constraints, physical and infrastructural constraints, ownership constraints, and valuation constraints.[190] In general, the following constraints and boosts can be distinguished:

(1) *The municipalities, as land developers, affect the firms' choice of where to establish themselves in two ways. The municipalities decide which locations will be developed for new business sites and, moreover, set conditions for establishing certain business parks based on the type and size of the companies.*

(2) *In contrast to the industrial real estate sector, the commercial real estate sector (office buildings) is driven not only by a productive demand, but by an investment demand as well. The inclination of firms to move to new buildings is, to a certain extent, determined by the willingness of the financial sector to invest in real estate (it is revealing in this respect that the degree in which office users move -- the financial sector invests to a larger extent in office buildings compared to industrial buildings -- largely exceeds the number of movers in the manufacturing industry).[191] Furthermore, for property developers, the driving force behind property development is the short-term gain from developing the building and selling it to either the final user or a financial institution. They are not concerned with the existing building stock; thus the*

---

189   See Chapter Two.

190   Valuation constraints may appear when methods of valuation are used incorrectly. 'Where methods of valuation are incorrectly used, land within conurbations may be on the market and appear available for industrial development, but is offered only at a price which potential users are unable to afford. (...) Until site owners come to terms with falling values and reduce their asking prices accordingly or the economy picks up enabling values to rise to meet owners' expectations, a valuation constraint can be said to exist' (Adams *et al.*, 1993: p. 57).

191   Note that a financial institution's decision to invest in property depends, among other things, on the returns that can be made on investments in other financial markets (government bonds, shares).

sooner buildings are written off, the better for them. We may assume that this facilitates firm's migrations to new buildings.

(3) *Both functional and technical ageing are characteristic to real estate. Meanwhile, firms may face difficulties if they intend to move to another building, on an alternative location. When they own the building, it can be problematic to sell their property.[192] As long as they cannot sell, it may be impossible for them to purchase new property. Firms renting office space probably find it less troublesome to relocate. However, a large gap may exist between the rent they pay and the actual level of rent. In both cases we speak of locational inertia (see Chapter Two). This brings us to another point.*

(4) *Apart from a shortage of available business sites, other typical characteristics of urban real estate markets may also frustrate the plans of companies to move to other locations. Particularly, fluctuations in property values (either impeding the purchase of new property or obstructing the sale of their own property) and the evolution of development costs and profit margins for the development industry (influencing the development strategies of the property developers) are relevant in this respect.*

(5) *On the other hand, a clear increase of property values -- especially when this means an enlargement of regional variations in property values -- may just bring about the decision of a firm to rake in the capital gains on their property and to move to another building. Adams et al. (1993: p. 52), for instance, refer to Massey and Meegan (1982), when they suggest that 'in some cases (...) firms may be glad to leave, if substantial sums can be obtained from the sale or development of an existing urban site.'*

(6) *Finally, characteristic to the production of property is that it has an allocation problem. A property developer's response to a demand for buildings is always delayed, because it takes a relatively long time to develop a new building. To avoid this problem, a developer may decide to build speculatively, but then he risks (temporary) vacancy and capital losses. The developer's decision whether or not to accept the risk depends, among other things, on his expectations with respect to the future demand for new buildings.*

The above inventory of relations between the real estate sector and the urban economy is not necessarily exhausting. Nonetheless, it shows that both constraints and boosts partially relate to the typical institutional organisation of the real estate market. The role of municipalities on urban land markets, the involvement of the financial sector with real estate development, the ownership relations on urban real estate markets, the fluctuations and regional variations in property values, the evolution of development gains and profit margins

---

192 Fothergill *et al.* (1987) have studied, with respect to the manufacturing industry, to what extent the problem of locational inertia actually exists in Great Britain and what the consequences are. In the Netherlands, this problem has not yet been. However, it may be expected that in the Netherlands it is of less concern, because the quality of the existing (industrial) building stock is probably better.

all refer to the institutional organisation of the real estate market. Below I will pay more attention to these points.

10.3. The British Experience: property-led urban regeneration policies

In the 1980s and early 1990s urban policy in Great Britain has primarily been based on urban regeneration through private-sector property development (Healey et al., 1992; Turok, 1992; Imrie and Thomas, 1993). The public sector tried to improve the economic performance of cities in Great Britain by attracting the property-development industry to rebuild the city. Various strategies -- from offering cheap building sites to public private partnerships -- can be followed, all in order to rouse the interest of potential investors and property developers. Obviously, the success of such a policy depends primarily on the response of the property-development industry to this challenge. Therefore, the first question that must be answered when evaluating this kind of urban policy is what was the actual response of the development industry? Did the development industry change its strategies? Second, which strategies were at the public sector's disposal to attract the development industry? Third, did the local economy benefit from property-led urban regeneration policies? As Turok wonders, 'can property act as an independent source of dynamism in the process of economic growth?' (Turok, 1992: p. 362). Finally, the implementation of public policy should always raise the question of whether the public money involved was spent effectively. So, has the property emphasis in British urban policy been the most appropriate way to activate the urban economy? What are the risks of this kind of strategy to the public benefit? What are the alternatives that are open to the public sector to stimulate urban economic growth?

These issues have given rise to a dispute on the nature and effectiveness of property-led urban regeneration policies, both with advocates (see especially Healey et al., 1992) and opponents (see Turok, 1992; Imrie and Thomas, 1993). To start with, there seems to be no controversy about the ways in which property -- in principle -- could contribute to urban economic regeneration: 'through the direct employment effects of construction-related activity, by accomodating the expansion of indigenous firms, by attracting inward investment, by revitalising run-down neighbourhoods, and by initiating area-wide economic restructuring' (Turok, 1992: p. 361). However, at this point their ways part. The authors do not agree on (1) the degree in which the public sector is able to affect these links positively, (2) the most effective way of public sector intervention directed at urban regeneration through private sector property development, (3) the side-effects that may appear as a consequence of the public sector's involvement with the property sector, and (4) the actual impact of property-led urban regeneration policies on the economy of British cities in the 1980s and early 1990s.

The book *Rebuilding the City* by Healey et al. (1992) is based on a positive perception of urban regeneration via the property sector. Its main concern is with the actual impact of property-led regeneration policies on urban economies and with the most effective way of public sector intervention directed at property-led urban regeneration. Healey (1992b) examines the potential impact of urban policy on local land and property markets using four models of the development process. Each of these models emphasises a different dynamic for land and property markets. They suggest, therefore, different driving forces for change in the development industry in a locality. To activate the development industry to rebuild the city, public-sector strategies must focus on the possibilities to set these driving forces in the right direction. Consequently, each of the models demands different policy measures. The first model is concerned with supply-side constraints on the production of land and property impeding supply to meet demand. It is assumed that the development process is driven by the demand for land and property for production and consumption. The supply side's response to this demand may, however, be limited by supply-side constraints. These constraints typically concern non-optimal site conditions and poor local infrastructural conditions, inadequate information and monopoly control by public-sector agencies. Healey argues that public policy based on the assumptions underlying this model can be of only limited use. '(...) It is blinkered by the preoccupation with public sector constraints on supply and fails to consider the range of possible constraints which may affect the building and development industry in a locality' (Healey, 1992: p. 26). Plausible constraints that are neglected in this model include the following: (1) tenure patterns, requiring legal support and resources for compulsory purchase; (2) land values may be high because of private sector expectations; (3) environmental problems; and (4) low levels of development activity in the past could lead to a slow local response to the release of supply-side constraints.

The second model focuses on landowners' struggles to capture a share of the surplus value generated in production. The driving force in the development process is believed to be the landowners' search to safeguard rates of return on land and property investment. 'The key issue is the problems landowners may face in conditions of urban decline, and how the strategy of urban regeneration through property development could help them' (*ibid.*: p. 27). The most appropriate public-policy interventions in this respect involve especially the reduction of supply of stock and the limitation of increases in supply. Moreover, landowners would benefit from environmental investments, infrastructure provision and so on, improving the overall conditions of an urban economy.

The third model highlights 'the competition between local and national/international networks, linking capital to development opportunities' (*ibid.*: p. 24). Its concern is with the institutional relations between 'those involved in the development process and the way these connect to other sectors of a local economy, and to regional, national and international financial and development interests' (*ibid.*: p. 30). The driving force behind the institutional dynamics of local property-development activity is, according to this model, the changing flows of finance into and out of the property sector. Healey suggests that regeneration strategies should concentrate on (1) encouraging more people in a locality to come forward to develop, or invest in development, and (2) increasing the density of local relationships, and hence the likelihood that local multiplier effects are generated.

Finally, the fourth model emphasises 'the dynamics of economic restructuring in a global production and consumption framework, and the role of finance capital and property as a financial investment in these processes' (*ibid.*: p. 24). It assumes that investment in the built environment is generated by the needs of production, of consumption, and of financial investment. Regeneration policy should also address the demands of finance capital. 'What this approach emphasizes more than the others is the need not only for a development strategy for the local economy, but for a strategic approach to managing the built environment. This needs to pay attention to amounts of stock in different categories, infrastructure opportunities and constraints, the location of major new investments, and the reconstitution of locales within the urban structure, in terms of their utilities, environmental qualities, and place in the value map' (*ibid.*: p. 33).

Healey's suggestions for public-sector strategies based upon the four models of the development process are not a blueprint for property-led urban regeneration policies. On the contrary, it follows from the above suggests that public sector strategies should explicitly be established on the specific local conditions. The driving forces behind property development must be identified. Healey's line of argument is a plea for a differentiated approach. Both spatial and temporal variations with respect to the organisational structure of the development industry in a locality, the structure of landownership, the relative significance of both producer and investor demand, the institutional relations that dominate in a city, the fragility of the local economy, etc. demand the adjustment of urban regeneration policies to the peculiarity of the situation. Obviously, the effectiveness of property-led urban regeneration policies depends on the success of the public sector to track the driving forces.

Turok (1993) does not question the potential positive economic effects of appropriate property development, but he warns against overenthousiastic expectations of urban policy, exclusively directed at the property sector. Is it worth the public money to facilitate private-sector real estate development and investments? Moreover, unwanted side effects may appear as a result of public-sector interventions in the property sector. One of the reasons for Turok's concern is his observation that 'the links between property and economic regeneration are universally poorly understood and there has been little detailed research on the subject (...)'. He claims that 'in practice it is often simply assumed that private-sector property development is synonymous with economic development, or that there is an inevitable one-way process leading from physical to economic regeneration and community prosperity (...)' (Turok, 1993: pp. 363-364). There is reason to believe that this assumption is false. For instance, empirical evidence suggests 'that the provision of property will lead mostly to local transfers of existing firms or will accomodate firms that would have moved into the region, anyway' (*ibid.*: p. 368). It can be added to this that property provision in one area may possibly even lead to physical dereliction in neighbouring areas. Next to even more limitations to property-led urban regeneration policies, there are also negative side-effects. Turok argues that 'the perceived need to establish a new image and favourable business aura in depressed urban areas has had several effects. Cities have ended up competing with each other for investment and tourism, spending large sums of money on promotion' (*ibid.*: p. 375). These arguments directly call into question whether public money is 'wasted' and could be used in better ways. Nevertheless, despite his different viewpoint, Turok comes more or less to the same conclusion as Healey does: 'finding the most appropriate position for property in urban policy will depend a great deal on the prevailing local circumstances' (*ibid.*: p. 377). That is, the effectiveness of public-sector intervention in the property sector depends greatly on temporal and spatial variations in physical, institutional and economic local conditions.

So far, I have discussed both the potential of and limitations to urban regeneration policies through private sector property development. This section, however, does not yet provide conclusions on the public sector's role on urban real estate markets or on the role of property development in the economic regeneration of cities. Section 10.5 will come back to this point. First, I will turn to the Dutch case.

10.4. The Dutch Experience: Conditions for Economic Growth

Compared to Great Britain, urban policy in the Netherlands has been less dominated by economic regeneration strategies. The urban renewal programme, primarily focussing on social housing, exceeded in size the public sector's involvement with the economic revitalisation of cities. In recent years the emphasis in urban policy has shifted somewhat towards a more economic approach: a policy of "renewing the neighbourhood" has been replaced by a wider policy of "renewing for the city" (Needham *et al.*, 1993: p. 38). Van der Knaap and Van der Laan (1993: p. 483) even argue that public sector policy has completely swung round: '(...) present policies have a too narrow economic perspective, which leads to an underestimation of present and future problems related to the labour and housing market.' However, according to Kreukels and Salet (1992b), Dutch cities have still not been discovered as potential sources of national welfare. In the VINEX Report -- the Dutch national planning report -- urban revitalisation was described as follows: 'the Cabinet lays emphasis on achieving good living and production surroundings, on utilising the available capacity in urban areas for living, working, recreation, and services, and on mixing these functions, all with the aim of maintaining and improving the physical conditions necessary for the city to function well' (MinVrom, 1990; quoted in Needham *et al.*, 1993: pp. 38-39). Needham *et al.* interpret this as: 'in practice this means trying to realize ambitious urban redevelopment schemes by means of public-private partnerships (ppp). In this way, the cities hope to present themselves as irresistibly attractive to firms, institutions and households' (p. 39).

A debate about the pros and cons of property-led urban economic regeneration policy, such as that in Great Britain, has never taken place in the Netherlands on the same level as in Great Britain. Nevertheless, public-sector strategies in Dutch cities have also been partially 'property-led.' Probably, if this debate should ever take place, the discussion would focus on similar points as the debate in Great Britain. It is not my intention, however, at least not in the present section, to discuss extensively the contents of (property-led) urban regeneration policy in the Netherlands (section 10.5 will attend to this point). Neither do I aim to compare the advantages and disadvantages of Dutch urban regeneration policy with the advantages and disadvantages of British policy with respect to the regeneration of cities.[193] I want to examine the role of the property sector with respect to the economy of Dutch cities -- this link is, of course, crucial in property-led urban regeneration policy.[194] Do the activities of the property sector contribute to urban economic regeneration or, oppositely,

---

193 For a detailed comparison of British and Dutch urban regeneration policies: see Kreukels and Salet (1992a).

194 Property-led urban regeneration is restricted to existing, obsolete urban areas. However, my concern here is broader, namely with the relations between the real estate sector and urban economic development in general.

does the typical functioning of the Dutch real estate market -- the strategies of the actors operating on this market -- just serve to obstruct urban economic growth? If the answer to this question is positive, we must also address a related issue, namely the most effective public-sector strategies to intervene in urban real estate markets, with the ultimate goal to generate economic growth. Note that at this point a close link exists with the previous chapter. For, it is aimed to assess the efficacy of the Dutch property system with regard to the degree in which it conditions the functioning of the urban economy.

The results of the research project commissioned by the Ministry of Economic Affairs (1994), *Room for Economic Activity,* make up a good starting point for the analysis of the relation between the real estate market and the economy.[195] As I mentioned above, one of the sections of this project (Ministry of Economic Affairs, 1994b) analysed the future need for business sites. The report concentrates on one specific aspect of that relation, namely the possible constraints that the land market may put up against economic growth. Will the available amount of business sites, both on national scale and split up in urban regions, be sufficient to meet the future demand for expanse as a consequence of the growth of the economy? In some situations, the demand for business sites has to compete, in this respect, with spatial claims for housing, recreational projects, infrastructural projects, etc. Moreover, the way in which potential business locations meet the standards that are required by the business sectors is the subject of the analysis. The ultimate goal of the study is to provide solutions for possible bottlenecks. Translated to the topic of the present section, the study by the Ministry of Economic Affairs concerns itself, essentially, with the strategies the public sector should use to intervene in the functioning of urban real estate markets. These public sector strategies are meant to remove potential obstacles to economic growth.

Room for Economic Activity contains a detailed analysis of the future demand for and supply of business locations. With respect to the supply of these business locations, the authors distinguish between the stock of business sites in different regions and between different types of locations (from seaport locations to high-quality locations for a special category of users, and from inner-city areas to locations on the urban fringe). Moreover, they judge the degree of 'solidity' of the local authorities' plans for new business locations. The supply is then confronted with the future demand for business locations. The report concludes that a shortage of business locations will probably appear in the majority of regions that have been distinguished, taking into consideration the future need both for office space and for buildings used by the manufacturing industry. To guarantee a sufficient supply of land for various economic activities in the future, the report recommends finding solutions for the following bottlenecks:

(1) the public sector's attention for and information about (changes in) demand and supply on land markets is inadequate;
(2) certain economic activities are increasingly excluded from establishment or expansion

---

195   Note that the report does not exclusively focus on public-sector strategies for the economic regeneration of existing urban areas. Its main concern is with the development of public-sector policy to take away any property-related obstructions to economic growth, both in existing urban areas and in new expansion areas. Nevertheless, the results of the report are certainly also valuable in the context of the present study, which is restricted to urban regeneration policy in existing urban areas. What I intend to emphasise here is the supposed relation between real estate sector activities and urban regional economic growth in this research project.

on attractive locations, mainly because of environmental objections;
(3) sometimes public sector policy creates an (unintended) scarcity of business locations, without recognising the needs of economic activities;
(4) a growing competition for expansion areas between different 'sectors' has arisen. Notably, the spatial claims by the housing sector reduces the potential amount of building land for business sectors;
(5) shortcomings in the planning system -- economic activities are sometimes put at a disadvantage in relation to alternative activities -- impede the smooth functioning of the land market;
(6) long-lasting development procedures slow down development processes and obstruct the realisation of new projects.

These recommendations are, in my opinion, too short-sighted. The analysis of future demand and supply on urban land markets does not take into consideration possible reasons -- with respect to the expected shortage of building land -- that are related to the characteristics of urban land and property markets. For instance, land-development costs, ownership constraints, infrastructural constraints, financial constraints or real estate development, etc. may all act as a constraint to new developments. From the above enumeration of bottlenecks, it can be gathered that in the report only constraints that are (unintentionally) caused by local public-sector policies are recognised. The report leaves aside completely the role of the real estate sector. Referring to the first chapter of the present study, we can conclude that it is apparently assumed in the Ministry of Economic Affairs report that the real estate market functions perfectly as a go-between. Throughout the chapters of this book I have argued that this assumption is false and may lead to incorrect public sector interventions in the real estate market. The Ministry of Economic Affairs chooses to influence the supply of building land, but completely passes over the way building land is supplied, price developments on the land market, ownership relations on regional/urban land markets, the strategies of the development industry with respect to land development, the degree to which private developers are prepared to develop real estate, the demands of finance capital with respect to real estate investments, and fluctuations in the profitability of real estate development.[196]

Our attention for the real estate sector's part in the urban/regional economy should particularly focus on factors that influence the strategies of private developers and investors, like uncertainty about future directions of public sector policy and on the rationality of their behaviour, on the impact of institutional changes - not only changes in government policy, but also structural changes in the strategies of private agencies - on the functioning of urban/regional land and property markets, and on institutional constraints (institutional inertia) that impede the smooth functioning of the real estate market. With respect to these institutional constraints I refer to, for instance, the inability of private developers in certain regions to respond in time to new development opportunities, the (financial) constraints on

---

[196] The housing market provides a good example of what can happen when the functioning of the real estate market is not sufficiently paid attention to in public sector policy. The early designation of the VINEX locations has led to undesired -- from a social point of view -- speculative behaviour of private developers on these locations.

firms to move to a new building, and the inability of municipalities to prevent speculative land purchases by private agencies in future expansion areas (combined with the financial risks these municipalities run).

The policy recommendations that follow from this analysis are in principle valuable in the pursuit of avoiding shortages of business sites. However, without more information on the causes of this shortage the effect of the recommendations is still dubious. The purpose of these recommendations is to facilitate the relocation of firms, in all sectors of the economy, and the migration/establishment of international firms to Dutch cities. This objective has in fact always dominated Dutch urban and regional economic policy. It is critical to an assessment of urban economic policy to realize that discrepancies are likely to appear between such a policy and public sector policy directed at tempting the property development industry to develop and invest in new real estate projects (while their ultimate perspective is identical). More precisely, the recommmendations by the Ministry of Economic Affairs may reduce the attractiveness of real estate development for developers/investors.

Finally, *Room for Economic Activity* must be criticized on one final point. Negative side-effects that are likely to appear are neglected. What will be the consequence of the relocation and inter-regional migration of firms in less-attractive regions? It may lead to capital losses for existing real estate owners and to the destruction of capital (since the economic life span of buildings will be reduced), it will result in new deprived business areas (that possibly must be revitalized with help of public money in the near future), and it will lead to an increased - and unwanted - competition between regions to attract firms, with winners, but also with losers. With help of the 'lessons' from the British experience I will now try to work out a number of recommendations meant to improve the efficacy of Dutch urban economic policy.

10.5. Synthesis: Public Policy, the Real Estate Sector and the Urban Economy

This final section brings together two issues. First, I intend to make a number of recommendations with respect to the directions for the public sector's property-led urban regeneration strategies, taking into account the limits to this kind of policy. I also intend to indicate the conditions that the internal dynamics of the real estate sector impose on the potential impact of urban economic regeneration policy in general. It is, furthermore, essential to specify -- regarding the chance of success of public sector policy -- the role of the property system. The latter point refers of course to the content of Chapter Nine, debating the efficacy of property systems.

This synthesis consists of a number of observations and conclusions. (1) First, it has been noted that the public sector, i.c. the local authorities, aims to induce urban economic growth. Stimulating local economic development is considered to be one of the public sector's strategies to generate national economic growth. (2) Second, the public sector, in its attempts to activate local economic development, often stimulates the real estate sector to develop and invest in new real estate projects. I have defined this as property-led urban regeneration policies. (3) Third, the public sector has several policy measures at its disposal to achieve this objective. Section 10.3 mentions four directions for public sector policy, ranging from a public policy directed at taking away supply-side constraints to the reduction of the supply of stock and the limitation of increases in supply to a public policy aiming to strengthen local institutional relations to a strategic approach to managing the built environment. The interventions of local authorities in the real estate sector vary according to the 'approach' that is followed. (4) Fourth, the chance of success of these differents approaches depends on *the nature of supply* in a locality (type and quality of the existing building stock, ownership relations, rental levels, type and quality of new buildings, location of both existing and newly developed buildings, etc.), *the nature of demand* (the size of demand for land and buildings), and the typical local/national *institutional organisation of the real estate market*. The latter point alludes to the organisational structure of the development industry, the strategies of market parties, government policy, rules and norms, and property rights.

(5) The considerations above lead me to conclude that a strategic approach to managing the built environment is the most promising way to stimulate real estate development. This approach recognises not only the nature of supply and demand (the amount, but also the type and quality, the location, etc), but also the various requirements of market parties, the significance of institutional relations, the relevance of the location to the profitability and costs of new developments, changes in real estate values and rental levels, and potential constraints; in short, the typical characteristics of the property system. Note, however, that such an approach is no guarantee for success. Crucial to urban management is the continual monitoring of the local real estate market.

(6) The typical characteristics of the property system must explicitly be considered as conditions to any form of public-sector intervention. Recall that the Dutch Ministry of Economic Affairs report (section 10.4), left these characteristics completely aside. Section 10.2 mentioned various situations in which the real estate sector can frustrate the successful implementation of public sector policy. On the other hand, the real estate market can also act as a boost to new real estate developments. In such a situation, the public sector can rather easily respond to private sector initiatives.

(7) Stimulating real estate development is one thing, generating economic growth via real estate development is another. Clear limits exist to the impact of real estate development on the urban economy (see Turok's argument in section 10.3). Therefore, it seems advisable to weigh the costs and benefits of public sector interventions in the real estate market and to compare them with alternative strategies to promote urban economic development.

(8) The above-mentioned points jointly call for a shift in Dutch public sector policy on urban real estate markets. The policy direction that underlies the Ministry of Economic Affairs research project -- always to take care of a sufficient supply of building land -- is too narrow in its approach. We need, rather, an urban economic policy that explicitly takes account of the functioning of the real estate market. I have emphasised that the public sector needs more information about the functioning of urban real estate markets and the nature of the relation between the real estate market and the urban economy.

(9) Related to the former point, I have argued that the implementation of both the Ministry of Economic Affairs' policy and the Ministry of Housing, Planning and the Environment's policy have imprtant implications for spatial restructuring processes in the Netherlands. However, both ministries interpret 'land' as an autonomous factor and take insufficiently into account the way land and property are *produced*. Moreover, it is essential

to the efficacy of public-sector policy that both ministries' policies, as far as spatial restructuring processes are affected, should be better geared to one another.

(10) Finally, the ultimate question that this chapter raises is whether we should favour a property system that incites local authorities, within one country, to compete with each other in their efforts to attract companies to their respective municipalities. This issue must be debated because not only is a considerable amount of public money spent on this policy (and, furthermore, that such a policy involves substantial financial risks for the public sector), but hand the benefits to local economic development and employment are at least dubious. Positive economic and employment effects in one locality -- the company's new home town -- are annulled by the negative effects in an other locality - the company's former home town. Moreover, urban regeneration via the property sector often leads to intra-regional migration (rather than the wished for interregional or international migration), with no positive regional employment effects at all. I certainly do not want to suggest that the public money that has been spent in the past on urban economic regeneration policy has been wasted -- indeed, numerous examples exist of successful urban revitalisation in Dutch cities -- but we must be aware of the fact that part of the public money has actually been a veiled subsidy to both the real estate sector (cheap building land, reduction of risks) and the companies that moved to new buildings (cheap business accomodation). Perhaps these veiled subsidies are necessary to guarantee the profitability of private-sector real estate development and/or to enable companies to move into new buildings that they need e.g. for production expansion, but the truth is that our information about the profitability of real estate development and the costs of business accomodation is incomplete. This line of argument immediately calls into question whether the *social efficiency* of public-sector investments in real estate development and in urban/regional economic development is sufficient. My arguments also lead to the conclusion that social efficiency will be improved if we take better account of the functioning of land and property markets and, related to this, of the factors that influence the efficiency of property-development processes (together with the willingness of the Ministry of Housing, Planning and the Environment and the Ministry of Economic Affairs to gear their activities better to one another).

SAMENVATTING

In deze studie is gezocht naar verklaringen voor processen van ontwikkeling en herontwikkeling die zich in steden, en met name in Nederlandse steden, voordoen. Met ontwikkelingsprocessen doel ik op de ontwikkelingen die zich voordoen op stedelijke onroerend-goedmarkten. Op deze markten worden bouwgrond en gebouwen ontwikkeld, worden grond en gebouwen verhandeld en verhuurd, en worden gebouwen uiteindelijk ook weer afgebroken, waarna de grond weer herontwikkeld kan worden. De studie richt zich met name op de wijze waarop grond en gebouwen ontwikkeld worden, op de aanbodzijde van de onroerend-goedmarkt dus - maar dan nog uitsluitend het aanbod van nieuwbouw en van bouwgrond. Wie zijn de bouwers en ontwikkelaars, met wiens geld worden vastgoedontwikkelingen gefinancierd, wat kost het, wie verdient er aan en hoeveel, welke strategieën worden door marktpartijen en overheden gevoerd en waarom, etc. Met betrekking tot de aanbodzijde van de onroerend-goedmarkt is vooral ingegaan op de wijze waarop het aanbod van grond en gebouwen in Nederlandse steden beïnvloed wordt door de organisatiestructuur van de onroerend-goedmarkt.

Een tweetal ontwikkelingen/constateringen vormen de aanleiding tot dit onderzoek. In de eerste plaats blijkt dat de factor "ruimte" een steeds belangrijkere plaats gaat innemen in het functioneren van stedelijke of regionale economieën. De aandacht richt zich op de vraag waar nieuwe economische activiteiten gerealiseerd dienen te worden, maar ook op de vraag of er nog wel voldoende ruimte beschikbaar is om toekomstige economische groei en woningbouw op te kunnen vangen en of de verschillende claims op de ruimte niet conflicterend zijn. Bij de beantwoording van die vragen wordt mijns inziens te weinig rekening gehouden met de wijze waarop die ruimte beschikbaar komt - de productie van bouwgrond dus - en óf die ruimte überhaupt wel beschikbaar komt. Bovendien wordt onvoldoende rekening gehouden met de productie van het gebouw zelf. Met andere woorden, de productie van grond en gebouwen en de wijze waarop die productie de voortgang van ruimtelijk-economische ontwikkelingen kan belemmeren verdient veel meer belangstelling.

In de tweede plaats is bekend dat veel gemeenten zich bij de uitvoering van stedelijk-economisch beleid juist richten op de vastgoedsector. Gemeenten stellen plannen voor nieuwe kantorenprojecten op, ze ontwikkelen nieuwe bedrijventerreinen, ze gaan samenwerkingsovereenkomsten aan met vastgoedpartijen om kantorenprojecten te ontwikkelen, en ze subsidiëren (met rijksgelden) vastgoedontwikkelingen door marktpartijen. Behalve dat de overheid de ontwikkeling van bedrijventerreinen, de ontwikkeling van kantorenprojecten in binnenstedelijke gebieden, en de woningbouw vaak met vrij aanzienlijke bedragen subsidieert, is zij in veel projecten - bijvoorbeeld bij de ontwikkeling van bouwgrond - vaak ook nog risicodrager. Dit roept de vraag op wat nu eigenlijk het maatschappelijk rendement is van deze overheidsinvesteringen.

De studie besteedt, zoals gezegd, vooral aandacht aan de betekenis van de institutionele context voor het functioneren van stedelijke grond- en vastgoedmarkten. Wat houdt de institutionele organisatie van de markt eigenlijk in, welke aspecten daarvan zijn belangrijk voor een discussie van marktprocessen, hoe komt die organisatiestructuur tot stand, welke veranderingen vinden er in plaats en waarom, in welke opzichten kan die organisatiestructuur, bijv. in internationaal opzicht, verschillen? De institutionele context is veel meer dan alleen overheidsbeleid. Bij de institutionele organisatie van een markt moeten we ook denken aan de samenstelling van bijv. de groep ontwikkelaars en bouwers op een stedelijke vastgoedmarkt, aan de verschillende strategieën van marktpartijen, aan allerlei relaties tussen marktpartijen die niet via de markt lopen (van pps-constructies tot informele netwerken), aan eigendomsverhoudingen, aan allerlei regels - niet alleen in de vorm van wetten, maar ook normen en waarden - die van invloed zijn op het marktproces, aan de betekenis van nieuwe ideeën, nieuwe technologieën, etc. Met betrekking tot de institutionele context moet ook aandacht besteed worden aan de rol die onzekerheid c.q. onvolledige informatie speelt in marktprocessen. Onzekerheid neemt een centrale plaats in de economie in. Veel marktprocessen worden sterk beïnvloed door de mate van onzekerheid. Denk maar eens aan de onzekerheid die er bestaat ten aanzien van de toekomstige opbrengsten van bijvoorbeeld commercieel vastgoed en de rol die dat speelt in de beslissingen die vastgoedontwikkelaars nemen ten aanzien van de ontwikkeling van nieuwe projecten.

Het belang van de institutionele organisatie van vastgoedmarkten komt nog het beste tot uiting als we kijken naar veranderingen die zich op deze markt voordoen in de loop der tijd, of als we kijken naar internationale verschillen in markt-performance. Zowel die veranderingen in de loop der tijd, als die internationale verschillen zijn vaak slechts goed te begrijpen als we ons richten op institutionele veranderingen en op institutionele verschillen. Om een voorbeeld te noemen: het feit dat Nederlandse gemeenten zich op de grondmarkt lange tijd tevreden hebben gesteld met de verkoop van bouwgrond tegen kostprijs, terwijl het zeker niet uitgesloten is dat de waarde van de grond op sommige locaties hoger was, heeft allerlei consequenties voor het functioneren van de grondmarkt. Als de grondprijzen bijvoorbeeld ineens zouden stijgen, zou onderzocht kunnen worden of die prijsstijging veroorzaakt wordt door een plotseling toegenomen vraag naar bouwgrond, met als gevolg schaarste, of dat er sprake is van een institutionele verandering. In dat laatste geval zouden bijvoorbeeld vele gemeenten er plotseling toe over kunnen zijn gegaan om marktprijzen te vragen voor bouwgrond op aantrekkelijke locaties, waar zij zich voorheen tevreden stelden met de kostprijs. Dat duidt niet alleen op veranderende strategieën van gemeenten, maar kan er bovendien toe leiden dat zich fundamentele veranderingen voordoen in de verdeling van ontwikkelingswinsten op de grondmarkt of dat marktpartijen eveneens hun strategieën wijzigen.

Om in staat te zijn om de invloed van institutionele factoren gedegen te analyseren heb ik gebruik gemaakt van de inzichten die institutioneel-economische theorieën opleveren ten aanzien van, onder andere, de rol van instituties, van institutionele verschillen en veranderingen, het verband tussen marktprocesses en allerlei processen die zich buiten de markt om voordoen. Met behulp van institutioneel economische theorie is een denkkader ontwikkeld dat het mogelijk maakt de institutionele organisatie van grond- en vastgoedmarkten, en de invloed daarvan op marktprocessen, te kunnen analyseren.

Het doel van de studie is drieledig. In de eerste plaats vindt een analyse plaats van de institutionele organisatie van stedelijke onroerend-goedmarkten, met name in Nederlandse steden; in de tweede plaats onderzoekt de studie de betekenis van institutionele veranderingen en van (internationale) verschillen in de institutionele context; en in de derde plaats analyseert de studie de invloed van de institutionele context op vastgoedontwikkelingsprocessen. Deze aspecten worden vooral onderzocht in relatie tot stedelijke grondmarkten en de koopwoningenmarkt in Nederland. De grondmarkt staan momenteel in de belangstelling, onder meer omdat de beschikbaarheid van bouwgrond een probleem dreigt te worden. Gemeenten in Nederland zien het als hun taak altijd voldoende bouwgrond aan te bieden. Die taak is momenteel echter minder gemakkelijk uit te voeren dan voorheen het geval was. Van verschillende kanten is gewaarschuwd dat, als er niets verandert, er een tekort aan nieuwbouwwoningen zal ontstaan, en dat de economische groei in sommige regio' zal stagneren, omdat er onvoldoende uitbreidings- en vestigingsmogelijkheden voor bedrijven zijn. De koopwoningenmarkt wordt gekenmerkt door, onder andere, een vrij sterke stijging van de huizenprijzen - met belangrijke consequenties voor huidige eigenaren, toekomstige eigenaren, en projectontwikkelaars. Daarnaast heeft het Rijk zich, in financieel opzicht, teruggetrokken van de woningmarkt, waardoor nu een aanzienlijk groter deel van de nieuwbouw ongesubsidieerd dient plaats te vinden. Het dreigende tekort aan nieuwbouwwoningen verdient meer aandacht. De vraag is of de oorzaak alleen gezocht moet worden bij een tekort aan bouwlocaties. Deze studie beargumenteert dat er meer aan de hand is.

De centrale probleemstelling voor het onderzoek luidt als volgt: "In welke zin wordt het functioneren van stedelijke grond- en onroerend-goedmarkten beïnvloed door de institutionele organisatie van de markt, wat zijn de gevolgen van die beïnvloeding voor de uitkomst van stedelijke (her-)ontwikkelingsprocessen, en welke veranderingen hebben plaatsgevonden in de institutionele context van stedelijke onroerend-goedmarkten?"

De studie is als volgt opgebouwd. Hoofdstuk Een geeft de maatschappelijke relevantie van het onderzoek weer. Er zijn onder meer een aantal vastgoedontwikkelingen in Nederlandse steden besproken waar sprake is van maatschappelijk ongewenste effecten. In die voorbeelden wordt duidelijk gemaakt dat *institutional constraints* daarin een belangrijke rol kunnen spelen.

Hoofdstuk Twee bespreekt relevante literatuur op het terrein van vastgoedonderzoek. Er is met name aandacht besteed aan institutionele analyses van stedelijke vastgoedontwikkelingen. Daarnaast zijn de *missing links* tussen stedelijk-economische theorievorming en vastgoedontwikkeling besproken. In het hoofdstuk wordt beargumenteerd dat in veel theoretische benaderingen van stedelijke dynamiek onvoldoende rekening wordt gehouden met de wijze waarop grond en gebouwen tot stand komen. Tegelijkertijd wordt echter ook naar een aantal studies verwezen waarin die ontwikkelingsprocessen juist wel centraal staan. Die studies vormen in feite de bouwstenen voor dit boek. Er worden een aantal thema's voor onderzoek in aangegeven, die ik als leidraad gebruikt heb bij deze studie. Daarbij gaat het om de betekenis van en veranderingen in verschillende kapitaalstromen op de vastgoedmarkt, om de veranderende strategieën van marktpartijen die betrokken zijn bij vastgoedontwikkeling, om de verschillende manieren waarop de overheid ingrijpt op vastgoedprocessen, en om de relatie tussen processen van vastgoedontwikkeling en stedelijk economische ontwikkeling.

In Part II (hoofdstukken Drie, Vier, en Vijf) wordt de theoretische basis van het proefschrift behandeld. In Hoofdstuk Drie wordt eerst aandacht besteed aan alternatieve verklaringen en analyses van vastgoedprocessen. Ik heb duidelijk proberen te maken dat het doel en object van studie van deze analyses verschilt van het perspectief dat in de huidige studie gekozen is. Hoofdstuk Vier gaat in op de stand van zaken met betrekking tot institutioneel-economische theorie. In het hoofdstuk is een *denkkader* ontwikkeld. Het denkkader, gebaseerd op institutioneel economische theorie, stelt vier thema's centraal die van belang zijn in het onderzoek naar de institutionele organisatie van de onroerend-goedmarkt: (1) de rol van informatieproblemen en onzekerheid in de markt, (2) de gevolgen van het feit dat het gedrag van verschillende actoren gekenmerkt kan worden door verschillende rationaliteiten, (3) de invloed van institutionele veranderingen op marktprocessen, en (4) de betekenis van padafhankelijkheid van een markt voor het functioneren van die markt. In Hoofdstuk Vijf wordt het theoretisch kader dan toegepast bij de analyse van onroerend-goedontwikkeling. Deze operationalisering heeft plaatsgevonden aan de hand van de zojuist genoemde thema's. Het doel van Hoofdstuk Vijf is om, met behulp van het institutioneel-economische denkkader, een aantal ontwikkelingen nader te interpreteren die van belang lijken te zijn voor het functioneren van stedelijke vastgoedmarkten.

Part III gaat in op de resultaten van een case study naar het functioneren van de grond- en woningbouwmarkt in Nederland. In deze case study is achtereenvolgens onderzocht de kenmerken van de organisatiestructuur van de Nederlandse woningbouwmarkt (hoofdstuk Zes), trends in woningbouwproductie en in de strategieën van de marktpartijen (hoofdstuk Zeven), en de (betekenis van) institutionele veranderingen die hebben plaatsgevonden in de afgelopen vijfentwintig jaar (hoofdstuk Acht). Het in hoofdstuk vier en vijf ontworpen denkkader is als leidraad voor het onderzoek gebruikt. De case study beoogt expliciet duidelijk te maken wat het belang is van de organisatiestructuur van de woningbouwmarkt voor de woningbouw, en dan met name de vrije-sector woningbouw. Een belangrijke aanleiding voor het uitvoeren van deze studie vormde het debat dat momenteel gevoerd wordt met betrekking tot de vermeende tekorten in woningbouwproductie. Er zijn argumenten aangevoerd dat de verklaring, als zouden deze tekorten uitsluitend samenhangen met het tekort aan woningbouwgrond, tekort schiet. Dieperliggende oorzaken, gerelateerd aan de rol van gemeenten op de grondmarkt, de strategieën van projectontwikkelaars, en structurele kenmerken van de woningbouwmarkt, spelen een minstens zo belangrijke rol. Door de gekozen opzet van de studie is het niet mogelijk de precieze betekenis van institutionele factoren in woningbouwontwikkelingen te bewijzen of te testen. Wél laat de studie zien dat in veel gevallen onderzoek naar bijvoorbeeld de strategieën van projectontwikkelaars en van overheden, naar de rationaliteit achter de beslissing van huiseigenaren te kopen of verkopen, naar de oorzaken achter allerlei institutionele veranderingen en de gevolgen ervan voor het functioneren van de markt een bijdrage kan leveren aan een beter begrip van vastgoedontwikkeling.

Part IV beoogt tenslotte tot een evaluatie van de studie te komen. In hoofstuk Negen is het Nederlandse *property system* beoordeeld op haar allocatieve doelmatigheid en op de efficiëntie van het productieproces (de productie van grond en gebouwen). In Hoofdstuk Negen ben ik ingegaan op de voorwaarden voor een doelmatig overheidsoptreden op stedelijke grond- en gebouwenmarkten en op de voorwaarden voor een efficiënt opererende onroerend-goedmarkt. Ik heb getracht duidelijk te maken dat juist het ruimtelijke-ordeningsbeleid van de overheid in sommige gevallen de efficiëntie van de grond- en gebouwenproductie niet ten goede komt. Bovendien heb ik enige kanttekeningen geplaatst, zonder daar overigens harde bewijzen voor te hebben, bij de strategieën van marktpartijen op de onroerend-goedmarkt. In hoofdstuk Tien zijn verschillende beleidsrichtingen besproken voor regionaal- en stedelijk herstructureringsbeleid. Deze bespreking heeft plaatsgevonden aan de hand van een analyse van de relaties tussen processen van vastgoedontwikkeling en regionaal-/stedelijke economische groei. Twee thema's staan centraal in dit laatste hoofdstuk. In de eerste plaats is aandacht besteed aan de vraag of een stedelijke herstructureringsstrategie *via de vastgoedsector* bijdraagt aan meer algemeen overheidsbeleid gericht op regionaal-/stedelijke economische groei. In de tweede plaats ben ik ingegaan op de verschillende manieren waarop gemeenten kunnen proberen vastgoedontwikkelingen te stimuleren. Door middel van deze twee thema's is nader ingegaan op, in de eerste plaats, de voorwaarden die vanuit de vastgoedsector gesteld worden aan een succesvol regionaal-/stedelijk economische beleid, en, in de tweede plaats, op het maatschappelijk nut van ruimtelijke (overheids-)investeringen. De uiteindelijke conclusie is dat het maatschappelijk nut van overheidsinvesteringen verbeterd zou kunnen worden door beter in te spelen op het functioneren van grond- en vastgoedmarkten en op de factoren die de efficiëntie van vastgoedontwikkelingsprocessen beïnvloeden. Daarnaast zou een betere afstemming tussen het beleid van het Ministerie van Economische Zaken en het Ministerie van VROM waarschijnlijk eveneens bijdragen aan een effectiever gebruik van overheidsgelden.

REFERENCES

Adams, C.D., A.E. Baum and B.D. MacGregor (1988) The availability of land for inner city development: a case study of inner Manchester. *Urban Studies*, 25 (1), pp. 62-76.

Adams, C.D. and H.G. May (1991), Active and Passive Behaviour in Land Ownership. *Urban Studies*, 28 (5), pp. 687-705.

Adams, C.D. (1991) Meeting the needs of industry? The performance of industrial land and property markets in inner Manchester and Salford, in: P. Healey and R. Nabarro (*eds.*) *Land and Property Development in a Changing Context*, Aldershot: Gower.

Adams, C.D., H.G. May, and T. Pope (1992) Changing strategies for the acquisition of re-siden-tial development land, *Journal of Property Research*, 9, pp. 209-226.

Adams, C.D, L. Russel, and C. Taylor-Russel (1992) The demand for industrial land: a North West case study. *Regional Studies*, 26 (6), 586-592.

Adams, C.D., L. Russell and C.S. Taylor-Russell (1993) Development constraints, market processes and the supply of industrial land. *Journal of Property Research*, 10, pp. 49-61.

Adams, C.D. (1994) *Urban Planning and the Development Process*. London: UCL Press.

Alexander, E.R. (1992) A transaction cost theory of planning. *Journal of the American Plan-ning Association*, Spring, pp. 157-173.

Alonso, W. (1964), *Location and Land Use*. Cambridge, MA: Harvard University Press.

Amin, A. and N. Thrift (1992) Neo-Marshallian nodes in global networks, *International Journal of Urban and Regional Research*, 16, pp. 571-587.

Amin, A. and N. Thrift (1993) *Globalisation, institutional thickness and local prospects*. Paper presented at workshop on 'Challenges in Urban Management', March 1993, University of Newcastle-upon-Tyne.

Amin, A. and N. Thrift (*Eds.*) (1994) *Holding Down the Global*. Oxford: Oxford University Press.

Badcock, B. (1994) The strategic implications for the Randstad of the Dutch property system. *Urban Studies*, 31 (3), pp. 425-445.

Balchin, P.N, J.L. Kieve and G.H. Bull (1988) *Urban land economics and public policy*, London: MacMillan.

Ball, M. (1983) *Housing Policy and Economic Power*. London: Methuen.

Ball, M., V. Bentivegna, M. Edwards, and M. Folin (*eds.*) (1985) *Land Rent, Housing and Urban Planning: A European Perspective*. London: Croom Helm.

Ball, M. (1985) Land rent and the construction industry, in: M. Ball, V. Bentivegna, M. Edwards, and M. Folin (*eds.*), *Land Rent, Housing and Urban Planning: A European Perspective*, London: Croom Helm.

Ball, M. (1986) The Built environment and the urban question, *Environment and Planning D: Society and Space*, vol. 4., pp. 447-464.

Ball, M. (1988) *Rebuilding Construction - economic change in the British construction industry*, London: Routledge.

Ball, M. and M. Harloe (1993) Rhetorical Barriers to Understanding Housing Provision: What the 'Provision Thesis' is and is not, *Housing Studies*, 7 (1), pp. 3-15.

Barkema, H.G. (1995) Prikkels en prestaties. *Economische Statistische Berichten*, (80), 8-3-1995, nr. 4000, pp. 228-230.

Barlow, J. and S. Duncan (1995) *Success and Failure in Housing Provision - European*

Systems Compared. Oxford: Pergamon Press.

Barras, R. (1983) A simple theoretical model of the office-development cycle, *Environment and Planning A*, 15, pp. 1381-1394.

Barras, R. (1984) The office development cycle in London, *Land Development Studies*, 1, pp. 35-50.

Barras, R. (1985) Development profit and development control: the case of office development in London, in: S.M. Barrett and P. Healey (*eds.*) *Land Policy: Problems and Alternatives.* Aldershot: Gower.

Barras, R. (1987) Technical change and the urban development cycle, *Urban Studies*, 24, pp. 5-30.

Barrett, S.M. and P. Healey (eds.) (1985) *Land Policy: Problems and Alternatives.* Aldershot: Gower.

Bassett, K. and J. Short (1980) *Housing and Residential structure: Alternative Approaches*, London: Routledge.

Bateman, M. (1985) *Office Development: a Geographical Perspective.* London: Croom Helm.

Beauregard, R.A. (1991) Capital restructuring and the new built environment of global cities: New York and Los Angeles. *International Journal of Urban and Regional Research*, 15, pp. 90-105.

Berg, L. van der (1985) *Urban Systems in a Dynamic Society*, PhD Thesis, Rotterdam: Erasmus University.

Berry, M. and M. Huxley (1992) Big Build: Property Capital, the State and Urban Change in Australia. *International Journal of Urban and Regional Research*, 16 (1), pp. 35-59.

Berry, J., S. McGreal, and B. Deddis (*eds.*) (1993) *Urban Regeneration, Property investment and development.* London: E. and F.N. Spon.

Blankenstein-Bouwmeester, A. and P. Lukkes (1984) *Institutionele beleggers op de markt voor onroerend goed.* Sociaal-geografische Reeks nr. 29. Groningen: University of Groningen.

Boekema, F. and E. van der Krabben (1992) Regio's, sectoren en vastgoed, *Stedebouw en Volkshuisvesting*, 73 (2), pp. 19-25.

Boelhouwer, P. and H. van der Heijden (1989) *Vrije-sectorwoningbouw: consequenties voor de ruimtelijke ordening, de volkshuisvesting en de bouwnijverheid.* Delft: Delft University Press.

Boelhouwer, P. and H. van der Heijden (1992) *Housing systems in Europe: Part I: A comparative study of housing policy.* Housing and Urban Policy Studies, No. 1. Delft: Delft University Press.

Boelhouwer, P. and H. Priemus (1990) Dutch housing policy realigned. *Netherlands Journal of Housing and Environmental Research*, 5, pp. 105-119.

Bos, C., J. Buit, K. Dobben, J. Walen, J., and M. Wingens (*Eds.*) (1987) *Successen en mislukkingen in de Nederlandse ruimtelijke ordening.* Amsterdam: PDI, University of Amsterdam.

Bovaird, T. (1992) Local Economic Development and the City. *Urban Studies*, vol. 29 (3/4), pp. 343-368.

Bovaird, T. (1993) Analysing Urban Economic Development. *Urban Studies*, vol. 30 (4/5), pp. 631-658.

Broek, P.J. van den (1988) *Overheid en bouwgrondprijzen, het beleid sinds de jaren vijftig.*

Amsterdam: Stichting voor Economisch Onderzoek.
Broek, P.J. van den and J. Schellevis (1994) *Woonwensen in ruimtelijk en economisch perspectief*. Amsterdam: Economisch Instituut voor de Bouwnijverheid.
Brouwer, H.J. (1989) The Spatial Restructuring of the Amsterdam Office-Market, *Netherlands Journal of Housing and Environmental Research*, 4 (3), pp. 257-274.
Brouwer, H.J. (1994) *Kantorenmarkt en Stadsstructuur*, Phd Thesis, Amsterdam: University of Amsterdam.
Brouwer, J. (1990) *Ruimte voor investeringen*. Delft: Waltman.
Brown, H.J., R.S. Philips and N.A. Roberts (1981) Land markets and the urban fringe: new insight for policy makers. *Journal of the American Planning Association*, 47, pp. 131-144.
Burger, J. (1990) *Bedrijfs- en overheidsbeleid in de woningbouw*. PhD Thesis, Rotterdam: University of Rotterdam.

Castells, M. (1973) *The Urban Question*, London: Edward Arnold.
Castells, M. (1989) *The informational city*, London: Basil Blackwell.
Chambert, H. (1988) *The Dynamics of Urban Development - Building, Housing and Planning in the Stockholm Region 1950-1985*. Paper presented at Seminar "Urban Politics and Urban Development, University of Utrecht.
Champman, K. and D.F. Walker (1991) *Industrial Location* (second edition). Oxford: Basil Blackwell.
Checkoway, B. (1980) Large Builders, Federal Housing Programmes, and Postwar Suburbanization. *International Journal of Urban and Regional Research*, 4, pp. 21-44.
Cheshire, P., S. Sheppard, A. Hooper and J. Peterson (1985) *The economic consequences of the British planning system*. Discussion Paper No. 29, Department of Economics, University of Reading.
Cheshire, P. and S. Sheppard (1989) British planning policy and access to housing: some empirical estimates, *Urban Studies*, 26 (5), pp. 469-485.
Clark, E. (1987) The rent gap and transformation of the built environment: case studies in Malmö 1860-1985. *Geografiska Annaler* 70B, 241-254.
Clark, E. and A. Gullberg (1991) Long Swings, Rent Gaps and Structures of Building Provision - the Postwar Transformation of Stockholm's Inner City. *International Journal of Urban and Regional Research*, 15 (4), pp. 492-504.
Coase, R. (1937) The Nature of the Firm, *Economica*, 4, pp. 386-405.
Conijn, J.B.S. and O.A. Papa (1987) *Institutionele beleggers op de woningmarkt*. Tweede Kamer 1987-1988, 19.623, No. 33. The Hague: SDU.
Corbridge, S., R. Martin and N. Thrift (*eds.*) (1994) *Money Power and Space*. Oxford: Basil Blackwell.
Cultureel Planbureau (1992) *Sociaal Cultureel Rapport 1992*. The Hague: SDU.
Cultureel Planbureau (1994) *Sociaal Cultureel Rapport 1994*. The Hague: SDU.

Dalen, H.P. van (1995) De ongrijpbare spaarder. *Economisch Statistische Berichten*, (80), 8-3-1995, nr. 4000, pp. 223-225.
Damme, E.E.C. van (1995) Marktwerking in theorie en praktijk. *Economisch Statistische Berichten*, (80), 8-3-1995, nr. 4000, pp. 236-238.
Davoudi, S. and D. Usher (1990) *Who is developing what in Tyne and Wear?* Urban Regeneration and the Development Process Project Paper No. 1, University of Newcastle-

upon-Tyne.

Dieleman, F.M. (*ed.*) (1985) *Toekomstverkenning Volkshuisvesting;* bijdrage aan de toekomst van de volkshuisvesting; een inventarisatie en programmeerstudie.

Dieleman, F.M. and S. Musterd (*eds.*) (1992) *The Randstad: A Research and Policy Laboratory*, Dordrecht: Kluwer Academic Publishers.

Dieleman, F. M. (1994) Social rented housing: valuable asset or unsustainable burden? *Urban Studies*, 31 (3), pp. 447-463.

Dieterich, H., D. Williams and B. Wood (eds.) (1993/4) *European Land and Property Markets, Netherlands, Germany, France, Sweden*. London: UCL Press.

Douma, S. and H. Schreuder (1992) *Economic Approaches to Organizations*. Hempstead: Prentice Hall.

Dowall, D.E. (1984) *The suburban Squeeze: Land Conversion and Regulation in the San Fransisco Bay Area*. Berkely, CA.: University of California Press.

Dreimuller, A.P. (1980) *Taak en plaats van de projectontwikkelaar in het bouwproces*. Amsterdam: Economisch Instituur Bouwnijverheid.

Duncan, S. (1989) Development gains and housing provision in Britain and Sweden. *Transactions Institute of British Geographers*, 14 (2), pp. 157-172.

Dunleavy, P. (1981) *The Politics of MassHousing in Britain 1945-1972*. Oxford: Clarendon Press.

Economisch Instituut voor de Bouwnijverheid (EIB, Conijn *et al.*) (1980a) *De financiering van investeringen in bouwwerken*. Amsterdam: EIB.

Economisch Instituut voor de Bouwnijverheid (EIB, Jansen) (1980b) *Structurele ontwikkelingen in de bedrijfstak bouwnijverheid*. Amsterdam: EIB.

Economisch Instituut voor de Bouwnijverheid (EIB, Bremer) (1991a) *Techniek, nieuwe materialen en arbeid in de bouwnijverheid*. Amsterdam: EIB.

Economisch Instituut voor de Bouwnijverheid (EIB) (1991b) *Ontwikkelingen in de bouwnijverheid tot en met 1996*. Amsterdam: EIB.

Economisch Instituut voor de Bouwnijverheid (EIB, H.M. Stijnen) (1992a) *De financiering van de nieuwbouw van woningen*. Amsterdam: EIB.

Economisch Instituut voor de Bouwnijverheid (EIB, P.J. van den Broek *et al.*) (1992b) *De bouw op weg naar 2000*. Amsterdam: EIB.

Economisch Instituut voor de Bouwnijverheid (EIB, P.J. van den Broek) (1992c) *Kantoren aan bod*. Amsterdam: EIB.

Economisch Instituut voor de Bouwnijverheid (EIB) (1994) *De verwachtingen voor de bouwproductie en de werkgelegenheid in 1994*. Amsterdam: EIB.

Eggertsson, T. (1990) *Economic Behaviour and Institutions*, Cambridge: Cambridge University Press.

Eggertsson, T. (1993) The economics of institutions: avoiding the open-field syndrome and the perils of path dependence. *Acta Sociologica*, 36: pp. 223-237.

Etzioni, A. (1988) *The Moral Dimension: Toward a New Economics*. New York: Free Press.

Evans, A.W. (1985) *Urban Economics: an introduction*, Oxford: Blackwell

Evans, A.W. (1987) *House Prices and Land Prices in the South East: A Review*, London: House Builders Federation.

Fainstein, S.S., N.I. Fainstein, and A. Schwartz (1983) *Restructuring the city: the political*

economy of urban redevelopment. New York: Longman.
Fainstein, S.S. (1990) Economics, politics and development policy: the convergence of New York and London. *International Journal of Urban and Regional Research*. 14 (4), pp. 553-575.
Fainstein, S.S., I. Gordon, and M. Harloe (*Eds.*) (1992) *Divided Cities*. Oxford: Blackwell.
Fainstein, S.S. (1993) *The City Builders*. Oxford: Blackwell.
Fainstein, S.S. (1994) Government programs for commercial redevelopment in poor neighborhoods: the cases of Spitalfields in East London and downtown Brooklyn, NY., *Environment and Planning A*, 26, pp. 215-234.
Faludi, A. and A. van der Valk (1990) *De groeikernen als hoekstenen van de Nederlandse ruimtelijke planningdoctrine*. Assen/Maastricht.
Faludi, A. and A. van der Valk (1994) *Rule and Order - Dutch Planning Doctrine in the Twentieth Century*. Dordrecht: Kluwer.
Fase, M.M.G. (1995) Het verdwenen geld. *Economisch Statistische Berichten*, (80), 8-3-1995, nr. 4000, pp. 239-241.
Feagin, B. (1987) *Houston: the free enterprise city*. New Brunswick, NJ: Rutgers University Press.
Fine, B. (1985) Land, capital and the British coal industry prior to World War II, in M. Ball, V. Bentivegna, M. Edwards and M. Folin (Eds) *Land Rent, Housing and Urban Planning*. London: Croom Helm.
Floor, H. and R. van Kempen (1994) *Wonen op maat: een onderzoek naar de voorkeuren en motieven van woonconsumenten en te verwachten ontwikkelingen daarin* (Deel 1: Theoretische uitgangspunten en probleemstelling). Utrecht: Rijksuniversiteit Utrecht.
Folin, M. (1985) Housing development processes in Europe; some hypotheses from a comparative analysis, in: M. Ball (*et al.*) *Land rent, Housing and Urban Planning; a European perspective*, London: Croom Helm.
Fothergill, S., M. Kitson, and S. Monk (1985) The supply of land for industrial development, in: S. Barrett and P. Healey: *Land Policy: Problems and Alternatives*. Aldershot: Gower.
Fothergill, S., S. Monk, and M. Perry (1987) *Property and Industrial Development*, London: Hutchinson.
Frances, J., R. Levacic, J. Mitchell, and G. Thompson (1991) Introduction, in: Thompson, G., J. Frances, R. Levacic, J. Mitchell, *Markets, Hierarchies and Networks, the coordination of social life*. London: Sage Publications.

Giebels, R., C.C. Koopmans, and F. Moolhuizen (1985) *De risico's voor gemeenten op de markt voor bouwrijpe grond*. Amsterdam: SEO.
Gloster, M. and N. Smith (1989) *Inner Cities - A Shortage of Sites*, London: Royal Institution of Chartered Surveyors.
Gool, P. van, R.M. Weisz, and P.G.M. Wetten (1993) *Onroerend goed als belegging*. Culemborg: Stenfert Kroese.
Gore, A. and D.J. Nicholson (1991) Models of the Land-Development Process: A Critical Review*Environment and Planning A*, 23, pp. 705-730.
Gosselings, J.H.W. (1990) *In wat voor wereld leven we?* Inaugural speech, Maastricht: University of Maastricht.
Granovetter, M. (1985) Economic Action and Social Structure: The problem of Embed-

dedness. *American Journal of Sociology*, 91 (3), pp. 481-510.
Granovetter, M. (1992) Economic Institutions as Social Constructions: A Framework for Analysis. *Acta Sociologica*, 35, pp. 3-11.
Granovetter, M. and R. Swedberg (*eds.*) (1992) *The Sociology of Economic Life*. Boulder: West-view Press.
Grootendorst, J. (1994) *De markthuur op kantorenmarkten in Nederland*. PhD Thesis, Amsterdam: Tinbergen Institute Research Series, University of Amsterdam.

Haila, A. (1988) Land as a financial asset: the theory of urban rent as a mirror of economic transformation. *Antipode*, 20, pp. 79-101.
Haila, A. (1990) The theory of land rent at the crossroads. *Environment and Planning D: Society and Space*, 8, pp. 275-296.
Haila, A. (1991) Four Types of Investment in Land and Property. *International Journal of Urban and Regional Research*, 15 (3), pp. 343-65.
Hamnett, C. (1994) Restructuring housing finance and the housing market, in: S. Corbridge, R. Martin and N. Thrift: *Money Power and Space*, Oxford: Basil Blackwell, pp. 281-308.
Harding, A. (1992) Property interests and urban growth coalitions in the UK, in: P. Healey, S. Davoudi, M. O'Toole, S. Tavsanoglu, D. Usher (*eds.*) *Rebuilding the City: Property-led Urban Regeneration*. London: E. and F.N. Spon.
Harloe, M., P. Marcuse, and N. Smith (1992) Housing for people, housing for profits, in: Fainstein *et al.* (*Eds.*) *Divided Cities*. Oxford: Blackwell.
Harrison, A.J. (1977) *Economics and Land Use Planning*, London: Croom Helm.
Hart, H.W. ter (1987) *Commercieel vastgoed in Nederland*. Deventer: Fed.
Harvey, D. (1978) The urban process under capitalism: a framework for analysis. *International Journal of Urban and Regional Research*, 2, pp. 101-131.
Harvey, D. (1982) *The Limits to Capital*. Oxford: Basil Blackwell.
Harvey, D. (1985) *The Urbanization of Capital*, Oxford: Basil Blackwell.
Harvey, J. (1992) *Urban Land Economics*. London: MacMillan.
Healey, P. and S.M. Barrett (1990) Structure and Agency in Land and Property Development Processes. *Urban Studies*, 27 (1), pp. 89-104.
Healey, P. and R. Nabarro (*eds.*) (1990) *Land and Property Development in a Changing Context*. Aldershot: Gower.
Healey, P. (1991a) Urban Regeneration and the Development Industry. *Regional Studies*, 25 (2), pp. 97-110.
Healey, P. (1991b) Models of the development process: a review, *Journal of Property Research*, 8, pp. 219-238.
Healey, P. (1992a) An institutional model of the development process, *Journal of Property Research*, 9, pp. 33-44.
Healey, P. (1992b) Urban Regeneration and the Development Industry, in: Healey *et.al.* (*eds.*) *Rebuilding the City: Property-led Urban Regeneration*. London: E. and F.N. Spon.
Healey, P., S. Davoudi, M. O'Toole, S. Tavsanoglu, S., and D. Usher (*eds*) (1992) *Rebuilding the City: Property-led Urban Regeneration*. E. and F.N. Spon, London.
Healey, P. (1993a) *Urban policy an property development - the institutional relations of real estate development in an old industrial region*. Newcastle: Dept. of Town and Country Planning, University of Newcastle upon Tyne.
Healey, P. (1993b) *Regional variations in the development industry - the significance for*

develop-ment activity, urban policy and planning policy. Paper presented at RICS Research Conference, London.
Healey, P. (1994) Urban policy and property development: the institutional relations of real-estate development in an old industrial region. *Environment and Planning A*, 26, pp. 177-198.
Heertje, A. (1973) *Economie en Technologische Ontwikkeling*. Leiden: Stenfert Kroese.
Helderman, J.K. (1993) *The re-ordening of the Dutch housing sector*, working paper 5, Research Programme 'Policy and Governance in Complex Networks, Rotterdam: Erasmus University.
Henneberry, J. (1988) Conflict in the industrial property market. *Town Planning Review*, 59 (3), pp. 241-262.
Hennepe, A.G. ter (1992) *Marktramingen voor de gebouwensector*. Naarden: BB&H Consultancy.
Hennipman, P. (1945) *Economisch motief en economisch principe*, Amsterdam: Noord-Hollandse Uitgevers maatschappij.
Hennipman, P. (1962) Doeleinden en criteria der economische politiek, in: J.E. Andriessen and M.A.G. van Meerhaeghe, *Theorie van de Economische Politiek*. Leiden: Stenfert Kroese.
Henry, N. (1992) The New Industrial Spaces: Locational Logic of a New Production Era? *International Journal of Urban and Regional Research*, 16 (3), pp. 275-396.
Hodgson, G.M. (1988) *Economics and Institutions*. Oxford: Blackwell.
Hooper, A.J. (1992) The construction of a theory: a comment. *Journal of Property Research*, 9, pp. 45-48.
Houghton, T. (1993) On the nature of Real Estate, Monopoly and the Fallacies of 'Monopoly Rent'. *International Journal of Urban and Regional Research*, 17, pp. 260-273.
Howes, C. (1989) Special Report Land Assembly: Private Sector gets a Boost. *Chartered Surveyor Weekly*, 19 January 1989, pp. 61-63.

Imrie, R. and H. Thomas (1993) The limits of property-led regeneration. *Environment and Planning C: Government and Policy*, 11, pp. 87-102.

Janssen, J.E. (1992) *Determinanten van prijzen voor bestaande koopwoningen*. Phd-thesis. Nijmegen: vakgroep Planologie, University of Nijmegen.
Jobse, R.B. (1987) The restructuring of Dutch cities. *Tijdschrift voor Economische en Sociale Geografie*, 78, pp. 305-311.
Jong, H.W. de (1992) *Dynamische Markttheorie*. Leiden: Stenfert Kroese.

Kemper, N.J. and P.H. Pellenbarg (1991) Bedrijfsverplaatsingen in Nederland. *Economische Statistische Berichten*, 6-3-1991, pp. 249-52.
Kempen, R. van (1992) *In de klem op de stedelijke woningmarkt? - huishoudens met een laag inkomen in vroeg-naoorlogse en vroeg-20ste-eeuwse wijken in Amsterdam en Rotterdam*. Utrecht: Stedelijke Netwerken.
King, R.J. (1989a) Capital Switching and the role of ground rent: 1 Theoretical problems. *Environment and Planning A*, 21, pp. 445-462.
King, R.J. (1989b) Capital Switching and the role of ground rent: 2 Switching between cir-

cuits and switching between submarkets. *Environment and Planning A*, 21, pp. 711-738.
King, R.J. (1989c) Capital Switching and the role of ground rent: 3 Switching between circuits, switching between submarkets, and social change. *Environment and Planning A*, pp. 853-880.
Kirzner, I.M. (1976) On the method of Austrian Economics, in: Littlechild, S. (*ed.*) (1990) *Austrian Economics* (3 vols.), ch. 30. London: Aldershot.
Kivell, P. (1993) *Land and the City, Patterns and Processes of Urban Change*. London: Routled-ge.
Klamer, A. (1995) De economie als anomalie. *Economisch Statistische Berichten*, (80), 8-3-1995, nr. 4000, p. 219.
Knaap, G.A. van der, and L. van der Laan (1993) Urban Revitalization in the Netherlands: Current Trends versus Actual Policies. *European Planning Studies*, 1 (4), pp. 483-497.
Knight, F.H. (1921) *Risk, Uncertainty and Profit*. Cambridge: The University Press.
Kortenoever, J. (1989) *Grondbedrijven in de branding van de ruimtelijke ordening*. Amsterdam: Universiteit van Amsterdam.
Krabben, E. van der (1991) *Een analyse van de Bosche onroerend-goedmarkt*, unpublished working Paper, Tilburg: University of Tilburg.
Krabben, E. van der (1993a) Kwaliteit van de gebouwde omgeving in het geding. *Rooilijn*, 26 (7), pp. 300-305.
Krabben, E. van der (1993b) Ruimtelijk-economisch beleid in nederlandse steden: het succes van gemeentelijk grondbeleid? in: F. Boekema (*ed.*) *Sociale Economie, markten, instituties en beleid*. Groningen: Wolters-Noordhof.
Krabben, E. van der and J.G. Lambooy (1993), A theoretical framework for the functioning of the Dutch urban property market. *Urban Studies*, vol. 30: 8, pp. 1381-1397.
Krabben, E. van der and J.G. Lambooy (1994), *An Institutional Economic Approach to Land and Property Markets*, Research Memorandum FEW 636, Tilburg: Tilburg University.
Krabben, E. van der and F. Boekema (1994), Missing links between urban economic growth theory and the functioning of property markets: economic growth and building investments in the City of 's-Hertogenbosch. *Journal of Property Research*, (11), pp. 111-129.
Krätke, S. (1992) Urban land rent and real estate markets in the process of social restructuring: the case of Germany. *Environment and Planning D: Society and Space*, 10, pp. 245-264.
Kreukels, A.M.J. and W.M.G. Salet (*Eds.*) (1992) *Debating institutions and cities: proceedings of the Anglo-Dutch Conference on Urban Regeneration*. The Hague: SDU.
Kreukels, A.M.J. and W.M.G. Salet (1992) Fragmentatie en orde van het stedelijk landschap; Een positiebepaling van het Britse en het Nederlandse stedenbeleid. *Beleid en Maatschappij*, (3), pp. 137-145.
Kruijt, B., B. Needham, and T. Spit (1990) *Economische Grondslagen voor Grondbeleid*. Amster-dam: Stichting voor Beleggings- en Vastgoedkunde.
Kruijt, B. and J.E. Janssen (1991) Een marktstemmingsindex voor vastgoed. *Economisch Statistische Berichten*, 23-1-1991.

Lake, R.W. (1983) *Readings in Urban Analysis: Perspectives on Urban Form and Structure*. New Jersey: Centre for Urban Policy Research.
Lambooy, J.G., P.C.M. Huigsloot and R.E. van der Lustgraaf (1982) *Greep op de Stad?*, Den Haag: Staatsuitgeverij - voorstudies en achtergronden WRR.

Lambooy, J.G. (1985) Urban Theory and Urban Planning, in: K.E. Haynes, A. Kublinski and O. Kultalakti (eds.) *Pathologies of Urban Processes*, pp. 409-425. Tampere: Finnpublishers.

Lambooy, J.G. (1993) The European City: From Carrefour to Organisational Nexus. *Tijdschrift voor Economische en Sociale Geografie*, vol. 84, 4, pp. 258-268.

Lie, R. and A. Bongenaar (1990) *Toplocaties: produktiemilieu en investeringsmilieu*. Amsterdam: Stichting voor Beleggings- en Vastgoedkunde, University of Amsterdam.

Lie, R. (1994) *Economische dynamiek en toplocaties, locatiekarakteristiek en prijsontwikkeling van kantoren in een aantal grote Europese steden*. Amsterdam: Tinbergen Institute Research Series, No. 63, University of Amsterdam.

Lin Leung, H. (1987) Developer behaviour and development control. *Land Development Studies*, 4 (1), pp. 17-34.

Logan, J.R. and H. Molotch (1987) *Urban Fortunes*. Berkeley: University of California Press.

Logan, J.R. and T. Swanstrom (Eds.) (1990) *Beyond the City Limits*. Philadelphia: Temple University Press.

Louw, E. (1994) *Vastgoedmarkt en ruimtelijke spreiding van kantoren*. Delft: Delft University Press.

Luithlen, L. (1992) Marxian concepts, capital accumulation and office property. *Journal of Property Research*, 9, pp. 227-246.

Lukkes, P., A.J. Krist, and P.J.M. van Steen (1987) *Kantorenmarkt, investeren en ruimte*. Zeist: Vonk Uitgevers.

MacGregor, B.D., A.E. Baum, C.D. Adams, S.C. Fleming, and J. Peterson (1985) *Land Availability for Inner City Development*, Working Paper in Environment Policy No 8, Reading: Department of Land Management and Development, University of Reading.

Machimura, T. (1992) The urban restructuring process in Tokyo in the 1980s: transforming Tokyo into a World City. *International Journal of Urban and Regional Research*, 16, pp. 114-128.

Markusen, J.R. and D.T. Scheffman (1978) Ownership concentration and market power in urban land markets. *Review of Economic Studies*, 45, pp. 519-26.

Massey, D. and A. Catalano (1978) *Capital and Land*. London: Edward Arnold.

McNamara, P. (1984) The role of local estate agents in the residential development process. *Land Development Studies*, 1, pp. 101-112.

Meer, J. van der (1989) *Wat beweegt de stad? - studie naar de stedelijke dynamiek in de Rotter-damse agglomeratie*. PhD Thesis, Rotterdam: University of Rotterdam.

MERIT (1990) *Diffusie van technologie en de ontwikkeling van de werkgelegenheid*. Maastricht: University of Limburg.

Mills, E.J. (1972) *Studies in the Structure of the Urban Economy*. Baltimore: John Hopkins Press.

Ministry of Economic Affairs (1994a) *Ruimte voor Economische Activiteit - verkennende analyse van de ruimtelijke ontwikkelingsmogelijkheden voor economische activiteiten* (publikatiereeks Dir.Gen. Economische Structuur, nr. 1) The Hague: Min.Ec.Affairs.

Ministry of Economic Affairs (1994b) *Vestigingslocaties in de toekomst, een confrontatie van vraag en aanbod* (BCI/NEI) The Hague: Min.Ec.Affairs.

Ministry of Economic Affairs (1994c) *Rijksnota's: concurrerende en complementaire ruimteclaims* (Kolpron Consultants) The Hague: Min.Ec. Affairs.

Ministry of Economic Affairs (1994d) *Milieuzonering rond economische activiteiten* (DHV/Heidemij Advies) The Hague: Min.Ec.Affairs.

Ministry of Economic Affairs (1994e) *Ruimte voor wonen 1995-2005* (Kolpron Consultants) The Hague: Min.Ec.Affairs.

Ministry of Economic Affairs (1994f) *Ruimte voor toerisme en recreatie* (Zandvoort Kappelhoff Advies) The Hague: Min.Ec.Affairs.

Ministry of Housing, Physical Planning and Environment (1989) *Nota Volkshuisvesting in de jaren negentig*. The Hague: SDU.

Ministry of Housing, Physical Planning and Environment (1990) *Fourth Physical Planning Memorandum Extra*. The Hague: SDU.

Ministry of Housing, Physical Planning and Environment (1992) *Vergelijkende studie naar volks-huisvestingssystemen in Europa*. The Hague: DGVH, MinVROM.

Ministry of Housing, Physical Planning and Environment (1992) *De kwaliteit van de woningvoorraad in het bestaand stedelijk gebied per 1990*. The Hague: DGVH, MinVROM.

Ministry of Housing, Physical Planning an Environment (1992) *Trendrapport Volkshuisvesting in de Jaren Negentig*. The Hague: SDU.

Ministry of Housing, Physical Planning and Environment (1992) *Woningbouw in de marktsector*. The Hague: DGVH, MinVROM.

Ministry of Housing, Physical Planning and Environment (1993) *Eigen woningbezit in cijfers 1993*. The Hague: DGVH, MinVROM.

Molotch, H. and S. Vicari (1988) Three ways to build: the development process in the United States, Japan and Italy. *Urban Affairs Quarterly* 24, pp. 188-214.

Morgan, E. (1990) A Shortage of Factories, in: Healey, P. and Nabarro, R. (*eds.*) *Land and Property Development in a Changing Context*. Aldershot: Gower.

Morrison, N. (1992) *The Commercial Redevelopment Process in Glasgow 1980-1991*. unpublished PhD Thesis, Centre for Planning, University of Strathclyde, Glasgow.

Muth, R. (1969) *Cities and Housing*. Chicago: Chicago University Press.

Nagelkerke, A.C. (1992) *Instituties en economisch handelen*. Tilburg: Tilburg University Press.

Nationale Woningraad (1994) *Wonen na 2000 - Wensen en Mogelijkheden*, Almere: Nationale Woningraad.

Needham, B. (1981) A neo-classical supply-based approach to land prices. *Urban Studies*, 18, pp. 91-104.

Needham, B. and B. Kruijt (1992) The Netherlands. in: B. Wood and R.H. Williams (*eds.*) *Industrial property markets in western Europe*. London: E. and F.N. Spon.

Needham, B. (1992) A theory of land prices when land is supplied publicly: the case of the Netherlands. *Urban Studies*, 29, pp. 669-686.

Needham, B., P. Koenders, and B. Kruijt, B. (1993) *The Urban Land and Property Market in the Netherlands - Country Report*. London: E. and F.N. Spon.

Needham, B. and R. Lie (1993) *The public regulation of property supply and its effects on private prices, risks and returns*, paper RICS Research Conference, London.

NIROV (1994) *Volkshuisvesting na de brutering*. The Hague: NIROV.

North, D.C. (1990) *Institutions, institutional change and economic performance*. Cambridge:

Cambridge University Press.

NVB (Nederlandse Vereniging van Bouwondernemers) (1993) *Thermometer van de Nederlandse koopwoningenmarkt*. Voorburg: NVB.

Oizumi, E. (1994) Property finance in Japan: expansion and collapse of the bubble economy. *Environment and Planning A*, 26, pp. 199-213.

Oude Veldhuis, M.C. (1992) *Stedelijke woningmarkten en de visie van marktpartijen*. Voorburg: NEPROM.

Pen, J. (1995) Een vak met een gat er in. *Economisch Statistische Berichten*, (80), 8-3-1995, nr. 4000, pp. 220-222.

Perry, M. (1986) *Small Firms and Economic Development*, Aldershot: Gower.

Piore, M. and C.F. Sabel (1984) *The second industrial divide*. New York: Basic Books.

Priemus, H. (1983) *Volkshuisvestingssysteem en Woningmarkt*. Delft: Delft University Press.

Priemus, H. (1984) *Verhuistheorieën en de Verdeling van de Woningvoorraad*. Delft: Delft University Press.

Pryke, M. (1991) An international city going 'global': spatial change in the City of London. *Environment and Planning D: Society and Space*, 9, pp. 197-222.

Pryke, M. (1994a) Looking back on the space of a boom: (re)developing spatial matrices in the City of London. *Environment and Planning A*, 26, pp. 235-264.

Pryke, M. (1994b) Urbanizing capitals: towards an integration of time, space and economic calculation, in: S. Corbridge, R. Martin, N. Thrift (*eds.*), *Money, Power, Space*. Oxford: Basil Blackwell.

Richardson, H.W. (1977) *The New Urban Economics*. London: Pion.

RIGO (1987) *Bouwkosten*. Tweede Kamer, 1987-1988, 19623, no. 35. The Hague: SDU.

RIGO (1991) *Marktwaarde woningbouwgrond in de marktsector*. Amsterdam: RIGO.

Robbins, L. (1935) *An Essay on the Nature and Significance of Economic Science*, (second edition), London: MacMillan.

Rouwendal, J. (1994) De regionale component van de woningmarkt, in: J. van Dijk and R. Florax (*eds.*) *Industriepolitiek, regionale clusters en de werking van markten*. Groningen: Geo Pers.

Sassen, S. (1991) *The Global City*. Princeton: Princeton University Press.

Schaar, J. van der (1987) *Groei en bloei van het nederlands volkshuisvestingsbeleid*. Delft: Delft University Press.

Schaar, J. van der (1991) Volkshuisvestingsbeleid: hoe lang nog? *Stedebouw en Volkshuisvesting*, 1991 (April), pp. 12-16.

Scott, A.J. (1988) *New Industrial Places*. London: Pion.

Scott, A.J. (1990), *Metropolis: from the division of labour to urban form*, Berkely: University of California Press.

Scott, M.F. (1991) *A New View of Economic Growth*. Oxford: Clarendar Press.

SEO (1987) *Grondprijzen voor de gesubsidieerde woningbouw*. Tweede Kamer, 1987-1988, 19623, no. 34. The Hague: SDU.

SEO (1993) *Het noodzakelijke weerstandsvermogen van woningcorporaties*. Amsterdam: SEO, University of Amsterdam.

Smith, M.P. (1988) *City, State and Market, the political economy of urban society*. Oxford: Basil Blackwell.
Solesbury, W. (1990) Property development and urban regeneration, in: P. Healey and R. Nabarro (*Eds.*) *Land and Property Development in a Changing Context*. Aldershot: Gower.
Stedebouw en Volkshuisvesting (1993) Commentaren op Trendrapport en Trendbrief. *Special issue*, 1993 (3).
Sykora, L. (1993), City in Transition: The Role of Rent Gap in Prague's Revitalization. *Tijdschrift voor Economische en Sociale Geografie (Journal of economic and scoial geography)*, 84, 4, pp. 281-293.

TAUW Infra Consult (1990a) *Kavelopbrengsten 1982 t/m 1988, ongewogen*. Deventer: TAUW.
TAUW Infra Consult (1990b) *Ontwikkelingen kavelprijzen nieuwe uitleg 1982-1988*. Deventer: TAUW.
Terpstra, P.R.A. (1987) *Het gemeentelijk grondbeleid*. Zeist: Vonk Uitgevers.
Terpstra, P.R.A. (1993) *Vastgoed en Grond, organisatie en beleid*. Bussum: Coutinho.
Theeuwes, J.J.M. (1995) Economie is oorlog. *Economisch Statistische Berichten*, (80), 8-3-1995, nr. 4000, pp. 242-244.
Thrift, N. (1994) Globalisation, Regulation, Urbanisation: The Case of the Netherlands. *Urban Studies*, 31 (3), pp. 365-380.
Thompson, G., J. Frances, R. Levacic, and J. Mitchell (*eds.*) (1991) *Markets, Hierarchies and Networks, the coordination of social life*. London: Sage Publications.
Topalov, C. (1985) Prices, Profits and Rents in Residential Development: France 1960-80, in: Ball et al. (*eds.*) *Land Rent, Housing and Urban Planning, a European perspective* London: Croom Helm.
Townroe, P.M. (1991) Rationality in Industrial Location Decisions. *Urban Studies*, 28 (3), pp. 383-392.
Turok, I. (1992) Property-led urban regeneration: panacea of placebo? *Environment and Planning A*, 24, pp. 361-379.

Vicari, S. and H. Molotch (1990) Building Milan: alternative machines of growth. *International Journal of Urban and Regional Research*, 14 (4), pp. 602-24.
Vreeze, N. de (1993) *Woningbouw, Inspiratie en Ambities*. Almere: Nationale Woningraad.

Wakker, P. (1995) Die verdraaide preferenties!. *Economisch Statistische Berichten*, (80), 8-3-1995, nr. 4000, pp. 231-232.
Weisz, R.M. and R. van Wettum (1988) *Onroerend-goed beleggingsmaatschappijen*. Leiden: Stenfert Kroese.
Whitehand, J.W.R. and S.M. Whitehand (1984) The physical fabric of town centres: the agents of change. *Transactions of the Institute of British Geographers*, 9, pp. 231-247.
Williamson, O.E. (1975) *Markets and Hierarchies: Analysis and Antitrust Implications*. New York: Free Press.
Williamson, O.E. (1985), *The economic institutions of capitalism*, New York: Free Press.
Williamson, O.E. (1992), Markets, hierarchies, and the modern corporation, an unfolding pers-pective. *Journal of Economic Behavior and Organization*, 17, pp. 335-352.

Wiltshaw, D.G. (1985) The Supply of Land. *Urban Studies*, 22, no. 1, pp. 49-56.
Wit, D.P.M. de (1993) *Portfolio Management of common Stock and Real Estate Assets*. PhD Thesis, Amsterdam: Tinbergen Institute Research Series, University of Amsterdam.

Zukin, S. and P. Dimaggio (*eds.*) (1990) *Structures of Capital: the social organisation of the economy*. Cambridge: Cambridge University Press.

Center for Economic Research, Tilburg University, The Netherlands
Dissertation Series

No.	Author	Title
1	P.J.J. Herings	Static and Dynamic Aspects of General Disequilibrium Theory; ISBN 90 5668 001 3
2*	Erwin van der Krabben	Urban Dynamics: A Real Estate Perspective - An institutional analysis of the production of the built environment; ISBN 90 5170 390 2

---

* Copies can be ordered from Thesis Publishers, P.O. Box 14791, 1001 LG Amsterdam, The Netherlands, phone + 31 20 6255429; fax: +31 20 6203395; e-mail: thesis@thesis.aps.nl